The Highland Bagpipe: Its History, Literature, and Music, with Some Account of the Traditions, Superstitions, and Anecdotes Relating to the Instrument and Its Tunes

W L. Manson

"THE CORONACH"

(*From the Painting by R. R. MacIan*)

The Highland Bagpipe

Its History, Literature, and Music

WITH SOME ACCOUNT OF THE

Traditions, Superstitions, and Anecdotes

Relating to

The Instrument and Its Tunes

BY

W. L. MANSON

*The tune with the river in it, the fast river and the courageous, that
kens not stop nor tarry, that runs round rock and over fall
with a good humour, yet no mood for anything
but the way before it.*—NEIL MUNRO.

TO

A. DEWAR WILLOCK

EDITOR OF THE

Glasgow Weekly Herald

WHO JUDICIOUSLY BLUE-PENCILLED

THE FIRST ISSUE OF THESE ARTICLES

AND ENCOURAGED THE WRITER TO

GIVE THEM TO THE PUBLIC IN THIS

MORE PERMANENT FORM

Preface.

THIS book was not written on a preconceived plan, drawn up from the beginning of the work. It "growed." It had its inception in a commission to write for the *Weekly Herald* half-a-dozen biographical articles on famous pipers. The necessary investigation produced a mass of material too interesting to be left unused, and the half-dozen articles of the original commission became twenty-seven, with very little of the biographical in them. These, after being finally recast, revised, and in several cases re-written, are now in the form of a book flung at an unoffending public. If the volume interests any one—well. If not— well. There is nothing more to be said on that point.

It were vain to attempt to acknowledge indebtedness to books or to men. Every available book bearing on the subject even in the most indirect way has been consulted, in many cases read. A great deal of the material used is of course common to all Highland literature, and one book cannot be quoted more than another. With men it is equally impracticable to give names. So many have helped, so many have written giving additional bits of information or suggesting improvements, so many have, in reply to requests, kindly supplied matter dealing with phases of the subject on which they have intimate knowledge, that one could not do justice to all without naming all. Still, while this may not be done, I cannot possibly refrain from saying that without the assistance given by Mr. Henry Whyte ("Fionn") in matters of Highland history and questions connected with the Gaelic language, the book could hardly have been published; while Mr. John Mac Kay, editor of the *Celtic Monthly*, in throwing open to me his valuable library of Celtic literature, did very much to lighten my labours. This, I think, is all I can safely say. If I said more, I would have to say so very much.

W. L. M.

GLASGOW, *April 27, 1901.*

Contents.

APPENDIX.

Illustrations.

The Highland Bagpipe.

CHAPTER I.

TUNING UP.

> "I have power, high power for freedom,
>   To wake the burning soul ;
> I have sonnets that through the ancient hills,
>   Like a torrent's voice might roll ;
> I have pealing notes of victory,
>   That might welcome kings from war ;
> I have rich deep tones to send the wail,
>   For a hero's death afar."

"A Hundred Pipers "—Scotland becoming Cosmopolitan—The War spirit of the Pipes—Regiments, not Clans—Annual Gatherings—Adaptability of Pipes—Scotch folk from Home—An aged Enthusiast—Highlands an Extraordinary Study—Succession of Chiefs—Saxon introduced—Gaelic printed—Highlands in 1603—The Mac Neills of Barra—Highland hospitality.

"WI' a Hundred Pipers an' a' an' a'" is a song that catches on with Highland people as well now as in the days when the piper was a power in the land. There is a never ending charm about the pipes, and there is a never ending swing about the song of the hundred

A

pipers, that stirs the blood of the true-born Celt, and makes him applaud vigorously in rhythm with the swing of the chorus. But it is because the song harks back to the time when one good piper was a man to be revered, and a hundred in one place a gathering to be dreaded—if they were all there of one accord—that it continues to hold its own. It expresses something of the grandeur that was attached to the national music, when the clan piper was second only to the chief in importance, and the pibroch as much a part of the clan life as the fiery cross, so it is accepted as the one outstanding bit of song that helps to keep alive the traditional glory of the Great Highland Bagpipe. Not that there is any immediate danger of that glory fading. It is but changing in character. Scotland has become cosmopolitan, and the fastnesses of the Highlands are no longer the retreats of wild cateran clans, whose peculiar habits and primitive ideas of social life helped to bind them together with ties of family strength, and at the same time to keep them unspotted from the Lowland and outside world that knew not the Gaelic and the tartan and the pipes. The *Piob Mohr* is not now an agency to be reckoned with by any one who wishes to explore the hills and glens, neither are there any little wars in Lorn or elsewhere, in which it can have an opportunity of leading Mac against Mac, or clan against clan. As a Highland war spirit, its glory has departed, and he would be a bold man who would say he was sorry for it. True, the Highland regiments who fight Britain's battles abroad still wear the tartan and march to the same old strains, but they are not now Highland clans. They are British battalions, whose empire, instead of being bounded by the horizon of a Scottish glen, is worldwide, and they march and wheel, and charge the enemy and

storm the heights in strict accordance with the orders of a
general who has his orders from Westminster. The only
gathering of the clans we have nowadays are the gatherings
in the halls of our big cities, where a thousand or two of
people bearing a common name meet under the presidency
of the next-of-kin of the chief of olden times, and drink, not
mountain dew, but tea, and have Highland or Jacobite
songs sung to them by people whose profession is singing,
and applaud dancers and pipers who dance and pipe because
it pays them to do so. This is very far removed from the
time when the *Piob Mohr* was in the zenith of its power,
though when one gets enthused with the atmosphere of such
a meeting, and forgets the slushy streets outside, and the
telegraph and the railway, and other nineteenth century
things that have made the Highlands impossible, the song
of the hundred pipers is quite sufficient to make the blood
course quicker, and to translate one for a moment to
other scenes and other times. But it is only for a
moment. The prosaic present comes back with a reality
that will not be denied, and one remembers with a sigh
that the song is but a sentiment, and that never more
will the gathering cries of the clans re-echo through the
glens, the fiery cross pass from hand to hand, or the peal
of the pibroch ring from clachan to clachan in a wild cry
to arms.

As an inspiration to the clansmen the bagpipe is no more,
but it remains an integral part of Scottish life and character. It is one of the peculiarities of the instrument that
it adapts itself to circumstances. When that phase of life
in which it was born and brought up, as it were, passed
away, it quietly but firmly declined to be moved into the
background. There is something of the stubbornness of the

old reivers about it, and just as the Highlander in his times
of greatest adversity stuck to his pipes, so the pipes seem
determined to stick to the Highlanders in spite of the ten-
dencies of latter-day civilisation. The love of the Highlander
for his pipes is too deep-rooted to vanish simply because
circumstances change.   When Rob Roy lay a-dying, and
when an old enemy came to see him, he had himself decked
out in his plaid and claymore, and when the interview was
over, " Now," said he, " let the piper play *Cha til ma tulidh*,"
and he died before the dirge was finished.   That spirit has
lived through the many changes that have taken place since
Rob Roy's day, and it lives in a modified form now.
Nothing will make a Scottish audience, especially a Scottish
audience far from home, cheer as the pipes will, and no
sound is so welcome at an open-air gathering, or to the
wandered Scotchman, as the wild notes of the national
instrument.   In the preface to one collection of Highland
music we are told of a well-known Edinburgh man, discreetly referred to as " W—— B——, Esq.," who was at the
time the most exquisite violinist in Scotland.   Even at the
venerable age of eighty-three, whenever he heard the
sound of the pipes he hastened to the place, and after
giving the itinerant player a handsome reward, he withdrew
to a passage or common stair near by and had what he
called " a wee bit dance to himsel'."   This does not seem a
very wonderful proceeding, though the story applies to
about forty years ago, for even now many a Highlander if
he is in anything like a private place, will begin to " Hooch "
and dance if he should happen to hear the pipes.   He
would never think of dancing to any other music—other
music is foolishness unto him.   Many things may and will
change, but it is hardly possible to imagine circumstances

which could dislodge pipe music from its honoured place as the national music of Scotland.

The preservation of the Gaelic, the kilt, and the pipes is the most notable feature in Highland history. Without his tartan, his language, and his music, the Gael would be only " A naked Pict, meagre and pale, the ghost of what he was.' But he has kept these, his distinguishing characteristics, and the Scottish Highlands of to-day is one of the most extraordinary studies in Europe, retaining as it does a language the most ancient, and the customs and music which distinguished it in ages the most remote, in spite of circumstances which might have proved too much for any social system whatever. The nature of the country did much to perpetuate these things. It was hilly, and, in the old days, inaccessible; the wants of the people were supplied among themselves, their manners were simple and patriarchal, and they had little intercourse with strangers except through trading in cattle and an occasional foray into the low country. So a spirit of independence and jealous pride of ancestry was cultivated, and in tradition, song, and music, the exploits of their forbears were celebrated. All this went to make Celtic Scotland a nation by itself, and its people a peculiar people. There is nothing in the political history of any country so remarkable as the succession of the Highland chiefs and the long and uninterrupted sway they held over their followers.

Somewhere about 1066 Malcolm Canmore removed his court from Iona to Dunfermline and introduced the Saxon language, and about 1270 Gaelic was entirely superseded in the Lowlands. Latin was used in all publications, and there were not many who could read what few books there were. Gaelic was not printed till 1567, centuries after it

had ceased to be the language of the court or of "society."
Then a book of John Knox's was issued in Gaelic, but it
was 1767 before the New Testament appeared in the Celtic
tongue.   When it did ten thousand copies were sold.
There was, of course, a vast store of poetry and literature
floating around in the minds of the people, passed down
from generation to generation ; but, with the exception of
two small collections, one by Rev. John Farquharson of
Strathglass in 1571, and the other by Alexander Mac
Donald, Ardnamurchan, about eight years later, it had all
to wait until 1759, when James Mac Pherson, the collector
of Ossianic poetry, compiled or wrote (whether he compiled
or wrote it is too delicate a matter to express a definite
opinion about in this place) the classics of the Highlands.
In spite of all these disadvantages, perhaps by reason of
them, the Highlands remained the Highlands until the
beginning of the present century.   The many years of
tribal warfare and of warfare with other peoples, did not
destroy the individuality of the race, it was the slow civilis-
ing process of later ages that made the Highlands less a
distinct nation than a province of the big British Empire.

Of the circumstances in the midst of which the pipes and
pipe music first got a hold on the affections of the Highland people we know but little.   There were harpers before
there were pipers, and probably bards before there were
harpers, but these did not record contemporary history or the
traditions of their age with any degree of fulness or accuracy,
if indeed they can be said to have recorded anything at all
who only told the next generation what they had heard
from the previous.   Writing in 1603 a traveller says of the
Highlanders :—

"They delight much in musicke, but chiefly in harps and clair-schoes of their own fashion. The strings of the clairschoes are made of brass wire, and the strings of the harps of sinews, which strings they strike either with their nayles growing long, or else with an instrument appoynted for that use. They take great pleasure to deck their harps and clairschoes with silver and precious stones; the poore ones that cannot attayne hereunto decke them with christall. They sing verses prettily compound, containing (for the most part) prayses of valiant men. There is not almost any other argument whereof their rymes intreat. They speak the ancient French language, altered a little."

As to the country itself, it was a mysterious, unknown land to all but the native. Ancient historians puzzled over its mystery, but could not fathom it. So they wrote under the shadow of the mysterious. Procopius, a Greek writer who flourished about A.D. 530, and wrote of the Roman Empire, speaking about the Highlands, says :—

"In the west, beyond the wall (Antoninus' Wall), the air is infectious and mortal, the ground is covered with serpents, and this dreary solitude is the region of departed spirits, who are translated from the opposite shores in substantial boats, and by living rowers. Some families of fishermen are excused from tribute in consideration of the mysterious office which is performed by these Charons of the ocean. Each in his turn is summoned at the hour of midnight to hear the voices and even the names of the ghosts, he is sensible of their weight, and feels impelled by an unknown but irresistible power."

Now we know how it was that the Romans could not conquer the Highlands. But we also know that the Highlanders were not, when the Romans came, the ignorant barbarians they are represented to have been, for Cæsar ascertained from them that the coast line of Britain was two thousand miles in length, an estimate not so very wide of the mark.

We are told by one fourteenth century historian that
"In Scotland ye shall find no man lightly of honour or
gentleness, they be like wyld and savage people ; " and by
another that " as to their faith and promise, they hold it
with great constancie," statements which are not at all con-
tradictory.   The once prevalent idea that a Highland chief
was an ignorant and unprincipled tyrant who rewarded the
abject submission of his followers with relentless cruelty and
oppression was entirely erroneous.   He might be naturally
ferocious or naturally weak, but in either case the tribal
system curbed excess, for the chief men of the clan were his
advisers, and without their approval he seldom decided on
extreme measures.   But though the sway of the chiefs was
thus mild in practice, it was arbitrary, and they themselves
were proud of their lot, their lands, and their dependents.
It is related of the lairds of Barra, who belonged to one of
the oldest and least-mixed septs in the Highlands, that as
soon as the family had dined it was customary for a herald
to sound a horn from the battlements on the castle tower,
proclaiming aloud in Gaelic, " Hear, oh ! ye people ! and
listen, oh ! ye nations ! The great Mac Neill of Barra
having finished his meal, the princes of the earth may dine."
The peasantry of the Highlands were always noted for
their hospitality.   " I have wandered," says Mr. J. F.
Campbell of Islay, than whom none knew the Highlands
better, " among the peasantry of many countries, and this
trip through the Highlands has but confirmed my old
impressions.   The poorest Highlander is ever readiest to
share the best he has with the stranger.   A kind word is
never thrown away, and whatever may be the faults of this
people, I have never found a boor or a churl in a Highland
bothy." Besides, the ancient Gaels were very fond of music,

whether in a merry or a sad humour. "It was," says Bacon, " a sure sign of brewing mischief when a Caledonian warrior was heard to hum his surly song." They accompanied most of their labours with music, either vocal or that of the harp, and it was among these chiefs and these people that the national music of Scotland took its rise. It is a matter of regret that its wild strains are now more frequently heard amid Canadian woods and on Australian plains than in the land where it was cradled.

CHAPTER II.

HARPERS, BARDS, AND PIPERS.

> " O'er all this hazy realm is spread
> A halo of sad memories of the dead,
> Of mournful love tales, of old tragedies ;
> Filling the heart with pity, and the eyes
> With tears at bare remembrance ; and old songs
> Of Love's endurance, Love's despair, Love's wrongs
> And triumphs o'er all obstacles at last,
> And all the grief and passion of the past."

Ancient musical instruments—Priestly harpers—Hereditary harpers
—Irish *versus* Scottish harpers—Royal harpers—Use of harp
universal—Welsh sarcasm—Mary Queen of Scots' harp—The
last of the harpers—" The Harper of Mull "—From harp to
pipes—The *Clarsach*—Pipes supplanting bards—The last clan
bard—Bardic customs—Bards' jealousy of pipes—The bard
in battle—Duncan Ban Mac Intyre—Two pipers scared—When
the pipes became paramount—The fiery cross—The coronach.

T HE harp was the immediate predecessor of the pipes ;
but in ancient times, and also contemporary with
the harp, there were other instruments. The *Complaynt of Scotland*, written in 1548, speaking of a company
of musicians, says :—

" The fyrst hed ane drone bagpipe, the next hed ane pipe made of
ane bleddir and of ane reid, the third playit on ane trump, the
feyerd on ane cornepipe, the fyfth playit on ane pipe made of ane
grait horne, the sext playit on ane recorder, the sevint plait on ane
fiddil, and the last on ane quhissel."

We cannot speak as to quality, but there was evidently no lack of quantity in these days.

The *Horn of Battle* was used by the ancient Caledonians to call their armies together. The *cornu* was blown by the Druids and their Christian successors, and St. Patrick is represented as carrying one. Ancient writers,

HARPER: ON A STONE AT MONIFEITH
From *Chalmers' Sculptured Stones of Scotland.*

indeed, lay particular stress on the musical ability of the Celtic priesthood, the members of which they describe as possessing extraordinary skill as harpers, taking prominent part with their instruments in religious ceremonies. The *cornu* in its rudest form was a cow's horn, and could sometimes be heard at a distance of six miles. The Irish Celts had various other instruments, but the harp was the favourite, both in Scotland and Ireland. The Hyperboreans,

who are believed to have been the aborigines of Britain,
were celebrated performers on the harp, accompanying their
hymns with its music ; and harpers were hereditary attendants on the Scottish kings and the Highland chiefs, from
whom they had certain lands and perquisites.   The cultivation of harp music reached the highest level in Scotland, the
players beating their masters, the Irish harpers, although
the class were more honoured in Ireland than in Scotland.
In Ireland none but a freeman was allowed to play the harp,
and it was reckoned a disgrace for a gentleman not to have
a harp and be able to play it.   The Royal household of
Scotland always had a harper, whose rank was much higher
than that of the ordinary servant, and the kings even were
not above playing.   James I. of Scotland, who died in 1437,
was a better player than any of the Scottish or Irish harpers.
In Scotland, however, the use of the harp ceased with the
pomp of the feudal system, while in Ireland the people retained for many generations an acknowledged superiority as
harpers.

It has been claimed for the harp that it is, or at least
was, the national instrument of Scotland.   It is admitted
that most of the Highland chiefs had harpers, as well as
bards, and that their music was esteemed as of no small
moment.   In several old Highland castles the harper's
seat is still pointed out, harps are mentioned in Ossian, but
not pipes ; there is a field in Mull called " The Harper's
Field," a window in Duntulm castle called " The Harper's
Window," it is a matter of history that Donald, Lord of the
Isles, was killed at Inverness by his own harper, after the
misfortunes which followed his incursion into Atholl ; and
there are many other references which prove the universal
use of the instrument.   But we have very few traces of

itinerant harpers in the Highlands resembling those of Ireland and Wales. In Wales it was the acknowledged national instrument. The pipes were known for some centuries, but the Britons never took kindly to them, a famous poet comparing their notes to

> "The shrill screech of a lame goose caught in corn,"

or a

> "Horrible, noisy, mad Irishman."

Weakness in the use of metaphor was evidently not a characteristic of Welsh poetry at this date. In Wales they "esteemed skill in playing on the harp beyond any kind of learning," but somehow the instrument never got the same hold on the national life of Scotland. If it had, it would not have been supplanted so easily as it was.

When the pipes actually superseded the harp in Scotland it is hardly possible to discover. We read that when Mary Queen of Scots made a hunting expedition into the wilds of Perthshire she carried a harp with her, and that that same harp is still in existence; that John Garve Mac Lean of Coll, who lived in the reign of James VI., was a good performer; and that once upon a time an English vessel was wrecked on the island and that the captain, seeing this venerable gentleman with his Bible in his hand and a harp by his side, exclaimed—"King David is restored to the earth"; and that the last of the harpers was Murdoch Mac Donald, harper to Mac Lean of Coll. Mac Donald received his learning from another celebrated harper, *Ruaraidh Dall*, or Blind Roderick, harper to the laird of Mac Leod, and afterwards in Ireland; and from accounts of payments made to him by Mac Lean, still extant, he seeems to have remained in the family till the year 1734, when he went to Quinish, in Mull, where he died in 1739.

This Murdoch Mac Donald was the musician who was immortalised by Tannahill as " The Harper of Mull." The story which inspired this song is quite romantic, and will bear repetition. The following abridgement is from Mr. P. A. Ramsay's edition of Tannahill's poems ;—

" In the island of Mull there lived a harper who was distinguished for his professional skill, and was attached to Rosie, the fairest flower in the island, and soon made her his bride. Not long afterwards he set out on a visit to some low-country friends, accompanied by his Rosie, and carrying his harp, which had been his companion in all his journeys for many years. Overtaken by the shades of night, in a solitary part of the country, a cold faintness fell upon Rosie, and she sank, almost lifeless, into the harper's arms. He hastily wrapped his plaid round her shivering frame, but to no purpose. Distracted, he hurried from place to place in search of fuel, to revive the dying embers of life. None could be found. His harp lay on the grass, its neglected strings vibrating to the blast. The harper loved it as his own life, but he loved his Rosie better than either. His nervous arm was applied to its sides, and ere long it lay crackling and blazing on the heath. Rosie soon revived under its genial influence, and resumed the journey when morning began to purple the east. Passing down the side of a hill, they were met by a hunter on horseback, who addressed Rosie in the style of an old and familiar friend. The harper, innocent himself, and unsuspicious of others, paced slowly along, leaving her in converse with the stranger. . Wondering at her delay, he turned round and beheld the faithless fair seated behind the hunter on his steed, which speedily bore them out of sight. The unhappy harper, transfixed with astonishment, gazed at them. Then, slowly turning his steps homewards, he, sighing, exclaimed—'Fool that I was to burn my harp for her !' "

It is said that Tannahill first heard this story at a convivial meeting, as an instance of the infidelity of the fair sex, whose fidelity he had been strenuously defending; notwithstanding that he himself was disappointed in the only love affair in which he was ever seriously engaged. The impression which the narrative made upon his mind led him to the composition of the song :—

> " When Rosie was faithfu' how happy was I !
> Still gladsome as simmer the time glided by ;
> I played my harp cheery while proudly I sang
> O' the charms o' my Rosie the winter nichts lang ;
> But now I'm as waefu' as waefu' can be,
> Come simmer, come winter, it's a' ane to me,
> For the dark gloom o' falsehood sae clouds my sad soul,
> That cheerless for aye is the Harper o' Mull.

> " I wander the glens and the wild woods alone,
> In their deepest recesses I make my sad moan ;
> My harp's mournfu' melody joins in the strain,
> While sadly I sing o' the days that are gane.
> Tho' Rosie is faithless she's no the less fair,
> And the thocht o' her beauty but feeds my despair,
> Wi' painfu' remembrance my bosom is full,
> An' weary o' life is the Harper o' Mull.

> " As slumbering I lay by the dark mountain stream,
> My lovely young Rosie appeared in my dream ;
> I thocht her still kind, and I ne'er was sae blest
> As in fancy I clasped the fair Nymph to my breast.
> Thou fause, fleeting vision, too soon thou were o'er,
> Thou wak'd'st me to tortures unequalled before,
> But death's silent slumbers my grief soon shall lull,
> An' the green grass wave o'er the Harper o' Mull."

The transition from the harp to the bagpipe was spread over about two centuries. In 1565 George Buchanan speaks of the Highlanders using both instruments, and during the seventeenth century the use of the harp declined

to such an extent that the number of professional harpers
was very small indeed. The civil wars largely accounted
for this, as the fitness of the bagpipe for the tumult of
battle gave it an easy superiority over the harp. Writing
at the beginning of the eighteenth century, Alexander
Macdonald, the Keppoch bard, said he preferred the pipes
to the harp, which he called *ceol nionag,* maidens' music.
When the bards thus openly avowed their liking for the
pipes, the transition period was over, for the harp was wont
to be their favourite instrument. The harp still exists as
the *clarsach,* which is being revived by Highland Associations, more especially in Glasgow, but, if the Irishism may
be permitted, the bagpipe is now " the harp of the Gael."

Besides supplanting the harp, the pipes also supplanted
the bards themselves. The bards were in their day a more
important body of men than the harpers, and naturally
much more relating to them has come down to posterity.
They existed from the remotest period of which there are
any records, and it was only in 1726 that, with the death of
Neil Mac Vuirich, the Clan Ranald bard, the race of distinctively clan bards became extinct. The race continued
to exist—bards exist to this day for that matter—but not
as clan bards, and after 1726 they were only public makers
of verse.

The bards, like the harpers, though to a greater extent,
wandered from house to house, keeping alive among the
people the memories of their wrongs, celebrating the valour
of their warriors, the beauty of their women, and the glory
of their chiefs. The calling was held in such high esteem
that after the fall of Druidism it was maintained at the
expense of the State. The bards, however, became so
numerous, overbearing, and extortionate that they lost

favour, many of them were killed by their enemies, and those left, shorn of their pride, but retaining their skill, occupied honourable positions in the retinues of their chiefs. In the heyday of their glory the bards summoned the clans to battle, and they moved about among the men inciting them to deeds of valour, their own persons being held as inviolable by friend and foe. The leaders looked to them to inspire the warriors, just as at the present day pipers are expected to supply enthusiasm to the regiment when on the eve of battle. The bard exhorted the clans to emulate the glory of their forefathers, to hold their lives cheap in the defence of their country, and his appeals, delivered with considerable elocutionary power and earnestness, always produced a profound effect. When the pipes began to be used, they took the place of the bard when the din of battle drowned his voice. and after the battle was over the bard celebrated the praises of the brave who had fallen and the valour of the survivors, while the piper played plaintive laments for the slain. The bards themselves did not always fight—they thought they were of more value as bards than as fighters. At the battle of Inverlochy, *Ian Lom*, the Lochaber bard, and the most celebrated of the race, was asked to share in the fighting, but declined. "If I go along with thee to-day, Sir Alasdair," said he, "and fall in battle, who will sing thy victory to-morrow?" "Thou art in the right, John," said his chief, "Let the shoemaker stick to his last." *Ian Lom*, however, is acknowledged to have been a brave man, and his attitude on this occasion is not considered a reflection on his character.

The bard, especially if he were also a musician, was always in great request at social functions, and in the absence of books he constituted the local library. The class

B

had naturally exceptional memories, and they became walking chroniclers of past events and preservers of popular
poetry and everyday history. They did not welcome the
pipes with any degree of enthusiasm. Instead, some of
them used all their arts to throw ridicule on the newer instrument. *Ian Mac Codrum*, the North Uist bard (1710-
1796), composed a satire on the bagpipe of one, *Domhnull
Bhan*, or Fair-haired Donald, which is exceedingly humorous
and sarcastic, and in the course of which he says :—

> " It withered with yelping
> The seven Fenian battalions,"

whatever they were. Then, he continued, the Gael loved
the pipes as Edinburgh people loved tea, although the
pipes had weakened for the first time

> " The strength of Diarmaid and of Goll."

The last bard known to have acted officially in battle
was Mac Mhuirich, or Mac Vuirich, the Clan Ranald
bard of the day, who recited at the battle of Harlaw,
in 1411. Mac Mhuirich was disgusted at the growing
popularity of the pipes, and composed a set of verses
descriptive of the bagpipe and its lineage, which are
more graphic, humorous and forcible than elegant or
gentlemanly. Duncan Ban Mac Intyre, the bard of
Glenorchy, has a poem on " Hugh the Piper," who,
it seems, had insulted the bard in some way. Hugh is
compared to a wicked dog barking at the passers-by,
and intent on biting their heels. He is to be hurled
out of the society of bards and pipers as a fruitless bough is
cut away from a flourishing tree, it is hinted that if he
would quit the country it would be a good riddance, he is

made the impersonation of all sorts of defects, and his musical efforts are compared to the cries of ducks, geese, and pigs. It should be added, however, that the same bard composed *Ben Dorain*, the most famous of his poems, to a pipe tune, dividing it into eight parts corresponding to the variations of the pibroch, and moulding the language into all the variations of the wild rhythm, so his spite must have been more at Hugh himself than at his music.

The antipathy of the bards to the pipes is easily understood. They had all along been the acknowledged inspired leaders of the people, inciting the clans to battle with their wild verses. The pipes with all their war spirit could hardly match this, which is culled from a battle song supposed to have been written on the eve of the invasion of England that terminated so tragically at Flodden :—

> " Burn their women, lean and ugly !
> Burn their children great and small !
> In the hut and in the palace,
> Prince and peasant, burn them all !
> Plunge them in the swelling rivers,
> With their gear and with their goods ;
> Spare, while breath remains, no Saxon,
> Drown them in the roaring floods. "

Neil Mac Mhuirich, the bard already mentioned, had been at a bards' college in Ireland, and brought back to his father's house not only stores of knowledge, but also the small-pox. Afflicted with the disease, he lay on a bed near the fire, where John and Donald Mac Arthur, two of the famous race of pipers, came in, and sitting down in front of his bed, began tuning their pipes. The discordant sounds raised the bard, and he, bursting with indignation, started railing at the pipes in a poetical and mock genealogy of the instrument. The poem itself is presentable in Gaelic, but in English it would be too much for the average reader. It emphasises strongly the bard's aversion to the pipes, comparing them and their music to many ridiculous things in nature and art. The pipers, who had intended to make the house their quarters for the night, were startled by the fierce invective coming from behind them, and on looking round and seeing the swollen and marked face of Neil, worked up into extraordinary excitement, terror took hold of them and they fled in consternation. The bard's father evidently sympathised with his son, for he waited patiently until the poem was ended, and then exclaimed " Well done, my son, your errand to Ireland has not been in vain."

When the pipes became paramount is about as difficult to determine as when they first threatened the position of the harp. They seem to have existed alongside the harp and the coronach and the fiery cross for a considerable time, as we have references to all these in the literature of the sixteenth and seventeenth and eighteenth centuries. John Mac Leod of Dunvegan, who lived about 1650, had a bard, a harper, a piper, and a fool, all of whom were most liberally provided for. We have got a blind harper, *Ruaraidh Dall,* harper to Mac Leod of Glenelg, and a blind piper, *Ian Dall,* piper to Mac Kenzie of Gairloch, each of whom excelled in his own sphere, and both of whom flourished about 1650, while, as we have seen, the bards and the pipers were often at loggerheads. The pibroch did not supersede the fiery cross at all, for, so long as the chiefs found it necessary to call the clans together, the goat was killed with the chief's own sword, the cross was dipped in the blood, and the clansman sent round.

The last battle at which a bard recited was fought in 1411, the last clan bard died in 1726, the last clan harper in 1739, when the hereditary pipers were in all their glory; the fiery cross was last used in 1745, when it travelled thirty-six miles through Breadalbane in three hours, and the coronach was superseded gradually by the lament of the pipes. The bards ceased to live as an order on the accession of the Kings of Scotland to the British throne, and there were no means provided at the Reformation for educating ministers or teachers for the Gaelic speaking part of the country. But all through the centuries covered by the dates given there were pipers. There are pipers still, not indeed clan pipers, but the class are recognised as peculiarly belonging to the Highlands, while harpers and bards have gone completely under in the great social revolution through which the Highlands have passed.

CHAPTER III.

THE TALE OF THE YEARS.

"No stroke of art their texture bears,
    No cadence wrought with learned skill,
And though long worn by rolling years,
    Yet unimpaired they please us still ;
While thousand strains of mystic lore
    Have perished and are heard no more."

The time of the Flood—Pipes in Scripture—In Persia—In Arabia—
In Tarsus—Tradition of the Nativity—In Rome—In Greece—
In Wales, Ireland, and Scotland—Melrose Abbey—In France—
In England—At Bannockburn—Chaucer—In war—First auth-
entic Scottish reference—Oldest authentic specimen—Became
general—Rosslyn Chapel—Second drone added—At Flodden—
"A maske of bagpypes"—Spenser—Shakespeare—James VI.—
A poetical historian—Big drone added—The '45—Native to
Scotland—The evolution of the Highlands.

*G*illidh *Callum* was (so goes the story) Noah's piper, and
(still according to the story) Noah danced to his
music over two crossed vine plants when he had
discovered and enjoyed the inspiring effects of his first
distillation from the fruits of his newly planted vineyard.
So the tune was named after the piper. This "yarn," to
give it the only appropriate name, can easily be spoiled by
anyone who tries, but the dance alluded to does seem to

have been originally practised over vine plants. Swords, however, came to be more numerous in Scotland than vines, and they were substituted. Some historians assert that the Celts are descended from Gomer, the eldest son of Japheth, son of Noah, a theory which would go far to support the *Gillidh Callum* story, for if there were Celts in the days of the ark, why should there not have been a piper? There is, however, just about as much to prove either story as there is to prove that

"Music first on earth was found
In Gaelic accents deep ;
When Jubal in his oxter squeezed
The blether o' a sheep,"

and that is little enough.

That the bagpipe is an instrument of great antiquity is an admitted fact, but whether it is one of those referred to in Scripture is another matter. The pipe without the bag is mentioned in I. Sam. x. 5, Isaiah v. 12, and Jer. xlviii. 36, but the pipe without the bag is not the bagpipe. There have been many attempts made to identify the instrument with one or other of those named in Scripture, and in histories of Scripture times, but these are all based on conjecture. An instrument is mentioned which was composed of two reeds perforated according to rule, and united to a leathern bag, called in Persian *nie amban*; and in Egypt a similar instrument is described as consisting of two flutes, partly of wood and partly of iron. Another traveller tells of an Arabian instrument which consisted of a double chanter with several apertures, and in 1818 ancient engravings were found in the northern states of Africa which seemed to prove that an instrument like the bagpipe had existed in Scripture times. The Chaldeans and Babylonians had two peculiar instruments, the *Sambuka* and the *Symphonia*, and some historians identify the latter as the *sackbut*, the alleged ancestor of the bagpipe. Others assert that a form of the bagpipe was used in the services of the Temple at Jerusalem, but this in any case, may be treated as the merest of conjecture.

The historical references to the instrument as having existed at all in these days are few and far between :—

385 B.C.—Theocritus, a writer who flourished about this date, mentions it incidentally in his pastorals, but not in such a way as to give any indication of what form it assumed.

200 B.C.—An ancient terra cotta excavated at Tarsus by Mr. W. Burchhardt, and supposed to date from 200 B.C., represents a piper with a wind instrument with vertical rows of reed pipes, firmly attached to him. The instrument has also been found sculptured in ancient Nineveh.

A.D. 1.—There is a singular tradition in the Roman Catholic Church to the effect that the shepherds who first saw the infant Messiah in the stable expressed their gladness by playing on the bagpipe. This is, of course, possible, but there is only the tradition and the likelihood that the shepherds would have musical instruments of some kind to support the theory. Albrecht Durer, a famous German artist of the 16th century, has perpetuated the idea in a woodcut of the Nativity, in which he represents one of the shepherds playing on the pipes, but his work is, naturally, founded on the tradition. The illuminator of a Dutch missal in the library of King's College, Aberdeen, has taken liberties with the tradition and given the bagpipe to one of the appearing angels, who uses it for playing a salute.

A.D. 54.—The cruel Emperor Nero was an accomplished musician, and a contorniate of his time has given rise to many assertions connecting him with the pipes. It is generally referred to as a coin, but it is in reality a contorniate or medal, which was given away at public sports. The sketch here reproduced (full-size) is from a specimen in the British Museum, and very little study will show that it

REPRODUCED FROM A CONTORNIATE IN THE BRITISH MUSEUM.

proves almost nothing relating to the bagpipe. The obverse bears the head of Nero and the usual inscription. On the reverse there seems to be the form of a wind organ with nine irregular pipes, all blown by a bellows and having underneath what is probably a bag. It is more closely related to the organ than to the bagpipe, and, as has been said, it proves nothing. Some writers call the instrument on which Nero played a flute with a bladder under the performer's arm, a description which does more to identify it as the bagpipe. It cannot have been considered a very honourable thing in Nero's day to play the pipes, for the emperor on hearing of the last revolt, that which cost him his throne and his life, vowed solemnly that if the gods would but extricate him from his troubles he would play in public on the bagpipe, as a sort of penance or thank offering probably. Perhaps history has made a mistake, and it may have been the pipes and not the fiddle Nero played on while Rome was burning. The medal, it may be added, is believed by the authorities at the British Museum to date from about A.D. 330, although it bears the impress of Nero.

That the instrument was in use among the Romans is indisputable. A historian, who wrote a history of the wars of the Persians, the Vandals, and the Goths, states that the Roman infantry used it for marching purposes, and he describes it as having both skin and wood extremely fine. The name it went by was *pythaula*, a word of Greek origin. which bears a striking resemblance to the Celtic *piob-mhala*, pronounced *piovala*. There is in Rome a fine Greek sculpture in *basso relievo* representing a piper playing on an instrument closely resembling the Highland bagpipe, the performer himself being dressed not unlike a modern Highlander. It is shown besides on several coins, but from the rudeness of the drawings or their decay the exact form cannot be ascertained. A small bronze figure found under Richborough Castle, Kent, represents a Roman soldier playing on the bagpipe, but his whole equipment is curious. The precise form of the instrument itself is questionable, and the manner of holding it, the helmet, the ancient purse on one side and the short Roman sword and dagger on the other, all furnish matter for debate. About 1870 a stone was dug from the ground near Bo'ness, on which was sculptured a party of Roman soldiers on the march. They were dressed in short kilts, and one was playing the bagpipe. The instrument was very similar to those of the present day except that the drones were shorter.

A.D. 100.—Aristides Quintilianus, who lived about this time, writes to the effect that the bagpipe was known in the Scottish Highlands in his day. This, however, may be set aside as a reference of no value seeing that the Highlands was then an unknown world to the Greeks. The Greeks of the same age knew the instrument as *Tibia utricularis*, and from the pipes, we are told, the Athenian shepherds drew the sweetest sounds. Other books again tell us that the Athenians rejected the pipes because they disturbed conversation and made hearing difficult. Still others —English be it noted—contain the sentence, "Arcadia in Greece : the bagpipe was first invented here," but the statement is not substantiated in any way.

A.D. 500.—In the sixth century the bagpipe is mentioned by Procopius, a Greek historian, as the instrument of the Roman infantry, the trumpet being that of the cavalry.

A.D. 800.—There is a picture of a primitive instrument copied from a manuscript of the ninth century. It consists of a blow pipe on one side of a small bag, with a sort of chanter having three or four holes and a beast's head instead of the usual bell-shaped end. The instrument was held extended from the mouth, and the bag, if any pressure was necessary, must have been elastic, as it could not be pressed in any way.

A.D. 1118.—Giraldus Cambrensis, the historian, mentions the pipes about this date as Welsh and Irish, but not as Scottish. But *The Complaynt of Scotland*, written in 1548, states that the instrument was a favourite with the Scottish peasantry " from the earliest periods." Another trustworthy record says it was in use in Scotland and Wales about the end of the twelfth century. Besides, Pennant in his *Tour* was told that it was mentioned in the oldest northern songs as the "soeck-pipe." There is little doubt it was cultivated to some extent in Scotland in the twelfth century.

A.D. 1136.—There are. or at least were, in Melrose Abbey, built in 1136, two carvings representing bagpipes, but they are not supposed to be of a date so early as the abbey itself. The first, that of an aged musician, is given in Sir John Graham Dalziel's *Musical Memoirs of Scotland,* published in 1849, but it cannot now he found in the abbey. If it existed when the book was written, it has succumbed since then to the action of the elements or the vandalism of the ignorant. The second, sketched on the spot, is one of those grotesque carvings which artists of early days, in what must have been a sarcastic humour, delighted in affixing to sacred buildings. It is a gargoyle in the form of a pig carrying a rude bagpipe under its head with the drone, the only pipe now remaining, on its left shoulder, and its fore feet, what is left of them, clasped around the bag. The mouth is open and the rain water off the roof runs through it. There is a tradition that as James IV. was not agreeing very well with the Highlanders the pig playing their favourite instrument was placed in the abbey as a satire. The chapel, however, on the outside of the nave of which the carving is, was built before the time of James IV. It is curious that all, or nearly all, the carvings on the outside of the abbey are ugly, some of them gruesome, while the figures on the inside are beautiful. This, it is supposed, was meant to convey the idea of Heaven inside and earth outside. In the architecture of the middle ages the gargoyle, or waterspout, assumed a vast variety of forms, often frightful, fantastic or grotesque. So the carving in Melrose Abbey may be simply the product of the artist's imagination. Besides, a French architect had a good deal to do

CARVINGS IN MELROSE ABBEY

with the abbey, so the designs may not all be emblematic of Scottish life of the date when they were made. In *Musical Memoirs of Scotland* it is stated that the instrument had two drones, one on each side of the animal's head, and a chanter which hung beneath its feet, these latter being placed on the apertures. The figure seems to have been very much worn away since this book was written.

A.D. 1200.—Coming down to ages of which we have better historical records, we find a drawing of the thirteenth century which shows a girl dancing on the shoulders of a jester to the music of the instrument in its simplest form, the chanter only.

A.D. 1300.—About the end of the thirteenth century the bagpipe in France was consigned to the lower orders, and only used by the blind and the wandering or mendicant classes. Polite society, however, resumed it in the time of Louis XIV. and Louis XV.

A.D. 1307.—Several payments to performers of the fourteenth and subsequent centuries are recorded. In the reign of Edward II. there is a payment to *Jauno Chevretter* (the latter word meant bagpiper) for playing before the king.

A.D. 1314.—The Clan Menzies are alleged to have had their pipes with them at Bannockburn, and they are supposed to have been played by one of the Mac Intyres, their hereditary pipers. The Clan Menzies claim that these pipes are still in existence, at least three portions of them—the chanter, which has the same number of finger holes as the modern chanter, but two additional holes on each side; the blowpipe, which is square, but graduates to round at the top; and the drone, of which the top half only remains. These relics, which are now preserved with great care, are supposed to be the remains of a set which were played to. the clan when they mustered at Castle Menzies, and marched to join the main body of the Scottish army at Torwood, and in front of them on the field of battle. There are said to be Mac Donald pipes in existence, which consist of a chanter and blowpipe only, and which, it is alleged, were played before the Mac Donalds at Bannockburn. This, most likely, also refers to the Menzies pipes, as the Mac Intyres, who are credited with having been owners of each, were at different times pipers to the Menzies and to the Clan Ranald branch of the Mac Donalds. Bruce's son, says another tradition, had pipes at Bannockburn. Sir Walter Scott represents the men of the Isles as charging to the sound of the bagpipe; and David Mac Donald, a Clan Mac Donald bard, who wrote about 1838, in a poem on the battle, says that when the bards began to encourage the clans, the pipers began to blow their pipes. There is, however, no historical proof that the instrument was used at the battle. Though horns and trumpets are mentioned by reliable historians, it is not till about two hundred years later that the bagpipe is referred to as having superseded the trumpet as an instrument of war.

A.D. 1327.—In the reign of Edward III. two pipers received permission to visit schools for minstrels beyond the seas, and from about that time till the sixteenth century the bagpipe was the favourite instrument of the Irish kerns.

A.D. 1362.—There is an entry in the Exchequer rolls of 1362 of forty shillings "paid to the King's pipers," which indicates the use of the pipes at that date.

A.D. 1370.—The arms of Winchester School, founded in 1370, show an angel playing a bagpipe, and a silver-mounted crosier, presented by the founder to the New College, Oxford, has among other figures that of an angel playing the bagpipe. Some enthusiast might surely have adduced the frequent connections of the instrument with angels as proof of its sacred origin.

A.D. 1377.—One "claryoner," two trumpeters, and four pipers were attached to the fleet of Richard, Earl of Arundel (Richard II). The bagpipe often appears in the English sculpture of the fourteenth and fifteenth centuries, and, of course, very frequently later.

A.D. 1380.—There are no English literary references to the pipes till the time of Chaucer, when the poet makes the miller in the *Canterbury Tales* play on the instrument:—

> " A baggepipe wel cowde he blowe and sowne,
>   And therewithal he broughte us out of towne."

So it seems that the company of pilgrims left London, accompanied by the strains of the bagpipe. It must have been in fairly general use, else the poet would not have worked it into his composition, but there are no means of discovering how long before this it had been in favour in England.

A.D. 1390.—At the battle between the clans Quhale and Chattan on the North Inch of Perth, Rev. James Mac Kenzie tells us in his *History of Scotland*, which is generally accepted as authoritative, the clans "stalked into the barriers to the sound of their own great war pipes."

A.D. 1400.—The bagpipe is supposed to have been first used officially in war in Britain at the beginning of the fifteenth century, quickly superseding the war-song of the bards.

A.D. 1406-37.—James I. of Scotland played on the "chorus," a word which some interpret as meaning the bagpipe. Besides we are also told that he played on " the tabour, the bagpipes, the organ, the flute, the harp, the trumpet, and the shepherd's reed." He must have been a versatile monarch. If he really wrote *Peblis to the Play*, the fact proves that if he did not play the pipes he was quite familiar with their existence, for he says :—

> " With that Will Swane came smeitand out,
>   Ane meikle miller man,
> Gif I sall dance have done, lat se
>   Blow up the bagpype than."

And also in another place :—

> " The bag pipe blew and they outhrew
>   Out of the townis untald."

Except that he gives us the first really authentic historical Scottish reference to the pipes, King James and his connection with the music is rather a puzzling subject.

A.D. 1409.—What is believed to be the oldest authentic specimen of the bagpipe now existing is that in the possession of Messrs. J. & R. Glen, of Edinburgh, which bears the date 1409. Except ·that it wants the large drone, which was added at the beginning of the eighteenth century, it is very much the Highland pipe of the present day. The following is a description of the instrument :—

" Highland bagpipe, having two small drones and chanter, finely ornamented with Celtic patterns carved in circular bands. The drones are inserted in a stock apparently formed from a forked branch, the fork giving the drones their proper spread for the shoulder. In the centre of the stock are the letters ' R. McD,' below them a galley, and below the galley is the date in Roman numerals, M:CCCC:IX. The letters both in the initials above the galley and in the numeral inscription are of the Gothic form commonly used in the fifteenth century. On the reverse of the stock is a triplet of foliageous scroll work. Bands of interlaced work en-

C

circle the ends of the forked part, which are bound with brass ferrules. The lower joint of one of the drones is ornamented with a
band of interlaced work in the centre. The corresponding joint of
the other drone is not original. The upper joints of the drones are
ornamented at both extremities with interlaced work and the finger
holes, seven in number, are greatly worn. The nail heads placed
round the lower part of the bell of the chanter are decorated with
engraved ornament. The bag and blowpipe are modern."

It should be added that very little is known of the story
of this old bagpipe, and the date carved on the stock is all
that justifies us in attributing it to the fifteenth century.
Also that its claims to antiquity are disputed by an instrument in the possession of the Duke of Sutherland, which is
said to have been played at the battle of Sheriffmuir.

A.D. 1411.—We have the statement of Rev. James Mac
Kenzie that at the Battle of Harlaw the Highland host
came down "with pibrochs deafening to hear." Mr. Mac
Kenzie, however, wrote at quite a recent date, and it would
be interesting to know his authority. We do know, of
course, that what is now a pipe tune was played at Harlaw,
but that in itself proves nothing, since the earliest known
copy of the music is not arranged for the pipes.

A.D. 1419.—An inventory of the instruments in St. James's
Palace, made in 1419, specifies "four bagpipes with pipes of
ivorie," and another "baggepipe with pipes of ivorie, the
bagge covered with purple vellat."

A.D. 1430.—From this time on till the Reformation the
bagpipe was fairly popular in the Lowlands of Scotland, and
it is most likely that its use became general in the Highlands about 1500.

A.D. 1431.—At the battle of Inverlochy in 1431, we are
told the pipes were played. This may have been supposed

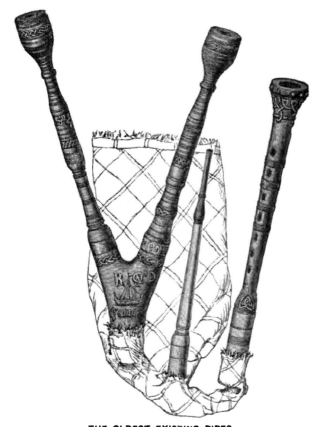

THE OLDEST EXISTING PIPES

(By permission of Messrs. J. & R. Glen and the Scottish Society of Antiquaries.)

from the fact that we have a pipe tune of that date, but it is probable enough.

A.D. 1440.—In Rosslyn Chapel, Midlothian, built in 1440, there are two figures represented as playing the pipes. The first, an angelic piper, is of a class of which specimens are to be found in various sacred edifices throughout England. It is in the Lady Chapel, and is not therefore much noticed by visitors. The other figure is one of a pair which are carved as if they were supporting one end of one of the arches of the roof. What meaning they were supposed to convey it is impossible now to determine, but the representation of the piper is obvious enough.

A.D. 1485-1509.—In Henry VII.'s Chapel at Westminster there is a grotesque carving representing a bagpipe. Similar carvings appear at Hull, Great Yarmouth, Beverley, and Boston.

A.D. 1489.—In July, 1489, we find there was a payment of £8 8s. to " Inglis pyparis that com to the Castel (Edinburgh) and playit to the king ; " and in 1505 another to " Inglis pipar with the drone." So the instrument must have been as much English as Scottish at that time.

A.D. 1491.—Here again we find the " Inglis " piper to the front. In August of this year a party of them received seven unicorns, that is gold coins, at Linlithgow for playing to the king. Both of these payments are recorded in the accounts of the treasurer of the Royal household.

A.D. 1494.—In the ninth year of Henry VII. there was paid to " Pudsey, piper on the bagpipes," 6s. 8d. Piping was not a short cut to fortune then more than it is now.

A.D. 1500.—At a sale of curios in London in the summer of 1899 a jug was disposed of on which there was a painting of a mule playing a bagpipe. The article fetched £200, but

ANGELIC
BAGPIPER
A.D. 1400-1500

BAGPIPER,
1400-1500

CARVINGS IN ROSSLYN CHAPEL

it cannot be proved that the painting dates from the sixteenth century, though that is the certified date of the jug.
About this time the second drone was added.

A.D. 1506-1582.—George Buchanan is the first to mention
the bagpipe in connection with Gaelic-speaking people, and
when he does mention it, it is solely as a military instrument. The harp was still the domestic musical instrument.

A.D. 1509-1547.—We have a curious set of wood-cuts of
the time of Henry VIII., one of which represents a piper
dancing to the *Dance of Death* clothed according to the
fashion of that time. He is dancing with a jester, who has
the tonsure of a monk and wears a sort of kilt.* We also
know of a suit of armour made for Henry VIII. on which
the figure of a piper is engraved.

A.D. 1513.—It is on record that John Hastie, the celebrated hereditary piper of Jedburgh, played at the battle of
Flodden. There is a painting of this date by the German
artist, Albrecht Durer, which represents a shepherd boy
playing to his sheep on the bagpipe, and another which
shows a piper leaning against a tree with a naked dirk at
the left side and a purse exactly like a sporran suspended in
front. Olaus Magnus, a Swedish prelate of the same century, affirms that a double pipe, probably the bagpipe, was
carried by the shepherds to the pastures that their flocks
might feed better.

A.D. 1529.—At a procession in Brussels in 1529 in honour
of the Virgin Mary, " many wild beasts danced round a cage
containing two apes playing on the bagpipes." This statement may be taken for what it is worth. It is difficult to
construct a theory that will explain it.

---

* See Chap. XV.

A.D. 1536.—In this year the bagpipe was played at church service in Edinburgh.

A.D. 1547-1553.—Among the musicians of Edward VI. at the Court of England was " Richard Woodward, bagpiper,"

GERMAN PIPER OF THE SIXTEENTH CENTURY
From the Painting by Albrecht Dürer.

who had a salary of £12 13s. 4d., not a princely sum. An entertainment was got up at court in this reign, part of which was a " maske of bagpypes." An artist " covered six apes of paste and cement with grey coney skinnes, which were made to serve for a maske of bagpypes, to sit upon the top of them like mynstrells as though they did play." The English of these ancient writers is often a bit obscure, but this seems to mean that there was an imitation of bagpipe playing by counterfeit apes. The Brussels incident of 1529 may probably be explained in the same way.

A.D. 1548.—Among the eight musical instruments mentioned in *The Complaynt of Scotland*, written in 1548, there are included " ane drone bagpipe " and " ane pipe made of ane bleddir and of ane reid." *

A.D. 1549.—A French officer describing warfare near Edinburgh in 1549, says " The wild Scots encouraged themselves to arms by the sounds of their bagpipes."

A.D. 1556.—In 1556 the Queen Regent of Scotland headed a procession in honour of St. Giles, the patron saint of Edinburgh, and she was " accompanied by bagpipers and other musicians."

A.D. 1570.—In 1570 three St. Andrews pipers were admonished not to play on Sundays or at nights.

A.D. 1579.—We next come across Spenser and Shakespeare. In the *Shepherd's Calendar*, Spenser makes a shepherd ask a down-hearted comrade :—

" Or is thy bagpipe broke that sounds so sweet ? "

And Shakespeare, whose genius touched on everything above the earth and under it, but who does not seem to have had a high opinion of the " sweetness " of the bagpipe, says of a character that he is as melancholy as a glib cat, or a lugged bear, or an old lion, or a lover's lute, or the drone of a Lincolnshire bagpipe. In another place he speaks of men

---

* See page 18.

who "laugh, like parrots at a bagpiper," and in yet another he infers that the instrument was more powerful than others then in use. " You would never," he says, " dance again after a tabor or pipe ; no, the bagpipe could not move you." He seems, however, to have known the utility even of his English pipes for marching purposes, for he concludes *Much ado about Nothing* with " Strike up, Pipers." This phrase, by the way, must surely have been taken from the play, for it is always held as referring more to the bagpipe than to any other instrument. Generally speaking, Shakespeare's references are more in the way of sarcasm than of praise.

A.D. 1581.—In 1581 we find James VI. returning from church at Dalkeith one Sunday with two pipers playing before him ; and, strangely enough, a little nearer the end of the century, we read, two pipers were prosecuted for playing on the Sunday. At various times between 1591 and 1596 pipers from the Water of Leith bound themselves strictly not to play on the Sundays. There was evidently one law for the king and another for the subject.

A.D. 1584.—A poetical historian describing a battle between the English and the Irish in 1584 says :—

> " Now goe the foes to wracke,
> The Karne apace do sweate,
> And bagg pipe then instead of trompe
> Doe lulle the backe retreate.

> " Who hears the bagpipe now ?
> The pastyme is so hotte,
> Our valiant captains will not cease
> Till that the field be gotte.

" But still thei forward pearse,
    Upon the glibbed route,
    And with thar weapons meete for warre,
    These vaunting foes they cloute."

Then, when the battle was over, the piper having been
killed :—

" The bagpipe cease to plaie,
    The piper lyes on grounde ;
    And here a sort of glibbed theeves
    Devoid of life are found."

It is difficult to see how an instrument like the present
Irish bagpipe could be of any use in war; but in 1601 a
traveller, visiting the same country, confirms the statement
that it belonged to the military.

In 1584 a man named Cockran " played on his bagpipe
in a dramatic performance in Coventry." An Irish bagpipe
has been seen in London theatres on various occasions, and,
of course, often enough in Scottish concert rooms. In 1798
a Mr. Courtney " played a solo on the union pipes in the
quick movement of the overture with good effect " in a performance founded on Ossian's poems.

A.D. 1594.—At the Battle of Balrinnes, a witch who
accompanied the Earl of Argyll referred in a prediction to
the bagpipe as the principal military instrument of the
Scottish mountaineers.

A.D. 1597.—In a court case at Stirling in 1597 we are
told that " W. Stewart brought into the kirkyard twa or
three pyperis, and thereby drew in grit nowmer of people to
dans befoir the kirk dur on tyme of prayeris, he being
always the ringleader himself." Mr. Stewart must have had
peculiar ideas of the fitness of things.

A.D. 1598.—An unpublished poem by Rev. Alex. Hume, minister of Logie, about 1598, contains the lines:—

> " Caus michtilie the warlie nottes brake
> On Heiland pipes, Scottes and Hyberniche."

So at this date there was a difference between the Highland pipes, the Lowland, and the Hibernian. The instrument was, in fact, becoming recognised as peculiar to the Highlands, in the one specific form at least.

A.D. 1601.—In 1601 Moryson, the traveller, visiting Ireland during a rebellion, says that " near Armagh a strong body of insurgents approached the camp of regulars with cries and sounds of drummers and bagpipes as if they would storm the camp. After that our men had given them a volley in their teeth, they drew away, and we heard no more of their drummers and bagpipes, but only mournful cries, for many of their best men were slain."

A.D. 1617.—When James I. came to Scotland in 1617 and decorated Holyrood with images of many kinds, he did not clear out the bagpipes from the Palace, jokingly remarking that as they had some relation to the organ they might remain.

A.D. 1623.—Playing on the " great pipe " was a charge made against a piper at Perth in 1623. The term great pipe would seem to indicate that the instrument was evolved from a previous kind, and is an argument in favour of the theory that the pipes were not " introduced " into Scotland, but are of native origin, and have been gradually developed up to their present condition.

A.D. 1650.—" Almost every town hath bagpipes in it," says a writer of the year 1650.

A.D. 1653.—In 1653 a woman pleaded for exemption from

censure because " English soldiers brought over a piper with them and did dance in her house." That, she thought, was sufficient excuse for any shortcomings in the management of her household.

A.D. 1662.—A Kirkcaldy man, who shot his father in 1662, sought liquor from an acquaintance to help to wile away his melancholy, and " there comes a piper, and this wretched man went and did dawnce." The music evidently was enough to dispel all the terrors of the law.

A.D. 1700.—About the beginning of the nineteenth century the big drone was added to the bagpipe, distinguishing it henceforth from the Lowland and Northumbrian.

A.D. 1741.—On a political occasion in 1741 the Magistrates of Dingwall were welcomed home by the ringing of bells, " while young and old danced to the bagpipe, violin, and Jewish harp." Rather a curious medley they would make. .

A.D. 1745.—Prince Charlie had a large number of pipers with him in his rebellion of 1745. After the battle of Prestonpans his army marched into Edinburgh, a hundred pipers playing the Jacobite air, " The King shall enjoy his ain again: " and when he marched to Carlisle he had with him a hundred pipers. Perhaps it was because of its prominence in his rebellion that the bagpipe was afterwards classed by the ruling powers as an instrument of warfare, the carrying of which deserved punishment.

A.D. 1775.—In this year we find the first reference to a professional maker of bagpipes. In the *Edinburgh Directory* for 1775, a book that could be carried in the vest pocket, " Hugh Robertson " is entered as " pipe maker, Castle Hill, Edinburgh." It was this same Hugh Robertson who made the prize pipes competed for at the meetings inaugurated by the Highland Society of London some time later, and an instrument of his make which took first prize at one of the competitions was recently in the possession of Mr. David Glen, Edinburgh. Where it now is cannot be discovered, as Mr. Glen parted with it to one of whose whereabouts he is not aware.

It is not necessary to trace the instrument farther down through the years. In Scotland, after it overcame the setback of the '45, it became more popular year by year until at last in 1824, we find an English traveller saying that " the Scots are enthusiastic in their love for their national instrument. In Edinburgh the sound of the bagpipe is to be heard in every street." The Lowland, the Northumberland and the Irish pipes lost favour, and the Lincolnshire—that referred to by Shakespeare—has been totally extinct since about 1850. The Great Highland Bagpipe is the only form that has held its own.

The early history of the Celts affords abundant room for controversy, and the origin of the pipes, their introduction into, or evolution in, the Highlands, will always be debateable matter. The weight of evidence, however, goes to show that the pipes and pipe music are far more likely to have been evolved out of the life of the Highland people than imported from any other country. The fact that the instrument is not mentioned in early Scottish history is no proof that it did not exist. Besides, we have now got away from the habit of trying to find the origin of things peculiarly Scottish outside of Scotland. It used to be the fashion to decry everything local to Scotland, and our clans, even, traced their origin to Norman and Norwegian sources. That time, however, is past, and now Highlanders pride themselves on an ancestry which, however far back it is

traced, is still Scottish. So with the pipes. They have
been in Scotland from all time, and it is in Scotland that
they have been brought to the highest degree of perfection.
The importation theory will not stand the test of inquiry.
If the pipes came from Norway, or Rome, or any part of the
Continent, or even England, how is it that in these places
they have deteriorated almost to the point of disappearance, while in Scotland they have been continually develop-
ing? Ireland, indeed, can put forward a good claim—
Christianity came from there, the peoples are the same,
and the relations between the two countries in early days
were very close—but there is less to uphold the claim than
there is to show that the pipes are native to the Highlands.
They are not mentioned in Ossianic poetry. In these times,
however, the pipes would be so subordinate to the harp that
their passing-by by the poet is a fact of little significance.
If the Celts were the original inhabitants of the Highlands,
and can be identified with the Picts—a theory for which
there is very strong argument indeed—there is surely nothing
more likely than that the pipes were always in existence
among the people. Robertson, in his *Historical Proofs of
the Highlanders*, shows clearly that there has never been a
radical change of race or customs in the Highlands, that the
music of the Great Highland Bagpipe has ever been peculiar
to the Gael of Alban, and that the Irish Scots must have
learned it from the Caledonian Picts. It is strong presumptive evidence in favour of his contention that in no other
country has the instrument been developed in the same way,
that it is one of the very few national musical instruments
in Europe, and that in no other country is there such a
quantity of peculiar music of such an age, composed solely
for the instrument, and fitted only for interpretation by it.

There is nothing in the music that connects it with any part of the Continent, or that shows that it was borrowed from any particular place. The pibroch cannot possibly have come from the Tyrol or Italy, neither can the reels and other popular melodies. The importation theory grew out of the ideas entertained of the rude and uncivilised state of Scotland at an early period, which was considered altogether incompatible with the delicacy of taste and feeling its poetry and music displayed. But the student of Highland history soon discovers that, with all the rudeness, there existed among the people just that delicacy of taste and feeling which found expression in the music, and he at once concludes that the music is a real growth of the home soil. The race were always in the land : why not their language, their music, their customs, in a more or less rude form ?

Passing from debateable ground, the result of our assorting of quotations seems to be that the first thoroughly authentic reference to the bagpipe in Scotland dates from 1406, that it was well known in Reformation times, that the second drone was added about 1500, that it was first mentioned in connection with the Gaelic in 1506, or a few years later, that it was classed in a list of Scottish musical instruments in 1548, that in 1549 and often afterwards it .was used in war, that in 1650 every town had a piper, that in 1700 the big drone was added, and that in 1824 the Scots were enthusiastic about the pipes. There is not the slightest doubt, of course, that the instrument was used in Scotland for many years, probably for centuries, before we can trace it, but previous to the dates given we have only tradition and conjecture to go by.

From 1700 till 1750 was perhaps the most critical time in the story of the Great Highland Bagpipe. The disaster at Culloden nearly spelt ruin for the pipes as well as for the tartan. The Disarming Act was very stringent, and the pipes came in for almost as strict a banning as did the kilt. The Jacobites were outlawed, the tartan was pronounced a mark of extreme disloyalty to the House of Hanover, and the life of a professed piper was hardly worth living. The Celt was crushed by the severity of his defeat and broken by the inrush of innovation that followed. Clanship, as such, ceased, and the chiefs, from being the fathers of their people, became the landlords. The Highlander lost his reckless passions, but he also lost his rude chivalry and his absorbing love for the old customs. Traditional history and native poetry were neglected, and theological disputes of interminable duration occupied much of the time formerly devoted to poetic recitals and social meetings. Poverty and civilisation did their work; taste for music declined, and piping died away. Absentee landlordism took the place of resident chieftainism, and Gaelic seemed likely to become a dead language, for the people seemed willing to let it die. The destruction of the crofter system completed the work of ruin begun by the destruction of the clan system. What this meant for Highland feelings and customs is vividly shown by the following extract from the writings of the elder Dr. Norman Macleod, *Caraid nan Gaidheal*, as he was called. The speaker is " Finlay the Piper."

" There, indeed, you are right; he was the man that had a kind heart. But this new man that has come in his place has a heart of remarkable hardness, and cares not a straw for the pipes or anything that belongs to the Highlands. He is a perfect fanatic in his passion for big sheep. It brings more enjoyment to him to look at a wether parading on green braes than to listen to all the pibrochs that ever were played. If I were to compose a pibroch for him, I would call it 'Lament for the Big Wether,' the wether that fell over the rock the other day, the loss of which almost drove him mad. It's not I that would be caring to say this to everybody; but as you happen to be with me on the spot there can be no harm in telling you how he treated the poor people here. There is not now smoke coming out of single chimney or sheiling in the whole glen, where you used to see scores of decent people working at honest work. This man would as soon give lodgment to a fox as to a poor crofter or a widow woman. You never heard in your life what a mangling and maiming he has made of the population of this glen. Not even a shepherd would he have from the people of the country; he brought them all in from the south. Even his shepherd's dog does not understand a word of Gaelic. Mactalla of the Crag has not sent back a single echo since good Donald went away. Everything must make way for the sheep. There is not a single brake now in which a bramble would grow; no tuft of brushwood on the slope where one could gather a nut; he has shaved the country as bare as the gable wall of a house, and as for sloes, where sloes used to be you may as well go and look for grapes. The birds, too, have left us; they have gone to the wood on the other side of the Sound; even the gay cuckoo cannot find a single stunted bush where it might hide. He has burnt all the wild wood that ran so prettily up the slope from end to end of this property. You won't gather as many sticks from the brushwood as would serve to boil a pot of potatoes, or as many twigs as would make a fishing basket. But no more of this; it makes my heart sick to think of it. Better to be talking of something else."

The new era dawned, however. The dawn came so slowly that it was hardly noticed. The rabid anti-Highland feeling died away, the powers that were took a sensible view of the situation, and in the reaction that followed the music of the pipes quickly regained its old position of pre-eminence. With this difference, however—it returned to popularity as a social instead of a military force, destined in the Highlands to be the pursuit of the enthusiast and the beloved of the common people, and in the British army only, the inspiration that leads men on to slay one another. In this respect the suppression of the rebellions of 1715 and 1745 marks a turning point in Scottish history, the importance of which has never been recognised. With Culloden ended the influence of old beliefs, and when, in 1782, the ban of the Disarming Act was removed, the people were ready for new ideas. A spirit of improvement and an enthusiasm for things Highland appeared, first modestly, then boldly, and under the auspices of a renovated society, without the environments of war and romance, a new order asserted itself. Competitions stirred up the more clever of the piping fraternity, and further popularised the music, books on Highland piping, written or compiled by leading pipers, began to appear, and with the publication broadcast of histories of the many tunes, the people began to take an intelligent and patriotic interest in the music. The Highlands is not now a barbarous and unknown land. It is classic ground, having been made so by the pens of clever writers, but the old instrument is still the emblem of the homeland to Highlanders all over the world, and, whatever dies out, many generations will not see the last of the pibroch.

CHAPTER IV.

The Make of the Pipes.

There's meat and music here, as the fox said when he ate the bagpipe.—*Gaelic Proverb.*

The "Encyclopædia" definition—The simple reed—Early forms—Simple bagpipes — The chorus — The *volynka* — Continental pipes—British pipes—The Northumbrian—The Irish—The Highland—Tuning—Modern pipes—Prize pipes.

"A wind instrument whose fixed characteristic has always been two or more reed pipes attached to and sounded by a wind chest or bag, which bag has in turn been supplied either by the lungs of the performer or by a bellows."

THIS is the encyclopædia definition, and generally speaking it is correct. But the bag is certainly an addition to the simple reed or shepherd's pipe. And if we wish to go further back we can go to the time when a schoolboy on his way to school pulled a green straw from the cornfield, and biting off a bit, trimmed the end and made for himself a pipe. "Many a pipe," says J. F. Campbell, "did boys make of straws in the days of my youth, and much discord did we produce in trying to play on the slender oaten pipe in emulation of John Piper." Boys being still boys, they still pull the green straws in the passing by, and no doubt if the pipes were not already in existence they would again grow out of this primitive pipe, slowly but surely. Without the bag the pipe is the most ancient of all instruments. It was quite natural that people should try to form sounds by blowing through a tube, and afterwards to vary the sounds either by varying the size or shape of the tube or by fitting into it some special mechanism. The pipe was well known to the Trojans, Egyptians, Greeks, and Romans, who had different kinds for different measures, and from contemporary writings we learn that the strain of blowing these early pipes was so great that the player had to bandage his lips and cheeks with a leathern muzzle. One ancient picture represents a player blowing a triple pipe, that is, three pipes joined at the mouth-piece, but separate futher down, a performance which must have made the need for some improved method of supplying wind very obvious. The name of the genius who first thought of having a reserve supply in a bag attached to the pipes, which would keep an equable current for the purposes of the music, while at the same time it would relieve the player's mouth of the continued strain of blowing, is lost to posterity, but in all probability the idea was originated at different places and at different times by different people. Mac Lean, in his *History of the Celtic Language*, considers the bagpipe as originally consisting of a bladder with drones and chanter of reeds and bulrushes, and affirms that he himself made and played on such an instrument. The first real bagpipe would, however, be a skin, most likely that of a goat or kid, and the invention of the valve in the mouth-piece would follow as a matter of course —that is, if the man who thought of the bag did not also think of having a bellows. There were no drones in the early pipes. St. Jerome, who lived in the fifth century, says

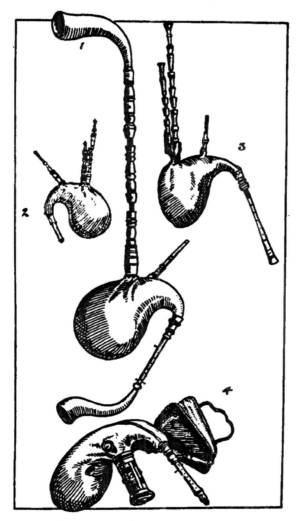

OLD GERMAN WIND INSTRUMENTS—A.D. 1619.

) *Large Bagpipe.* (2) *Dudey or Hornpipe.* (3) *Shepherd's Pipe.* (4) *Bagpipe with Bellows.*

that at the synagogue, in ancient times there was a simple species of bagpipe, consisting of a skin or leather bag, with two pipes, through one of which the bag was inflated, the other emitting the sound. This was the first real bagpipe and it was also, it may be added, the germ of the organ, for the bagpipe is but the organ reduced to its simplest expression.

There was an ancient instrument, called the chorus, which seems to have been closely related to the bagpipe. The chorus was composed of the skin of an animal, which was inflated by a pipe in the back of the neck, and had another pipe issuing from the mouth. That it was not exactly the same as the bagpipe is evident from the fact that it was called *alterum genus cori* to distinguish it from the instrument composed of a bag specially manufactured with mouthpiece and pipe, which was known as *unum genus cori*. Giraldus Cambrensis, one of the most authoritative writers of the twelfth century, assigns the chorus to Scotland, but says nothing of its construction, although he credits the country with superior musical skill. Some ancient writers class the chorus with stringed instruments, and assert that it has no connection whatever with the bagpipe. Living as we do at the beginning of the twentieth century, we cannot possibly decide such a delicate point. And it does not matter much that we cannot.

Those who hold that the instrument was originally imported into Scotland believe that the parent of the Scottish bagpipe was an instrument known as the *volynka*, found in some provinces of the Russian Empire and ascribed more particularly to the Finns, who called it *pilai*. It was a rude instrument, consisting of two tubes and a mouthpiece, all apart, inserted in a raw, hairy goatskin. It was not held in high esteem, for when the Czar degraded the Archbishop of Novogorod in 1569 he alleged that the worthy father was " fitter for a bagpiper leading dancing bears than for a prelate." But no less than five different kinds of bagpipes were known on the Continent in the seventeenth century, some of them with very high qualities as musical instruments. They were :—

I. The *cornemuse*, a simple instrument inflated by the mouth, with a chanter having eight apertures for notes, but without any drones.

II. The *chalemie*, or shepherd's pipe, used by peasants at festivals, and also in country churches. It was inflated by the mouth, had a chanter with ten holes, and had also two drones.

III. The *mussette*, which was inflated by a bellows. It had a chanter with twelve notes, besides other apertures and valves opened by keys, and with four reeds for drones, enclosed in a barrel. It was a complicated instrument, and elaborately made. In one instance, we read, the bag of the *mussette* was made of velvet embroidered with *fleurs de lis*. It was, however, the " class " variety of the bagpipe, and was played before Royalty. The *mussette* was said to sound most sweetly, " especially in the hands of Destouches, the Royal Piper." So they had a royal piper in those days and the pipes were honoured.

IV. The *surdelina* of Naples, an instrument with two drones, two chanters, and numerous keys.

V. The Italian peasant's bagpipe, having two chanters, each with a single key, and one drone.

In Germany the instrument was known as the *sackpfeife*, in Italy as the *cornamusa*, in Rome as *tibia utricularis*, in Lower Brittany as *bignou*, and other Continental names for it were *tiva, ciarmella, samponia* or *samphoneja* and *zampugna.*

There was besides the simple combination of reed and bladder, so simple that it could be made by the shepherd boy himself, without the aid of tools and without any special aptitude for mechanics. From it spring all the others which demand the skill of the finished artisan and the help of turning laths and latter-day implements. The Italian bagpipe, which was made familiar in Britain through the wandering *pifferari*, was a very rude instrument, consisting of a goat's skin, with an enormous drone, on which the player performed by means of a mouth tube, another player making the melody on a separate chanter. A visitor to Naples in 1824 describes a musician in a sheepskin coat, with the wool outwards, playing a bagpipe, of which the bag consisted of " the undressed skin of a goat inflated by one of the legs in its original shape." How anything could be inflated by the leg of a goat he does not stop to inform us, but as the bagpipe now used in Italy is very agreeable and also presentable, though limited in power, it must have been improved considerably since 1824. That it did exist in a more finished condition is evident from the statement of another traveller, made in 1850, that he had heard the national music of Hungary played at Pesth on the *dudelsack*, " a genuine bagpipe, with a fine drone, adorned in front with a goat's head, and covered with a goat's skin." It is not clear whether he means that the bag or the drone was adorned in front with the goat's head, but most likely it was the bag, and the head would be in its original relation to the skin of the goat. The *sackpfeife* (bagpipe) and *chalemie* (shepherd's pipe) seem to have been intimately associated with the wandering minstrels of Germany from time immemorial, and under the name of *dudey* or *dudelsack*, is still well known to the German peasant.

There are three recognised kinds of bagpipes in the British Islands :—

I. The Northumbrian bagpipe.

II. The Irish bagpipe.

III. The Great Highland Bagpipe.

THE NORTHUMBRIAN BAGPIPE

The Northumbrian bagpipe is in two forms, one like the Highland, but of smaller dimensions and milder tone, and the other a miniature of this, and having the same relation to it as a fife has to a German band. The Lowland bagpipe of Scotland may be identified with the Northumbrian, but it is looked on rather contemptuously by the devotees of the Highland, because, in their opinion, it merely imitates other instruments, and is not fitted to perform what they consider the perfection of pipe music—the pibroch.

The Northumbrian and the Lowland pipes were easily carried about, and were much gentler than the great Highland, but

they did not resemble those used on the Continent. They
had the same tone as the Highland, but were less sonorous,
and were blown by a bellows put in motion by the arm
opposite to that under which the bag was held. In this
latter respect they were similar to the Irish, and like them
they had the drones fixed in one stock and laid horizontally
over the arm, not borne on the shoulder. The real Lowland bagpipe, however, never got farther than two drones.
A new form of the Northumbrian was played until very
lately, perhaps still is. It also was a bellows instrument,
and had several keys on the chanter, which gave it a
chromatic scale. A peculiarity of its fingering was that
only one hole was uncovered at a time, the end of the
chanter being kept shut. Although the Great Highland
Bagpipe has now surpassed the Lowland, the latter is not
quite extinct, and a few years ago there were, even in Aberdeenshire, at least two performers on it. In the Borders of
Scotland there were probably many more. The Northumbrian pipes, it may be added, were often wholly formed of
ivory, and richly ornamented with silver. The bag was
covered with cloth or tartan, and fringed or otherwise
adorned. The compass of the old Northumbrian small
pipe chanter was only of eight notes (one less than that of
the Highland); but with a few keys to produce semi-tones,
all the old Northumbrian airs could be played. The
modern chanter has been lengthened by the addition of
keys until the scale extends from D below the treble clef
to B above it.

The Irish bagpipe is the instrument in its most elaborate
form. It also is supplied with wind by a bellows. The
drones are all fixed on one stock, and have keys which are
played by the wrist of the right hand. The reeds are soft

and the tones very sweet and melodious, and there is a harmonious bass which is very effective in the hands of a good player. Some of the drones are of great length, winding as many as three times the length of the apparent tube. The player is seated with one side of the bellows tied firmly to his body, the other to his right arm, the drones under his left leg, and the end of the chanter resting on a pad of leather on his knee, on which it is tipped for

the purpose of articulating many of the notes. The bag is made of goat's skin and is rendered pliable by means of bees' wax and butter. Originally it, like that of the Highland pipe, was filled by the mouth, but it was changed so as to be filled by the bellows. In later instruments several finger keys were adapted to a fourth tube, whereby a perfect chord could be produced, and thus the instrument was rendered fit for private apartments, where as the Highland and the Lowland were only suitable for the open air.

The sweetness of the sound, the result of the smallness and delicacy of the reeds and the prolongation of the pipes; the capacity of the instrument, the result of the many keys, and the capability of the chanter; have earned for the Irish pipes the title of the Irish organ. The compass of the instrument is two octaves. Like the Lowland, the Irish bagpipe is fast dying out, but there is in Glasgow at least one player, an old man, bent with years, but devoted to his pipes, who takes his stand near the top of the classic High Street, and can always depend on a small but select audience, to appreciate his rendering of Scotch and Irish airs on the bagpipe of Erin. Both the Irish and the Northumbrian pipes have, it may be added, been elaborated until they have almost ceased to be bagpipes.

And lastly, we have the "Great Highland Bagpipe." In this instrument a valved tube leads from the mouth to an air-tight bag which has four other orifices, three large enough to contain the base of three fixed long tubes termed drones, and another smaller, to which is fitted the chanter. The three are thrown on the shoulder while the latter is held in the hands. All four pipes are fitted with reeds, but of different kinds. The drone reeds are made by splitting a round length of " cane " or reed backward from a cross cut near a knot or joint towards the open end. They thus somewhat resemble the reed in organ pipes, the loose flap of cane replacing the tongue, and the uncut part the tube or reed proper. They are set downward in a chamber at the base of the drone, so that the current of air issuing from the bag tends to set the tongue in vibration. The drone reeds are only intended to produce a single note, which can be tuned by a " slider " on the pipe itself, varying the length of the consonating air column.

The chanter reed is different in form, being made of two approximated edges of cane tied on to a metal tube. It is thus essentially a double reed, like that of the oboe or bassoon, while the drone reed roughly represents the single beating reed of the organ or clarionet. The drone reed is an exact reproduction of the " squeaker " which children in the fields fashion out of joints of tall grass, probably the oldest form of this reed in existence.

The drones are in length proportional to their note, the longest being about three feet high. The chanter is a conical wooden tube, about fourteen inches long, pierced with eight sounding holes, seven in front for the fingers and one at the top behind for the thumb of the right hand. Two addi-

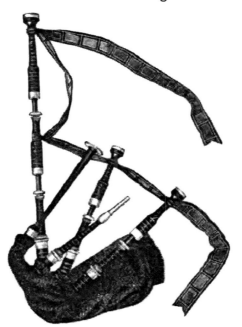

THE GREAT HIGHLAND BAGPIPE

tional holes bored across the tube below the lowest of these merely regulate the pitch, and are never stopped; were it not for them, however, the chanter would require to be some inches shorter, and would consequently have a less pleasing appearance.

The two smaller drones produce a note in unison with the lowest A of the chanter, and the larger an octave lower. The indescribable thrill which the bagpipe is capable of imparting is produced by a sudden movement of the fingers on certain notes, which gives an expression peculiar to the pipes, and distinguishes the pibroch from all other music. The drones, as has been said, are tuned by means of " sliders " or movable joints, and this tuning, or preparation for playing, which generally occupies a few minutes of the piper's time before he begins the tune proper, is heard with impatience by those not accustomed to the instrument. It gave rise to the saying, applied to those who waste time over small matters, " You are longer in tuning your pipes than playing your tune." It cannot, however, be helped so long as this instrument remains exactly as it is. The piper's warm breath goes almost directly on to the reeds, and the consequence is that no sooner does he get his pipes in tune than he starts to put them out of tune—by blowing into them. What is needed is some contrivance that will prevent this, by cooling the air before it reaches the chanter. There are several contrivances in use among leading players, each generally the invention of the man who uses it, but none has come into general favour. Highlanders are a conservative race, and they are not willing to make any changes on their much-loved instrument. It would, however, be well if they would take this matter into consideration, and do something to render unnecessary that preparatory tuning which many people find so unpleasant— that is if it is possible to prevent the reeds getting wet while wet breath is blown into the instrument. The bellows of course gets over the difficulty, but we hardly wish to see a bellows attached to the Highland Bagpipe. It would not then be Highland.

The Highland bagpipe is louder and more shrill than any other, probably because it was all along intended for use as an instrument of war, and pipe music is known to have been heard at a distance of six miles, and, under specially favourable circumstances, of ten miles. The Duke of Sutherland has a bagpipe which was played on in the '45, and could be heard at a distance of eight miles.

Modern pipes are generally made of black ebony or cocoa-wood, the ferrules or rings being of ivory. Sometimes the pipes are half-mounted in silver, that is the high ferrules in ivory and the low in silver. The drones of the best makers have the inside lined with metal, where there is friction in the tuning slide. The bag is formed of sheep-skin, in which are securely fastened five pieces of turned wood called stocks. These receive the ends of the chanter, the mouth-piece, and the drones. The chanter reed is formed of two pieces of Spanish cane, placed side by side. The tops of these are worked down to a fine edge, and the bottoms are tied with fine hemp to a small metal tube. The blow-pipe has on its lower end a valve, which prevents the return of the wind to the mouth. The drones pro-vide a background or additional volume of sound, which gives body to the music. The big drone is fitted with two, and the others with one tuning slide each. The drones are interchangeable, so that the big drone can be placed in the right or left stock to suit a right or left-handed player. When the bag is filled with wind the pres-sure of the player's arm must be so regulated that there is always just sufficient force of air to bring out the notes clearly without interfering with the steady action of the

drones. The bag is held well under the arm, the big drone
rests on the shoulders, and the others are suspended from it
by ribbons and silk cords. The bag is generally held slightly
in front, so that the short drones rest on the shoulder.
When on full-dress parade a banner flies from the big drone,
with the arms of the regiment or chief as a motto. The
drones are generally placed on the left shoulder, but many
players place them on the right. The whole instrument is
kept in position by the tension of the bag. The instruments used by present-day pipers are the full set, the half-
set or reel pipes, and the practising chanter.

The bagpipe had originally but one drone. A second
was added about 1500, and a third about 1800. Bagpipes
with one drone are still used occasionally, and so late as the
winter of 1899 an itinerant player might sometimes be seen,
late at night, playing for coppers at Jamaica Street corner,
Glasgow, on such an instrument. The two drone pipes were
barred at competitions owing to some supposed advantage
they gave to the player, and they appeared last in 1821.

The pipes awarded as prizes at competitions under the
auspices of the Highland Society of London are almost
always of cocoa wood, having armorial bearings and a silver
plate inscribed with the name of the successful competitor.
The bagpipe is the result of an evolution process, and if
this process continues we may yet see it further improved,
and the instrument made so that it will commend itself not
only to Highlanders themselves, but to lovers of music
generally. A great deal of the prejudice against the pipes
is, however, caused by the ignorance of their critics, and
perhaps if people criticised less and understood more we
would not hear so much of the shortcomings of the instrument.

CHAPTER V.

With an Ear to the Drone.

" What needs there be sae great a fraise
　Wi' dringing, dull, Italian lays;
　I wadna gie our ain strathspeys
　For half a hunder score o' them ;
　They're dowf and dowie at the best,
　Dowf and dowie, dowf and dowie,
　Dowf and dowie at the best,
　[Wi' a' their variorum ;]
　[They're dowf and dowie at the best,]
　Their *allegros* an' a' the rest.
　They canna please a Scottish taste
　Compared with Tullochgorum. "

Dr. Johnson—Inspiration of Scottish music—Professor Blackie—
Highland music simple—Scottish airs once Highland—Age of
Highland music—Capability of the bagpipe—How it has suffered
—Peculiarities of the pibroch—Pipe music not fitted for inside—
How it troubled the pressman—Chevalier Neukomm—Professor
Blackie again—A Chicago jury's opinion—An ode to the pipes.

D R. JOHNSON, who was in several ways a bundle of
contradictions, found at least one thing in Scotland
that he enjoyed. When on his tour through the
Hebrides, he was on various occasions entertained by the
bagpipe music of his host's piper, and he liked nothing better
than to stand behind the performer and hold the big drone
close to his ear while the instrument was in full blast. He
was not so affected as some of his country men and women

E

now-a-days, who say the sound of the drone is unpleasant, forgetting, or ignorant of, the fact that it is simply the bass A of their fine church organs sounded continuously by a reed on a wind instrument. But to them the organ is refined and represents culture, while the bagpipe is the barbarous instrument of a barbarous people, whose chief end is to act as custodians of a part of the country that provides good sport after the Twelfth, but is best forgotten all the rest of the year. So they scoff at the national music and the national instrument of Scotland, with the spirit of prejudice, half affected, half real, which induces John Bull to deny his neighbour north of the Tweed the possession of any good thing. And besides, as Gilbert says :—

> " A Sassenach chief may be bonnily built,
>   Wear a sporran, a hose (!) a dirk and a kilt ;
>   He may in fact stride in an acre of stripes,
>   But he cannot assume an affection for pipes."

The Scots were always a musical people. Their national airs, if nothing else, prove this. But music to Scotsmen, still more to Highlanders, was always more than music; it was something which inspired and intensified all their thoughts, and, combined with the impassioned lays of the bards, was to them their principal intellectual food. The bards, whether leading their countrymen with naked bodies and bared broadswords, against their foes, or reciting in the festive hall, endeavoured by means of the choicest language, wedded to the tenderest and boldest music, to impart to their listeners all that was noble and heroic. With harp and voice they poured forth music and words that stirred the very depths of courage and fervour in the enthusiastic nature of the Gaels. And the music which they composed was, like the people, rugged but whole-hearted, " the music of the great bens, the mysterious valleys, and of deep crying unto deep," a music which showed that the people who could live on it were not a people of sordid and sensual tastes, but a people who were by nature and circumstances fitted to appreciate the grand, the awe-inspiring, and the true. They traversed daily a country of the wildest and most diversified scenery, mountains and forests and lochs, their minds partook of the sublimity of their surroundings; they mused continually with glowing imagination on the deeds of their forefathers and their own exploits, and the music to whose rhythm they were bred was but the reflex of their character and life. " That is what makes all your Celtic music so good," wrote Professor Blackie. " It is all so real; not tricked up for show, but growing out of a living root."

Highland music was always different from Lowland, in that it was based largely on memories of the past, and connected by undying tradition with events that had left their impress on the country or the clan. It was always simple and unaffected, and the Highlander always preferred the simple strains of his countrywomen and the grandeur of the pipes in their native glens to the finest opera. Besides he liked variety, as the existence of marches, pibrochs, quick-steps, laments, reels, jigs, and strathspeys testify, and he was equally at home with the grave, the gay, or the melancholy. The melancholy, however, was the predominating note. One can recognise a Gaelic air among a thousand. Quaint and pathetic, it moves on with the most singular intervals, the movement self-contained and impressive, especially to the Celt.

Scottish music as it now exists has been derived largely from the Highlands. No man did more to acclimatise

Celtic music in the Lowlands than Burns. By wedding
Highland airs to his own incomparable poetry he gave them
a new lease of life, albeit he helped to destroy them under
their old names while preserving them under the new.
The music of "Scots Wha Hae," "Roy's Wife," "Auld
Lang Syne," "Of a' the Airts," and "Ye Banks and Braes,"
has no counterpart across the Border or among the Saxon
race. It is the ancient inheritance of the Celt, made
national by the genius of a national poet.

The age of Highland music is another guarantee of its
excellence. It has stood the test of time, the severest of all
ordeals. We have not much English poetry which can, with
any certainty, be ascribed to a date earlier than the time of
Chaucer, but the Scots were celebrated for musical genius
since the beginning of history, genius which, an early historian says, could not be found elsewhere on this side of the
Alps. We have, for instance, a "Song of the Druids,"
though, to tell the truth, we cannot prove its Druidical
origin; we have "Somerled's Lament," composed on an
event which took place in 1164, though not necessarily at
that date; we have a piece of pipe music composed in the
middle of the battle of Inverlochy in 1427; the "Rout of
Glenfruin," which refers to a desperate engagement between
the Mac Gregors and the Colquhouns in 1602; and a
"March to the Battle of Inverlochy," and "The Clans'
Gathering;" both composed on the battle fought at Inverlochy in 1645. These do not prove that the pipes themselves were capable at that time of rendering such music,
but they prove that the music existed. There are some
pipe tunes—*Cogadh na Sith* and *A Ghlas Mheur*—for instance, so ancient that their origin cannot be traced, but
they have, by means of their own merits, and in spite of the

want of the printing press, lived all through the centuries.
In the beginning of the twelfth century, Giraldus Cambrensis said of the music of the Irish Celts that it was
above that of any nation he had ever known, and in the
opinion of many, Scotland at that time far surpassed Ireland, even while her people were sunk in misery and
barbarism.

As to the question whether people of good musical taste
can appreciate the music of the great Highland bagpipe, it
is a fact that people who have the keenest appreciation and
intense enjoyment of the music of such composers as Mozart
and Handel, of the great singers and great musicians, can
at the same time enjoy a pibroch or a strathspey when
played by a master hand. Mendelssohn on his visit to the
Highlands was favourably impressed by the pibroch,
and introduced a portion into one of his finest compositions.
The pibrochs are remarkable productions ; all the more
remarkable that they were composed by men who, we may
safely assume, were of an humble class, and not blessed in
any way with the advantages of education—least of all with
those of a musical education.

The great Highland bagpipe is not fitted for executing
all kinds, or even many kinds of music. Its compass is
only nine notes, from G second time treble clef to A, first
ledger line above clef. The scale may be called a
" tempered " one. The C note being slightly flattened
admits of a greater variety of keys than could otherwise be
used, and for its own purposes the scale is perfect. The
notes are G natural, A, B, C, D, E, F sharp, G natural,
and A. It is this G natural, or flat seventh, which gives
the scale its peculiar character. The A is that of any other
instrument in concert pitch. The so-called imperfection of

scale, together with the somewhat harsh tone, is the cause
of the unpleasant effect on the accurately sensitive ears of
those accustomed to music in the natural diatonic scale, but
these also account for the semi-barbarous, exciting stimulus
the instrument exercises on the minds of Highlanders,
especially on the battlefield.   The chanter of the Highland
bagpipe has an oboe or bassoon reed broader than that of
the other kinds, whence that loudness of sound for which it
is known.   This is a valuable quality in a military instrument, and when heard at a sufficient distance, when the
faults of scale are not so noticeable, the music is very
agreeable.   Besides, compass and variety are not always
the highest qualities of music, and, although the chanter of
a bagpipe is almost devoid of expression and beyond the
performer's control, the suitable execution of simple airs is
equally practicable, and of equal value with music obtained
from other instruments.   Simple airs may be performed on
simple instruments, and a master hand can bring from imperfect materials results better than those produced by the
amateur with materials of the highest class.   But we should
not expect from one instrument the music proper to
another, or blame the one because it fails to please those
who are used to the other.   The bagpipes have all along
been subject to the criticism of the stranger, who knew
neither them nor their people, but who came to criticise
and went away to scoff, not remembering that a Highlander
suddenly imported into a London drawing-room would
have as poor an opinion of the music there as the Londoner
has of his.   They have suffered too from the well-meaning
efforts of their friends.   Some have invented contrivances
and modifications for bringing the instrument nearer to
all-round music.   Others have adapted for the pipes pieces

never intended for them, and which only show up their deficiencies, in the hope of bringing the music nearer to the pipes. Neither has succeeded to any great extent, and neither is likely to succeed. The Mac Crimmons of Skye, the greatest masters of the bagpipe, never violated the principle of using only music specially composed, and they succeeded beyond all others in demonstrating the powers of the instrument. Those who have since departed from their principle have failed to justify the departure, but they have proved, what they might have known before they began, that an instrument cannot produce what it is not constructed to produce. The Highland bagpipe is the exponent of Highland music, and of that only.

And there is enough and to spare without invading the realms of other instruments. There are reels, strathpeys, and marches out of number, and there are, above all things, pibrochs, or, to give the proper spelling, *piobaireachd* ("pibroch" is simply an attempt made by Sir Walter Scott to spell the word phonetically, so as to make it pronounceable to his south country readers ; but it has come into such general use that its correctness passes unquestioned.)* The word does not, properly speaking, denote any class of tune —it means pipe-playing—but it is generally applied to a class which in itself includes three classes—the *cruinneachadh* or gathering, the *cumhadh* or lament, and the *failte* or salute. The pibroch has been called the voice of uproar and misrule, and its music that of real nature and rude passion. It is the great specialty of the Highland bagpipe,

---

* The proper name of "classic" pipe music in the Gaelic is *Ceol Mor*, the Great Music, a word which includes gatherings, laments, and salutes.

and no piper is considered a real expert unless he is a good pibroch player. It is the most elaborate of the compositions devised for the pipes, and is difficult to define otherwise than as a theme with variations. Dr. Mac Culloch, a rather cynical traveller, who wrote books on Scotland in 1824, which still pass as standard, considered it " of an extremely irregular character, containing a determined melody, whereon, such as it is, are engrafted a series of variations rising in difficulty of execution, but presenting no character, as they consist of commonplace, tasteless flourishes, offensive to the ear by their excess, and adding to the original confusion instead of embellishing the air which the ground may possess." " It has," he adds, " neither time, rhythm, melody, cadence, nor accent, neither keynote nor commencement nor termination, and it can therefore regulate nothing. It begins, goes on, and ends, no one knows when or how or where, and if all the merit of the bagpipe is to depend on its martial, or rather its marching, utility, it could not stand on a worse foundation." But Dr. Mac Culloch, strangely enough, himself says a little later:—

" The proper music of the bagpipe is well worthy of the instrument. They are really fit for each other, and ought never to have been separated. The instrument has suffered in reputation, like the ass in the fable, from making too high flights. It is, properly speaking, a military weapon (*sic*), and the pibroch is its real business."

A pibroch is generally in triple or quadruple time, although many are in two-fourth and six-eighth time. It begins with the *urlar* or groundwork of the composition and its doubling. Then comes the high A or thumb variation, after which the music proceeds :—

(1) *Siubhal,*	with its doubling and trebling.		
(2) *Leum-luath,*	Do.	Do.	Do.
(3) *Taor-luath,*	Do.	Do.	Do.
(4) *Taor-luath fosgailte,*	Do.	Do.	Do.
(5) *Taor-luath breabach,*	Do.	Do.	Do.
(6) *Taor-luath a mach,*	Do.	Do.	Do.
(7) *Crun-luath,*	Do.	Do.	Do.
(8) *Crun-luath fosgailte,*	Do.	Do.	Do.
(9) *Crun-luath breabach,*	Do.	Do.	Do.
(10) *Crun-luath a mach,*	Do.	Do.	Do.

It is finished up with the ground or *urlar* as at the beginning.

The pibroch is not a mere voluntary, played as the taste of the performer may dictate, though it seems so to those unacquainted with the nature of the music, especially when the player is inexperienced. All, however, are not so ignorant or confused as the listener of a story told by the late Duke of Gordon. A piper in a North of England town had played a pibroch which wonderfully excited the attention of his hearers, who seemed equally astonished at its length and the wildness and apparent disconnection of its parts. Unable to understand it, one of the spectators at the conclusion anxiously asked the piper to " play it in English."

The pibroch is properly a " pipe tune," and its most legitimate form is the " gathering." The gathering is a long piece of music composed on the occasion of some victory or other fortunate circumstance in the history of a clan, which, when played, is a warning to the troops to turn out. The lament and salute originated in a similar way, but should be used on specific occasions only. The three classes are now, however, treated as one, propriety being frequently so much discarded that the pieces are called marches, an entirely unwarranted change, considering the nature of the music.   The bagpipe has its military music mostly composed for itself, and generally employed by regimental pipers for marching purposes, and there is no necessity either for using pibrochs as marches or for adapting for regimental purposes the music of other instruments as has been done to far too large an extent.

Bagpipe music has also suffered greatly in popular estimation through the efforts of well-meaning but mistaken people to lift it out of its proper place and graft it on to city life and inside entertainments.   It is not pleasant chamber music even to Highland ears unless played on chamber pipes.   There are times and circumstances for everything, and there are few pleasures that will admit of being transplanted out of their own sphere.   The " Haughs o' Cromdale " was a grand thing at Dargai, and a sonata by Paderewski is all right before a fashionable audience in a big city, but to exchange them would only make both ridiculous.   The old pipers could indeed so regulate their instruments as to make the music almost as sweet as that of the violin, but sweetness is not the outstanding feature of the bagpipe, and it is not fitted for private houses or any but the biggest of public halls. The hills themselves are its appropriate concert room, and among them it pervades the whole atmosphere, and becomes part of the air until one can hardly tell whence it comes. It makes rhythm with the breeze and chimes in with the rush of the torrent, and becomes part of the world in which it is produced.   It suits the bare heath, the solitary cairn, the dark pass, the silent glen, and the mountain shrouded in mists as no music ever did or can do, and it is at its best floating across the silent loch or over the mountain stream, or round the rugged hillsides. It is a military and an outdoor instrument, and there is no justification for comparing pipe music with classical productions. It is like comparing taties and herring with wine jellies, or hoddin' grey with broad cloth.

Playing within doors is a Lowland and English custom. In the Highlands the piper was always in the open air, and when people wished to dance to his music, it was on the green they danced. The pipe was no more intended for inside than are firearms. A broadside from a man-of-war has a fine effect when heard at a proper distance, but one would not care to be sitting by the muzzles when the guns went off. That the large pipes are still used in halls for entertainment purposes is accounted for by the strength of association, as much as by their appropriateness. Highlanders would not consider a gathering at all complete unless they had their pipers present—a feeling which is easily understood, and which no one wishes to see die out. But that does not alter the fact that, in a small apartment at any rate, they are entirely out of place. The writer is not likely soon to forget one experience of his own, which helped to confirm him in this opinion. It was in one of the big Glasgow halls at a Highland gathering, where I was, in a professional capacity, doing a " special " of several columns for a Highland paper. To catch that week's issue, my " copy " had to be posted before I slept, so, as soon as the chairman had finished his speech, I adjourned to one of the very small rooms behind the platform to " write up " while the musical part of the programme proceeded, expecting to be pretty well through before the turn of the next speaker came. But the " association pipers " were there before me, and what must they do but shut all the doors to keep the

sound from reaching the platform, and start practising the
marches and reels they were to play later on, marching from
end to end of the little apartment.   In five minutes the big
drone seemed to be vibrating all through my anatomy, while
the melody danced to its own time among the crevices of
my brain.   It was impossible for me to take my fingers out
of my ears—a position which did not lend itself to rapid
writing or careful composition.   But the pipers did not
think anything about it (they had in fact stopped conversation and started playing because they "did not wish to
disturb me"), and I soon made an excuse to go out.   I tried
the artistes' room, but the soprano was doing up her hair,
the comic man was arranging his somewhat scanty habila-
ments, the old violinist was telling funny stories, and I
seemed so obviously out of place that I could not possibly
start working.   Next I tried the stair, but the draught was
too much for me.   Then I tried the concert hall itself, but
the applause was so frequent that the desks were always
rattling.   So I came back to the pipers, and braved it out
for half an hour, after which I went back to the concert
hall and did it on my knee.   Anything more indescribably
disagreeable than that half-hour in the ante-room it is
difficult to imagine, and there seems, when I think of it now,
to have been no relation whatever between that "music"
and the harmonies which used to float across the bay in the
days long ago, when the piper at the big house tuned his
pipes and played to the gentry as they sat at dinner, the
while we boys lay prone on the grass and drank in all the
twirling of his notes.   But in the one case there was a mile
of sea between and rocks and fields around, and a blue sky
above.   In the other, I seemed to be caged in with some
mad thing that hammered at every panel for freedom.

It was the Chevalier Neukomm, a very distinguished musician, who said, when asked for his opinion, " I don't despise your pibrochs ; they have in them the stirrings of rude, but strong, nature. When you traverse a Highland glen, you must not expect the breath of roses. You must be contented with the smell of heath. In like manner Highland music has its rude, wild charms."

And our own Professor Blackie puts it even better when he says :—

" The gay ribboned bagpipes moaning away in melancholy coronachs, or rattling like hailstones to the clash of claymores on the backs of the fleeing Sassenachs. In this case at least—

' 'Tis distance lends enchantment to the sound.'   .

On this point no Highlander of good taste will disagree with you. The bagpipes belong to the open air as naturally as heather belongs to the hills and salmon to the sea-lochs. Men do not mend pens with Lochaber axes, or employ scene painters to decorate the lids of snuff-boxes."

As to the man who practises the ordinary pipes in an ordinary city apartment, with but the thickness of a brick dividing him from neighbours on either side, he is the worst enemy of his craft and worthy of all execration. The wise enthusiast will get a smaller set made for home use, having the lower part of each drone and the top of the chanter turned large enough to fit the stocks of the full-size pipes, so that one bag and the stocks in it does for both sets. These will not sound so loud as to disturb neighbours, and the performer can enjoy himself as well as with pipes of full size. It must have been of neighbours of a player on the large pipes that the Chicago jury was composed which tried an action for damages in 1899. A Scottish society was parading the streets to the martial skirl of the pipes, when they met a horseman, whose horse took fright and bolted, throwing the rider through a shop window. The subsequent action turned on the question of whether or not the pipes were musical instruments, and the jury decided that they were not. After which it may be well to conclude with the following verses by Mr. Patrick Mac Pherson, New York, contributed to the *Celtic Monthly*, always remembering the open air and giving allowance for the poet's license :—

"Away with your fiddles and flutes,
  As music for wedding or ball,
Pianofortes, clarionettes, lutes—
  The bagpipe surpasses them all.

"For polkas, the waltz, the quadrille,
  There's nought with the pipes can compare ;
An anchorite torpid 'twould thrill,
  Such glorious sounds in the air.

"So tuneful, harmonious, and sweet !
  The very perfection of art,
Lends wings to the tardiest feet,
  And joy to the sorrowing heart.

"Upheaved, the fair dancers would feel
  Like birds, poising light on the wing,
As nimbly they trip in the reel,
  And roll off the steps of the fling.

"No requiems grand I assail,
  Like Handel's Dead March, played in 'Saul,'
But yet I maintain that the Gael
  In coronachs vanquishes all.

"In music, in warfare, in song—
  With bagpipes and banners unfurled,
Like a torrid simoom borne along,
  The Highlanders lighten the world."

CHAPTER VI.

THE "LANGUAGE" OF THE PIPES.

"Wild as the desert stream they flow,
  Wandering along it's mazy bed ;
Now scarcely moving, deep and slow,
  Now in a swifter current led,
And now along the level lawn
With charming murmurs softly drawn."

Have the pipes a language ?—A wild, fanciful notion—How it got a
  hold—How much of it is true ?—The reed actually speaking—A
  powerful influence—The power of association—Neil Munro—
  Descriptive Highland airs—*A Cholla mo Run*—Military stories
  —In South Africa—An enthusiastic war correspondent.

IN this chapter we would walk warily, knowing that we
are on dangerous ground. The question is, Has the
bagpipe a language more than any other instrument ?
Can it speak to the heart of the Highlander more than any
other instrument can speak to hearts that know it, and the
music which it discourses, and the associations of that music ?
Through the great bulk of what has been written about the
bagpipe there runs this idea of its power, this wild, fanciful
notion that it has an actual language and that those who
understand that language can converse by its means. Some
have even attempted to analyse the music, and to discover
the alleged secret, while others have held that *canntaireachd*,
fully dealt with in the next chapter, was in reality a

language and not merely a very rude system of musical notation. And this notion of the speaking power of the pipes got such a hold on the imaginative people of the Highlands that, although personally each of them did not understand how the thing was possible, many of them accepted it as truth and believed the stories illustrating the subject, which ultimately became part of their traditional literature. It seems like sacrilege to disturb the ideas which have been accepted as absolute truth for centuries, but there is no doubt whatever that of the speaking power of the pipes about seventy-five per cent. exists in the vivid imaginations of the retailers of Highland tradition. It was indeed in the chanter-reed of the pipes that, after a long search, and after great difficulties, Baron von Kempelen, a distinguished Continental mechanic and musician, discovered the nearest approach to the human voice. He believed it was possible to get an approximation of language by some mechanical contrivance, and he was able to convert the reed to the elements of a speaking machine, and through its aid and with many appliances he obtained letters, syllables, words, and even entire sentences. But all the same, the bagpipe cannot speak any more than it can fly. If it has ever in all its history conveyed, by means of an extemporised tune, information to people at a distance definite enough to enable them to alter all their battle tactics, we require better historical proof of the incident than is to be got of any of the stories to be given here.

While, as a simple matter of fact, it is true that the bagpipe cannot speak, it is equally true that its music exercises a strangely powerful influence over the Celtic mind. The race are, or at any rate were, of a peculiarly imaginative temperament. This, taken along with the fact that their music always had strong associations, explains a great deal. Many of the pibrochs were composed without premeditation, under the influence of exuberant joy or the wildest sorrow or despair. Consequently, when, under favourable circumstances, they were again played by master hands, they roused up the old memories, and did really, though not literally, speak to the listeners. The construction of the pipe also helps. It is the only instrument since the days of the old Highland harp which represents the Gaelic scale in music, and it is this that makes the pipe appeal so naturally and so intensely to the Gael. To him, especially if from home, it speaks of the past of his own race, and of the days of his youth. In this lies its special charm :—

> " When he hears the bagpipe sound
> His heart will bound like steed for battle."

Pipe music has many voices, and it expresses many of the emotions which are given vent to by language that can be printed. Neil Munro, as enthusiastic a Highlander as any man, does not believe in the " speaking " theory, but he believes in the descriptive character of the music. As witness —

" The tune with the river in it, the fast river and the courageous, that kens not stop nor tarry, that runs round rock and over fall with a good humour, yet no m 'od for anything but the way before it."

The tune that, as *Paruig Dall* said, had " the tartan of the clan it." And—

" Playing the tune of the ' Fairy Harp,' he can hear his forefolks, plaided in skins, towsy-headed and terrible, grunting at the oars, and snoring in the caves ; he has his whittle and club in the ' Des-

F

perate Battle' (my own tune, my darling!), where the white-haired
sea-rovers are on the shore, and a stain's on the edge of the tide; or
trying his art on Laments he can stand by the cairn of Kings, ken
the colour of Fingal's hair, and see the moon-glint on the hook of
the Druids."

Most of the old Highland airs were composed on particular occasions, or for the purpose of conveying particular
feelings.   One, for instance, is designed to express the succession of emotions in the mind of an Ardnamurchan crofter
while tilling his soil in an unpropitious season and hesitating
whether to emigrate or attempt to pay his landlord the
triple rent a rival had offered.   Another commemorates the
arrival of Prince Charlie at a farm-house in Skye, where one
of his followers was sent forward to see if he was likely to
find friends there.   To a Highland ear the tune expresses
the first hesitating, half-whispered questions of the mes-
senger, then his confidence as he finds the goodwife favourable, and finally his composed feelings on finding that he
was among friends.   Another was composed on an occasion
when the Mac Kenzies attempted to obtain possession of the
lands of Mac Donell of Glengarry.*   The chief of the Mac
Kenzies had his men and allies assembled at different points,
one party being concealed in a church at Beauly, and, tradition says, this church was burned over the heads of a worshipping congregation by friends of the Mac Donells.   But
the pibroch contradicts this, for when the tune is properly
played the listener in fancy hears the flames rustling and
blazing through the timbers of the church, mingled with
the angry remonstrances and half-smothered shouts of the
warriors, but there is no representation of the more feeble

---

* See Index under *Gilliechroist.*

plaints of women and children. Had these been among the victims, their cries would surely have formed the burden of the tune.*

Many other instances of descriptive pipe music are to be found. The pibroch of *Daorach Robbi* contains the keenest satire ever levelled at the vice of drunkenness. The ludicrous imitation of the coarse and clumsy movements, the maudlin and staring pauses, the helpless imbecility of the drunkard as he is pilloried in the satire with the ever-recurring sneering notes, *Seall a nis air* (Look at him now) are enough to annihilate any person possessing the least sensibility, who, while hearing them, is conscious of having been in the position described, even for once in his life. *Gillidh Callum* is a striking contrast to *Daorach Robbi*. The total abstainer could hardly find a better text than the latter, while the man who advocates temperance only would be strongly supported by the former, which illustrates enlivening virtues of the fruit of the vine without its degrading effects. So with most pipe music. It describes something, and in this respect is second only to the recitative of the bards. It is, of course, necessary that performer and listeners should be Highland themselves. No one who is not versed in the poetry and music of the Highlands can impart to others, or appreciate for himself, the spirit of romance and pathos and love and sorrow and martial sentiment which is in the music, just as no actor can play well unless he enters into the spirit of the play. To the enthusiast for Highland music, the feelings aroused by other instruments are general and undefined, and common to

---

* It should be stated that the best authorities now agree that there never was a church burned at the place referred to.

Frenchman, Spaniard, German, or Highlander, but the bagpipe is sacred to Scotland. Gaelic itself has a sentiment
that cannot be expressed, and so with its music. It appeals
to us, but we cannot express it, and only those who know it
understand it.

And now for one or two of these stories where the pipes
are alleged to have spoken. The best known is that of
A Cholla mo Run, or "The Piper's Warning." * The
piper and friends were entrapped in Duntroon Castle, while
Coll Citto, his master, and his followers were away at Islay,
and the enemy laid an ambush to entrap the returning party.
The piper one day saw Coll's boats returning, and he knew
that unless something was done they would sail right into
the ambush. So he asked leave to go out on to the battlements and play a tune. This was granted, and the piper
played extempore music, which to those in the boats
meant :—

> " Coll, O my dear, dinna come near,
>   Dinna come near, dinna come near ;
>   Coll, O my dear, dinna come near,
>   I'm prisoner here, I'm prisoner here."

and more to the same purpose. Coll instantly took warning, turned his boats and fled. But the Campbells, in whose
custody the piper was, also understood, and, some accounts
say he had his fingers cut off, others that he was killed on
the spot for his bravery in warning his friends. All agree
that he spoke to Coll in the boats across an expanse of
water by means of the pipes alone, and the tune has ever
since been associated with the incident in which it
originated.

---

* See Index under *A Cholla mo Run.*

Then there is the story of "Women of this Glen," *
alleged to have been instrumental in warning some of the
Mac Ians on the eve of Glencoe, and several others very
similar.

Some stories come from wars of a less remote date. A
Scottish regiment, we are told, on a sunbaked plain in India,
was being mowed down by some mysterious disease. The
doctors could not tell what it was, but the kilties were being
swept off by it, one by one. At last it was discovered.
Away on the outskirts of the camp, in the short still gloaming of the Eastern evening, a group of the men had
gathered round the regimental piper. Their heads were
buried in their hands, and big hot tears rolled through their
fingers. And the weird, wae strains of "Lochaber no
more," played more melancholy than ever, filled the air.
They were dying of homesickness, and the bagpipe spoke to
them of home and all that was there. Another Scottish
regiment had been at the Cape for a long time, and the
officers found that the bagpipe so affected the men as to
make them unfit for duty. The men were homesick, and
their music intensified this feeling, and it had to be stopped
for a time. The men of course knew the tunes, and what
they meant, but there is nothing to show that the same
tunes played on another instrument would not have had the
same effect.

We had the old idea revived in all its beauty by one of
the ablest of the war correspondents in the recent South
African War. Mr. Julian Ralph, of the London *Daily Mail,*
in a letter to his paper, spoke eloquently of the services rendered to the Highland Brigade by their pipers, and of the

---

* See Index under *Bodatch nam Briogais.*

way in which the pipes spoke to the men and the men
listened to the pipes.   He was a stranger to the music, and
at first he was not impressed by it.   But gradually he came
to like it, and to miss it when he was not within the range
of the notes.   Here is how he tells of the pipes speaking to
the men :—

"Then off strode the fresh player with the streamers floating
from his pipes, with his hips swaying, his head held high, and his
toes but touching the earth.   Once I heard a man say, 'Gi' me the
pipes, Sandy ; I can tell ye what naebody has said,'—at least, those
were the strange words I thought that I distinguished."

After General Wauchope was killed along with so many
of his men at Magersfontein, the soldiers were for a time
gloomy and dispirited.

" ' It's the pipes that make them so,' said an officer.   ' The pipes
are keeping them a great deal resentful, and still more melancholy.'
' The pipes ?   What have the pipes to do with their feelings ?'

" ' Eh, man ?   Don't you know that the pipes can talk as good
Scots as any man who hears them ?   Surely 'tis so—and 'tis what
the pipes are saying, first in one player's hands and then in another's,
that keeps the men from forgetting their part in the last battle.'

" Once, as the days passed, when I saw this officer again at leisure,
I went to him for an explanation of his surprising disclosure.   I
had been trying to learn the language of the pipes in the meantime,
but I acquired no more understanding than a dog has of English
when he distinguishes between a kindly human tone and a cross one.
I could tell when a tune was martial and when another was mournful.   When a gay one rang out—if any had—I would not have
mistaken it for a dirge.   To some this may seem a very little learning, but I had begun by thinking all the tunes alike.

" 'Yesterday,' said my friend the officer, 'we'd a little match
between men who had some skill at embroidering the airs of the old
ballads with trills of those grace-notes that they call warblers, but
this contest was broken up by a rugged son of the hills who, after

asking for the pipes, flung from them a few strong, clear notes which gained the attention of all who are born to a knowledge of the music that speaks. I am not one of those, but I called my soldier-servant up and asked him what was being played.' 'Well, sir,' said he, ' that's Mac Callum—a great museecian he is. And hark, sir ; he has the right of it and boldly he is telling every one his thoughts. He says that every man kens that the gran' general who's dead was as cunning and skilfu' in war as ony man above him, and 'tis late in the day—now that he's laid away and dumb—to put blame on him as if he were an ignoramus and a butcher, like some others. And now, oh ! brawly ye're tellin' it, Mac Callum—he says there may be scheming and plotting in high places but no skullduggery o' ony sort, however it is gilded, will ever deceive ane single true chiel o' the Highlands.' "

" ' And then,' said my gossip, ' the pipes passed to the hand of another man, and my servant—seeing me about to move away— touched my arm and bade me wait, as this new player was another adept with the pipes. ' He's grand at it,' said he ; ' well done, Stewart. He's saying, sir, that the reason none will heed those who blame our grand leader that's gone is that there's men of rank among us—and of proud blood—that'll stand up to any man at home and swear that when our fallen chief came back with his orders for the battle he complained of them sorely, but he said, ' No better could he get,' and when he lay down in his blanket his head was full of the trouble that was coming on him—he not being able to learn what he needed to know against the morrow.'

"There was more of this recital of what the pipes had spoken to the regiment, but it would only be irritating a sore to repeat it. The pipers spoke even more plainly as the bold outpourings of one incited bolder from another. At last there were suggestions, by pipes grown mutinous, of sentiments which, happily, have seldom been spread within the British Army. But what I have told suffices to illustrate my sole point, which is that the gift of eloquent speech in chords and trills is born with the master-pipers.

"I never saw my officer-friend again for more than a nod or a word in passing. But on one day the pipes next door rang jubilantly, and man after man applied himself to them with ginger in his touch. Each blew triumphant, thrilling, heart-stirring chords, and every piper swaggered at his work with such a will as to send his aproned kilt to and fro with what seemed a double swing to each beat of the time.

"I said to myself, 'They have learned that Hector Mac Donald is coming to be their new brigadier, and the pipes are assuring them that every Highlander may be himself again, certain of victory and new glory under a leader second only to the one they have lost.' I still believe my conjecture was right.

"And I know from living next door, as it were, that the cloud of gloom that had hung over the brigade was dispelled almost with the suddenness of its horrid appearance.

"After that the kilties began to make in this war a continuation of their glorious record in so many lesser wars in the time that was."

All of which is very fine writing, but one cannot get rid of the idea that Mr. Ralph was the victim of an elaborate joke. The speaking theory was new to him and he accepted it in all its amplitude. There is no report of what his officer-friend said when he read Mr. Ralph's article—if he ever did read it.

The simple truth about the "language" of the pipes seems to be that a Highland listener gets from the pipes what, in a more or less degree, anyone gets from the music he loves—a stimulant for his emotion and imagination, nothing more. He is an emotional being, and his imagination, aided and abetted by the sorrows and the joys of many generations—which affect his disposition though he knows it not—and by the many associations of particular tunes or styles of playing, runs riot when he hears the pipes, and to him they speak as no other instrument ever can speak. A primitive instrument working on the feelings of a primitive people has a much more direct and intense psychological effect than on a sophisticated people who have scores of different cunning instruments and myriads of airs, a fact which should always be remembered when the "language" of the pipes is discussed. After all it depends much more on the listener than on the instrument. In our appreciation of any music, and in the effect it has on us, there is involved all that we ourselves have been, seen, heard, thought, and—sometimes—forgot. A plaintive love air brings up the old days, the sunny weather, the sweethearts of our youth, all the store of associations that are buried in us, and—who knows?—all the loves and hates, the joys and sorrows of our dead fathers, modified or intensified by our own personal character. Therefore to us that plaintive air is the sweetest of music. To the Highlander the bag-pipe conveys the fine rapture a high-class audience gets, or at least professes to get, from Sarasate's violin and Paderewski's piano. To him it has a direct message, but to the rest of the world it is what a violin is to him, probably less. But as for an impromptu tune conveying intelligence like spoken language—ah well, we must draw the line somewhere.

CHAPTER VII.

THE LITERATURE OF THE PIPES.

" I hin-do, ho-dro, hin-do, ho-dro, hin-do, ho-dro,
 hin-da, ho-dra, hin-do, ho-dro, hin-da, chin-drine,
. hin-do, ho-dro, .hin-do, ho-dra, hin-do, ho-dro, hin-do,
 ho-dro, hin-do, ho-dro, hin-da, chin-drine, hin-do, ho-dro,
 hin-do, ho-dro, hin-da, hin-da, hin-do, chin-drine."

Ancient music lost—Transmission by tradition—Druidical remains
—Systems of teaching—No books—" Unintelligible jargon "—
Canntaireachd—The Mac Crimmon System—The Gesto Book—
A scientific system—A tune in *Canntaireachd*—Pipers unable to
explain—Earliest printed pipe music—Mac Donald's books—
More recent books—Something to be done.

FOR long, the music of the pipes was so much a part of
the life of the people that no records of tunes were
necessary. But there came a time when interest in
these things waned somewhat, and it was then that the
want of printed or written records were felt. By reason of
that want, we now know little or nothing of truly ancient
Scottish music. Perhaps we have not lost much, but in any
case it would have been interesting to know the musical
tastes of our forefathers away back in the early centuries.
We are quite willing to believe that some of the exquisite
melodies still existing were handed down to us by Gaelic
progenitors, and are as old as the race itself, but the fact

remains that we cannot trace any of them for more than two or three centuries, nor tell whether or not they are older than the first mention of them we have in authentic history. That many of the tunes were composed on incidents or battles four and five hundred years back does not prove that the tunes themselves are as old as the events they commemorate. Composers then, as now, chose their subjects irrespective of dates. The pipes were in fairly common use about the middle of the seventeenth century, probably for centuries earlier, and when they were in use, there must have been music for them. But we have not that music now, thanks to the blank which occurred between the decay of the system whereby music was taught orally and the introduction of the educational system of later centuries. Clanship isolated the people into small communities and prevented a general knowledge of music from being spread abroad, and it could not very well be committed to paper when the people knew of no system of signs which would represent it. So the only method of preserving the tunes was their transmission from one generation of pipers to another, a method which rendered it very easy for the unscrupulous to re-baptise or paraphrase old tunes, and pass them off as their own, and also left the tunes to change gradually as they passed from performer to performer. Then, again, the decay of the Gaelic made it necessary to give English names to Gaelic tunes, and a number of the finest Highland airs have been wedded to the songs of such poetical giants as Burns, Hogg, Tannahill, and Cunningham, and their identity completely lost. Gaelic itself has been kept pure enough through traditional generations, but the conditions which applied to the music did not apply to the language. The language was the heritage of an entire

people, their daily bread, as it were; the music was cultivated only by a class of the people, and was far more subject
to change than the language.

It is alleged that the chanting of Druidical precepts in
Pagan times was imitated by the early Christians, and some
remains of Druidical songs, with music attached, were said
to have been in existence so late as 1830, but there is now
nothing to show what were the qualities of Highland music
prior to the dates of tunes which are well authenticated. The
music of the pipes is ancient, without a doubt; it passed
through a long evolution process, and it has changed but
little since we have known it committed to paper. That is
about all that can safely be said on the point.

Before people learned to express their thoughts by marks
on paper, they carried the music in their heads. The music
teacher nowadays gathers his books and his scales and his
instruments around him; then he gathers his pupils; then
he expounds the theories on which the system of music is
based; then he shows how these theories work out in actual
practice, and then he proceeds to learn his pupils how to
practice them. All of which makes the learning of music a
"special subject," and goes to instil into the heads of the
non-musical the idea that they, too, by reason of having
passed through all the courses, must needs understand music.
Whereas all the time it is only the theory of music, as
taught in the text-books, they understand. This in itself is
not a bad thing, if people incapable of anything higher
would be content with it, and not pose as authorities. But
the tendency of our educational system is, or at least was
very recently, towards the production of a race of pedants,
and the creation of a dead level of mediocrity in which the
common person thinks he is as clever as the genius, and the

genius is too modest to hold his head higher than that of the common person. In the old days, when the difficulties were insurmountable to the common person, genius shone forth all the brighter. There was little of the literature of the pipes in these days, and a piper's ear was his best teacher. Consequently the great pipers stood head and shoulders above the common crowd—giants because of their genius and life-long study. It is quite likely that the raising of the level of the mass, even at the expense of genius, may be a good thing, but that is another matter.

Two hundred years ago there were few, if any, books bearing on the subject, and were it not for the powerful memories of the hereditary pipers of the different clans, and their devotion to their art, but little even of the music of that time could have been preserved. The hereditary pipers were walking storehouses of Highland musical knowledge. They taught their pupils by ear and off the fingers. Taking them out to the hillside, they first learned them to chant words with the tunes in a sort of "unintelligible jargon," then to finger the chanter silently from memory, then to play the chanter, and afterwards to play the pipes themselves. This system, if such it could be called, required as its very groundwork the possession on the part of the pupil of an ear for music, a natural aptitude for pipe music, a devotion to the music peculiar to the Highlands, and an intimate know-ledge of and reverence for all the circumstances which en-twined themselves into the histories of the various tunes. Without these qualifications no man could be a great piper, and the hereditary pipers were very chary about beginning to train anyone who did not promise to come up to their expectations.

The "unintelligible jargon" just referred to is perhaps the most curious thing in all the history of pipe music. The words are not a fair description, for it was intelligible enough to the initiated, but from the point of view of others, no other phrase is suitable. It was, in short, a system whereby known and fixed sounds in the shape of syllables represented sounds in the shape of notes of music known to the teacher, but unknown to the pupil, in such a way that when the pupil, after being taught, heard a number of the syllables repeated by word of mouth, he could at once reproduce their prototypes as a bit of pipe music. There were no signs about it whatever, no noting of the syllables—that is in the early stages of the system—and it is difficult for us who can hardly imagine music without conjuring up a book before the mind's eye, to grasp the idea. The transmission of music by a system of language signs is peculiar to the pipes, and no full parallel to *Canntaireachd*, as it has been called, is to be found in any other country. By this "unintelligible jargon" of syllables the hereditary pipers trained their pupils, without the aid of any scales or other notations, and in this form the tunes were chanted all over the Highlands. To this day many pipers will give the syllabic wordings of tunes, and several of the more expert can play the pipes direct from such a notation. The different teachers of piping—they were always clan pipers—had different systems, but all were based on the principle of arbitrary and known sounds, representing certain notes, and a succession of these, of course, a tune. The system of the Mac Crimmons, hereditary pipers to Mac Leod of Dunvegan, and the most famous teachers and players, became most popular, as they had by far the largest number of pupils, and a reference to it will serve to illustrate the subject.

Some time or other—the date cannot be fixed—the system was committed to paper, and in 1828 Captain Neil Mac Leod of Gesto published a book, giving the notation in actual type. It is perhaps the most remarkable book that has ever been issued in connection with any musical instrument. Though to the ordinary reader it is absolute nonsense, so late as 1880, Duncan Ross, the Duke of Argyll's piper, who

CAPTAIN NEIL MAC LEOD OF GESTO
(From a Photograph in the possession of Dr. Keith N. Mac Donald, Edinburgh.)

learned his art orally in Ross-shire from the chanting of John Mac Kenzie, Lord Breadalbane's piper, himself a pupil of the Mac Crimmons, could read and play from it at sight, and as he is still alive can, I suppose, do so to this day. In the same year, Ross, the Queen's piper, chanted a tune in articulate words, and, when compared with the Mac Crimmon language, the notes were found to be identical in length and rhythm, although the words were different. It was the same tune expressed by a different set of words, and the experiment proved that the old pipers did not teach in a haphazard style, but according to fixed rules. The Mac Crimmons, in particular, wrote down their tunes, and Captain Mac Leod himself took down from the dictation of John MacCrimmon, one of the latest of the race, a collection of airs, as verbally taught at the "college" at Dunvegan, which he incorporated in the "Gesto" book. After this it is not so difficult to believe that a piper, when he heard the instrument, could imagine it was a language, and know what the player meant him to understand. When education came, and the notation was printed, it was seen that it was a system scientifically constructed, and one from which an expert could read music at sight, just as a pianist can play from the staff, although he has never seen the piece before. At least three different systems existed in the Highlands seventy years ago, and Donald Cameron, Seaforth's famous piper, and the acknowledged successor of the MacCrimmons, though practically an illiterate man, could read ordinary music, and also had a system of his own.

The "Gesto" Book contains twenty pibrochs, and is now very rare. It was reprinted some years ago by Messrs. J. & R. Glen, Edinburgh. Captain Mac Leod had a large manuscript collection of Mac Crimmon pibrochs, as noted by the pipers themselves, part of which was very old, and part more modern. Of these he only published a few as an experiment. The verse given at the head of this chapter is part of the tune *Gilliechroist*, the first line being interpreted :—

"Yonder I see a great smoke."

The tune afterwards proceeds with " variations," which complicate the wording considerably, and make it appear even more unintelligible. Here again is the *urlar* or groundwork of " The Prince's Salute " in the notation of the Mac Crimmons :—

" hi o dro hi ri, hi an an in ha ra,
  hi o dro ha chin, ha chin hi a chin,
  hi o dro hi ri, hi an an in ha ra,
  hi o dro ha chin, ha chin hi chin,
  hi o dro hi ri, hi an an in ha ra,
  hi o dro ha chin, ha chin hi a chin,
  hi o dro hi ri, hi an an in ha ra,
  hi o dro ha chin, ha chin hi chin."

It is impossible to discover whether the pipers built up their tunes, as tunes are now-a-days built up from a certain scale, or simply used the syllables as convenient signs to represent certain fixed notes. Perhaps no better illustration of the subject is to be found than a pamphlet published in 1880 by Mr. J. F. Campbell, of Islay, the compiler of *Popular Tales of the West Highlands,* and entitled *Canntaireachd.* An interpreter of the notation who could play it at sight, could not explain it to Mr. Campbell. " It was like asking a thrush to explain the songs which Mother Nature had taught him " :—

" A party, of whom three were good musicians and the fourth was used to play upon human nature, met, the interpreter came, we chose a word in a tune and, asked—

" ' What is *hirrin !* '

" ' That is *hirrin,*' said the piper, and played three notes deftly with his little finger by striking a note on the chanter once. Two were open notes ; one closed.

" ' Do you know the name of the fingers ?' said the teacher.

" ' Yes,' said I, ' that's *ludag,* the little finger.'

G

" ' Well,' said the artist, ' that's *hirrin,*' and he played the passage several times to show how it was done with the little finger.

" ' Is *hirrin* the name of the little finger of the right hand, or the name of the hole in the chanter, or the name of the note ; or what else is it ? '

" ' No,' said the master, ' that's *hirrin,*' and he played that word over again cleverly with the same little finger. Then he continued—

" ' Old John Mackenzie taught me that in Ross long ago ; and he learned it over the fire in the Isle of Skye. We used to sit and listen to him, and learn what he said and sang, and learn to finger in this way.' Then the piper played silently with his fingers, and every now and then he blew the chanter and sounded a passage a breath long from the book, which he read easily, but could not explain—and that's *hirrin*—and if any of the party ever hear that particular combination of three notes again the name of it will be remembered. It means three notes combined.

" Compared to a book of poetry, it thus appears that each tune is like a song, and *hirrin* is like a word in a line which keeps its place and its time in the tune. That much we learned from our interpreter. He had learned by rote certain articulate syllables combined as words which for him meant passages in a particular pipe tune. For the ignorant residue of mankind they meant nothing."

There Mr. Campbell had to stop, for further light on the subject he could not obtain. " The pipers' language," he says, " is not founded upon a systematic combination of vowels and consonants to make words, like C E D, D E C, D E D. It is not a set of names for notes, like Do, Re, Mi, Fa, Sol, La, Si, Do. Each tune has a different set of words made of different syllables. Only nine notes can be sounded on the instrument, and more than sixty syllables occur in a book of twenty tunes." Mr. Campbell must have been unaware of the assertion of some enthusiasts that 3,000,000 combinations can be practised on the pipes, or he would not have written that last sentence. Proceeding, he

says, " it seems that something natural to human songsters
has been spelt with the Roman alphabet, so that words of
one, two, three, four, six, and eight syllables, do in fact
suggest accent rhythm and tune, high and low notes and
whole tunes, which can be learned by rote, written and read,
as if the tunes were songs in an unknown tongue. This is
in fact a language and its music."

Persevering in his researches Mr. Campbell got Ross, the
Argyll piper, his brother, and a skilled pianist to help him.
He opened the Gesto book at the tune called " The End of
the Little Bridge ;" Ross read the tune and sounded the
signs on a chanter, while his brother chanted at intervals
sounds which both brothers had learned from oral chanting
and could play on a pipe. The musician with his eyes on
the book played his notes with his left hand on the piano,
as he heard them from the pipers, and wrote them with his
right on music paper, according to his own system. By this
means one combination of sounds was translated from the
pipers' written language into another system of musical
notation, and the result was music, showing that the hereditary pipers, whatever is the secret of their system, had a
system. Were there only as many different syllables as
there are possible notes on the chanter, the matter would
have been easily understood. As it is, the Gesto book is
the only book of its kind in existence. In all countries of
the world, the natives chant tunes to certain strings of
syllables, and to this day we have the " Fal de ral " choruses
to a certain class of songs. In the Highlands alone these
apparently nonsensical sentences stood for actual living
music, were written as such, and, in the Gesto book, printed.
But the system which in a continuance of the congenial
atmosphere of clanship and hereditary pipers and schools of

piping, and ignorance of what is now called popular education, might have developed into an exact science, has been
smothered by nineteenth century progress, and is now known
only to piping enthusiasts and students of the antique in
our national life.   Various attempts have been made to
construct a theory which would explain the system, but none
is thoroughly satisfactory.

Leaving the mystery of *Canntaireachd*, we come to the
time when pipe music was first written in ordinary notation.
The piece known as " The Battle of Harlaw " was played at
that encounter in 1411 ; but it is significant that the oldest
copy of the music extant, supposed to date from 1620, is
not adapted for the bagpipe. The earliest known attempt
to write pipe music in ordinary notation was made in 1784
when Rev. Patrick Mac Donald, Kilmore, Argyllshire,
included in a collection of Highland Vocal Airs four pipe
tunes.   In 1803 the same author published a " Treatise "
on the bagpipe, written by his brother, Mr. Joseph Mac
Donald.   This contained one tune, suited for beginners.
Some time after the '45—it must have been a considerable
time—Mr. Donald Mac Donald, bagpipe maker, Edinburgh,
was employed by the Highland Societies then existing to
collect and note down as many pibrochs as he could find.
In these days the mysteries of correct time were known to
few and those of metre to fewer ; but Mac Donald started
with a brave heart, and to him as much as to the hereditary
pipers the Highlands is indebted for the preservation of
much of its pipe music.   He collected mostly in the west
country, and it is noticeable that the great majority of tunes
now existing are west country tunes.   The east Highlands,
doubtless, had its own pipe music, but for want of a collector most of the airs have been lost. " Craigellachie,"

the gathering of Clan Grant, is the only notable exception. Mac Donald's first volume contained twenty-three pibrochs, but the exact date of its publication is unknown. In 1806, we are told in Angus Mac Kay's book, Donald Mac Donald was voted the thanks of the judges at the annual competition in Edinburgh for having "produced" the greatest number of pipe tunes set to music by himself. His book, however, does not seem to have been published then, for from internal evidence (there is no date) it is obvious that it did not see the light before 1816. In the volume he promised to give histories of the tunes when he published a second instalment. A long time after he sent the manuscript of his second volume to Mr. J. W. Grant of Elchies, then in India, with a plaintive letter asking him to accept it as no one had shown so much interest in it as he had, and the publication of the first volume had nearly ruined him. The manuscript is now in the possession of Major-General C. S. Thomason, R.E., a grandson of Mr. Grant, and, it is hoped, will yet be published.

Of a later date, we have the book published in 1838 by Angus Mac Kay, piper to the Queen. It was a pretentious volume, containing sixty pibrochs, with histories of the tunes, the lives of the hereditary pipers, and other interesting matter. It will always be a puzzle to students of pipe music why Mac Donald and Mac Kay included in their books so many poor pieces and left out some of the best. Ross's collection, which appeared long after, contained some which one would have thought Mac Kay or Mac Donald might have had. Messrs. Glen, Edinburgh, published a collection dated 1854, and there are besides the publications of Mac Phee, Mac Lachlan, Gunn, Henderson, Mac Kinnon, Bett, and others, all issued later. Most of these, however,

appear to have been based largely on Mac Donald's and
Mac Kay's books. Mr. David Glen of Edinburgh has, it
may be added, published recently the old pipe music of the
Clan Mac Lean, compiled under the supervision of the Clan
Mac Lean Society of Glasgow.

The Gesto collection of Highland music, edited by Dr.
Keith Norman Mac Donald, and dedicated to the Mac
Leods of Gesto, is perhaps the most outstanding publication in which the music of the pipes has been adapted for
the piano. It was published in 1895. Dr. Mac Donald's
avowed object was to supply a collection free from all
adulteration, and to preserve the music as it was sung and
played by the Highlanders themselves. The book, while
not containing everything that is good in pipe music, undoubtedly contains a larger selection of the best than any
other. There are songs, pibrochs, and laments ; marches,
quicksteps, and general martial music ; and also reels and
strathspeys, numbering in the aggregate about three hundred and forty tunes ; and all over, the book is perhaps
more interesting and comprehensive than any that has been
issued. A second edition was published in 1898.

In 1896 Major-General Thomason, already mentioned,
issued for private circulation a small volume. In this he fore-
shadowed a larger, which has since been published.* Major-
General Thomason is the possessor not only of the manuscript
of Donald Mac Donald's proposed second volume, but also of
all the manuscript music left by Angus Mac Kay. Besides,
he spent many years in collecting pibrochs from all possible
sources, and at the present time he believes that he has almost
every pibroch known to be in existence. He has spent much

---

* Messrs. S. Sidders & Co., Ball Street, Kensington, London.

time and labour editing his collection, and the result is the
volume referred to, which is published under the title of
Ceol Mor (the proper title of real pibroch music). Besides
being an extraordinarily diligent collector of tunes, Major-
General Thomason was imbued with the idea of rendering
the reading of pibrochs more easy. He took notes of the
difference in times and the different styles of playing, and
became so proficient that he could note any strange tune
from the playing of another piper. It was only a step
further to decide that the signs which he could note down
as the tune was being played would serve as a notation from
which the tune could be replayed. He invented, in fact, a
system of shorthand for pipe music, and then he set about
endeavouring to publish a book printed after his own system, in the hope that pipers would learn it in preference to
the old and cumbersome system. By this means he believes
he will further popularise bagpipe music, but the ordinary
notation has now got so firm a hold that it will be difficult
to convince pipers that it will pay them to learn another.
Like ordinary shorthand systems, *Ceol Mor* is doubtless capable of improvement; but the idea opens up an altogether new field in the literature of pipe music, and as the
book contains some two hundred and eighty tunes—the
result of thirty years' collecting—it is to be hoped that it
will prove a success.

After all it is not so much more books that are needed as
a thoroughly standard work including all that is best in
pipe music set in some uniform style. There is, however,
no getting away from the fact that this cannot be done with
any hope of financial success. The jealousies of musicians
come in the way, and pipers will have some new tunes, even
although it is well known that these, as a rule, are worth-

less. Nothing short of an encyclopædia containing everything that has ever been composed would please everybody, and this would require to be sold for a few shillings. Then there are the difficulties of copyright—different persons or publishers claiming different tunes or settings of tunes. Still, with anything like a common desire to promote the best interests of national music, these difficulties could to a large extent be overcome. There never was a more opportune time than the present, there being so many pipers and the ability to read music being almost universal. Meantime pipers are struggling along with many tunes and a good many books with a lot of irregularities and inconsistencies scattered through them. There is certainly room for improvement, and if pipers and publishers, or some of the Highland societies—say in Glasgow—took the matter up in earnest, something could be done to set up a standard of some kind that would give the music of the pipes its proper place.

CHAPTER VIII.

The Pipes in Battle.

" Fhairshon swore a feud
    Against the Clan MacTavish,
Marched into their land,
    To plunder and to rafish.
For he did resolve
    To extirpate the vipers,
With four-and-twenty men
    And five-and-thirty pipers."

A Culloden incident—Ancient Celts in battle—The harper and
bard superseded—First mention of pipes in battle—First
regimental pipers—In the navy—Prince Charlie's pipers—An
" instrument of war "—A MacCrimmon incident—Power of
pipes in battle—A Magersfontein incident—Byron's tribute—
Position in actual battle.

PROFESSOR AYTOUN in these cynically humorous
lines, from the " Bon Gaultier Ballads," would have
us believe that the piper was more important in
times of war than the actual fighting man. He was important, no doubt, but hardly in the proportion of thirty-
five to twenty-four. The Duke of Cumberland, a man whom
Highlanders, and more especially those with Jacobite lean-
ings, do not hold in very high reverence, was making ready
to meet Prince Charlie at Culloden, and when he saw the

pipers of the clans who supported him preparing their musical instruments, he asked somewhat testily, " What are these men to do with such bundles of sticks. I can get far better implements of war than these." " Your Royal Highness," said an aide-de-camp, " cannot get them better weapons. They are the bagpipes, the Highlanders' music in peace and war. Without these all other instruments are of no avail, and the Highland soldiers need not advance another step, for they will be of no service." Then Cumberland, who was too good a tactician to underrate the value of anything, allowed the pipers to take their part in the fight. It is difficult to believe, although the story is given on good authority, that he was so ignorant, but we know that a general who did not understand the music of his different regiments would now-a-days be considered very deficient indeed. Officers of our day not only understand about the music, they fully appreciate its value. This is particularly true of the officers of Highland regiments who, as a rule, do all they can to foster a love for the pipes, knowing quite well that

> " Its martial sounds can fainting troops inspire
> With strength unwonted and enthusiasm fire."

The use by the Celts of the bagpipes in battle fits in beautifully with all we know of the ancient people. Their demeanour in the actual fight was always remarkable. In old times they did not fight as they do now, with weapons deadly at long distances from the enemy, and to use which in a uniform style they are disciplined. Each warrior fought for his own hand, with his own claymore, subject, after the fight began, to no system of rules. Before the battle a strange nervous excitement, called by ancient writers, *crith-*

gaisge, or "quiverings of valour," came over him. This was followed by an overpowering feeling of exhilaration and delight, called *mir-cath*, or "the joyous frenzy of battle." It was not a thirst for blood, but an absorbing idea that both his own life and fame and his country's good depended on his efforts, and a determination to do all that could be done by a resolute will and undaunted spirit. The *mir-cath* has been seen in a modified form on several occasions in modern warfare, but only when the Highland soldier has a chance of charging with the bayonet. Then that shout which precedes an onset no foe can withstand is heard, and the Highlanders forget themselves and rush forward like an irresistible torrent.

The harp was originally the national musical instrument of the Highlands, but its strains were too soft and melting for the clash of arms, and the utmost efforts of the harper would fail to rouse the vengeful fervour of the Gaelic heroes. The pibroch's shrill summons, telling the sad tale of devastated straths and homeless friends, with notes that had often led them to victory aforetime, was needed to gather them to the fray ; it drowned with its piercing tones the wailings of the bereaved, and called in maddened ardour for revenge on the enemy. It was perhaps a descent when the pipes had to be substituted for the voice of the bard, and it was certainly a descent when the pipes as a domestic instrument superseded the soft and soothing harp. But the two changes were inevitable, and the first is not so great as it seems. The pipes almost spoke to the people, and their music was but another language in which their deeds and those of their ancestors were being preserved.

The bards, who preceded the pipers as an inspiring military force, seemed themselves not only susceptible to the influence of the *mir-cath*, but capable of imparting it to others. Before the battle they passed from clan to clan, giving exhortation and encouragement in wild recitative strains, and rousing the feelings of the warriors to the highest pitch of frenzy. When the noise of fighting drowned their voices, the pipes, after they became general as military instruments, kept the enthusiasm alive. Both bard and piper helped when the battle was over to celebrate the deeds of those who had survived and the honour of the brave who had fallen, the piper's part of the work being more often the playing of laments for the departed. By these means, death was robbed of its terrors, for the honouring of the dead who died nobly naturally produced a magnanimous contempt for the last enemy. The pipes, from their first introduction, had no rival as an instrument of war. That they were used as such in ancient times we have historical proof. Among the Highlanders the bagpipe is supposed to have superseded the war-song of the bards about the beginning of the fifteenth century. We have the tradition of the Clan Menzies that it was used at Bannockburn, but though we grant that on many occasions

> " The Menzies' pipers played so gay,
>   They cheered the clan in many a fray,"

as the family chronicler tells us, we can hardly accept the evidence of tradition alone, when it is backed up by little or nothing from history. The first mention of military bagpipe music is given in accounts of the battle of Glenlivck, in 1594, but it is not until after 1600 that we find pipers mentioned as men of war by reputable historians. In 1627, says the Transactions of the Society of Antiquaries in Scotland, a certain Alex. MacNaughton of that ilk was commissioned by King Charles I. to " levie and transport twa hundredthe bowmen " to serve in the war against France. On January 15th, 1628, he wrote to the Earl of Morton, from Falmouth, where his vessel had been driven by stress of weather. In a postscript he said :—

" My L.—As for newis from our selfis, our bagg pypperis and Marlit Plaidis serwitt us in guid wise in the pursuit of ane man of war that hetlie followit us."

The English of the postscript is, like the spelling, a little shaky, and I am not going to explain how it was possible to pursue " ane man of war that hetlie followit us," or whether the pipers frightened the enemy or, as a cynical writer observes, " merely supplied the wind for the sails " and helped the ship away. The quotation, however, proves conclusively that there were soldiers in these days who wore the tartan—" Marlit Plaidis " is decidedly poetic—and had bagpipers in their company. " Besides," continues the Transactions, " the piper Allester Caddel was followed by a boy," his gillie presumably, and there were also " Harrie M'Gra, harper, frae Larg," and " another piper."

In 1641, Lord Lothian, writing from the Scottish Army at Newcastle, puts in a word for the pipers :—

" I cannot out of our armie furnish you with a sober fiddler ; there is a fellow here plays exceeding well, but he is intollerably given to drink ; nor have we many of those people. Our armie has few or none that carie not armes. We are sadder and graver than ordinarie soldiers, only we are well provided of pypers. I have one for every company in my regiment, and I think they are as good as drummers."

They were evidently better than fiddlers, anyhow.

In 1642 there were regular regimental pipers, and it is believed that the 21st Royal Scots Fusiliers, then the North

British Fusiliers, was about the first regiment which had them. When the town of Londonderry was invested in 1689 by James VII., two drums, a piper, and colours were allotted to each company of infantry, each troop of horse had a trumpet and a standard, and each troop of dragoons had two trumpets, two hautbois, and a standard. When the figures relating to the strength of the army are analysed, it is found that each regiment must have had fourteen pipers, fifty-six drums, five trumpets, and fourteen hautbois —that is, if the bands were at full strength.

That pipers were not always confined to the land forces is shown by an advertisement in the *Edinburgh Courant* in 1708, asking for " any person that plays on the bagpipes who might be willing to engage on board a British man-of-war." British and Dutch ships are known to have been lying in Leith Roads at the time, which accounts for the advertisement. A harper is mentioned as being in the navy as early as 1660, so music was not a new thing on board a man-of-war.

Although drummers were used in Highland regiments before 1745, the pipers outnumbered them very much, for whenever one was found who could play the pipes, the clans compelled him to follow them. Prince Charlie is said to have had thirty-two, who played before his tent at meal-time, and that their instrument was considered a weapon of war is proved by the fact that although a James Reid, one of the pipers who was taken on the suppression of the rebellion, pleaded that he had not carried arms, and was not, therefore, a soldier, the Courts decided that the pipe was a warlike instrument, and punished the performer just as if he had carried a claymore. When, after the battle of Prestonpans, the Prince entered Edinburgh, we read that—

" As he came marching up the street,
The pipes played loud and clear,
And a' the folks came running out
To meet the Chevalier."

At the time of the rebellion the pipers had come to be
highly respected members of the clans. Almost as much so
as the bards were in their day. In 1745 the Mac Leods
marched into Aberdeenshire and were defeated at Inverurie.
Mac Crimmon, the great piper from Dunvegan, and master
of the celebrated Skye " college," was taken prisoner after a
stout resistance, and the following morning it was found
that not one of the pipers of the victorious army played
through the town as usual. When asked the reason of their
extraordinary conduct, they answered that while the Mac
Crimmon was in captivity their instruments would not
sound, and it was only on the release of the prisoner that
they resumed their duties. The Mac Crimmons were then,
however, so well known all over the Highlands that the
action of the other pipers can hardly be considered
remarkable.

Many and many a time has the efficacy of pipe music in
rallying men and leading them on to victory been proved.
At Quebec in April, 1760, when Fraser's regiment were
retreating in great disorder the general complained to a
field officer of the behaviour of his corps. " Sir," the officer
replied, warmly, " you did very wrong in forbidding the
pipers to play this morning ; nothing encourages the Highlanders so much in the day of battle, and even now they
would be of some use." "Then," said the general, " let
them blow like the devil if that will bring back the men."
The pipers played a favourite martial air, and the Highlanders, the moment they heard it, re-formed, and there

was no more disorder.   When the regiment raised by Lord
MacLeod in 1778, called the 73rd or MacLeod's Highlanders,
was in India, General Sir Eyre Coote thought at first that
the bagpipe was a " useless relic of the barbarous ages and
not in any manner calculated to discipline troops."   But
the distinctness with which the shrill sounds made themselves
heard through the noise of battle and the influence they
seemed to exercise induced him to change his opinion.   At
Port Novo in 1781, he, with eight thousand men, of which
the 73rd was the only British regiment, defeated Hyder
Ali's army of twenty-five battalions of infantry, four hundred Europeans, from forty-thousand to fifty thousand
horse, and over one hundred thousand matchlock men, with
forty-seven cannon.   The 73rd was on the right of the first
line, leading all the attacks, and the general's notice was
particularly attracted by the pipers, who always blew up the
most warlike strains when the fire was hottest.   This so
pleased Sir Eyre Coote that he called out—" Well done,
my brave fellows, you shall have a set of silver pipes for
this."   And he was as good as his word, for he gave the
men £50, and the pipes which this bought had an inscription testifying to the high opinion the general had of the
pipers.   At the battle of Assaye, again, the musicians were
ordered to lay aside their instruments and attend to the
wounded.   One of the pipers who obeyed this order was
afterwards reproached by his comrades.   Flutes or hautbois,
they told him, they could well spare, but for the piper, who
should always be in the heat of the battle, to go to the rear
with the whistles was a thing unheard of.   The unfortunate
piper was quite humbled, but he soon had an opportunity
of playing off the stigma, for in the advance at Argaun
shortly after, he played with such animation that the men

could hardly be restrained from breaking the line and rushing to the charge before the time.

Of a different nature is a story told of the Seaforth Highlanders. On the 12th of August, 1793, as the grenadiers of Captain Gordon's company at Pondicherry were on duty in the trenches, exposed to a burning sun and a severe cannonade from a fortress near by, Colonel Campbell, field officer of the trenches, ordered the piper to play some pibrochs. This was considered a strange order to be made at such a time, but it was immediately complied with, and, says the writer of the chronicles of the regiment, " we were a good deal surprised to perceive that the moment the piper began, the fire from the enemy slackened, and soon almost entirely ceased. The French all got upon the works, and seemed more astonished at hearing the bagpipes than we with Colonel Campbell's request." It was a new kind of warfare, and again justifies the use of the appellation " weapon " instead of " instrument " used by the court which tried the Jacobite piper in 1746.

We all know the story of Lucknow, and though we know that, as a matter of history, it is entirely discredited, we cannot deny its extreme probability, and the intense effect the sound of the pipes in the distance would have had on the fainting men and women in the Residency. Something like the Lucknow story is that of Prince Charlie, who, when the clans were slow in gathering to his standard at Glenfinnan, retired to a hut and rested, disheartened and anxious. When at noon on the 19th of August no appearance was made he became hopeless, but in the afternoon the sound of the pipes made themselves heard, and shortly after the clans appeared. This is the moment which the

authoress of the well-known song, "The March of the
Cameron Men," has described :—

> " Oh proudly they walk, but each Cameron knows
>   He may tread on the heather no more,
> But boldly he follows his chief to the field,
>   Where his laurels were gathered before.

> " I hear the pibroch, sounding, sounding,
>   Deep o'er the mountain and glen,
> While light springing footsteps are trampling the heath,
>   'Tis the march of the Cameron men."

A good instance of the power of the pipes to rally men
is told of the fateful battle of Magersfontein, during the
present war in South Africa.   When, at one stage, it seemed
as if " retreat " had been sounded, a piper tried to tune his
pipes, but his lips were too dry.   A major handed him his
own water bottle, and immediately afterwards, " Hey,
Johnnie Cope " rang out.   The men gathered round the
piper as he stood there playing, marking time with his foot,
and the tide was turned.   The soldiers were sifted back into
regiments and companies, and something like order was
evolved out of chaos.

Foreigners do not understand how a certain kind of music
can have such a powerful effect on men, and even our friends
south of the Cheviots have been known to sneer at it, but
the facts are too stubborn to ding, and they are acknowledged by men of the highest military experience.   Perhaps
there is no nobler tribute to their power and military
beauty than that of Lord Byron, himself an Englishman:—

> " And wild and high ' The Cameron's Gathering ' rose,
>   The war note of Lochiel, which Albyn's hills
> Have heard, and heard, too, have her Saxon foes :—

How in the noon of night that pibroch thrills,
Savage and shrill !   But with the breath which fills
Their mountain pipe, so fill the mountaineers
With the fierce native daring which instils
The stirring memory of a thousand years
And Evan's, Donald's fame rings in each clansman's ears. "

The Highland soldier has proved on many a hard-fought field the inspiring influence of

" Those thrilling sounds that call the might
Of old Clan-Alpine to the fight,"

but in all the great battles fought and won by Highlanders since 1689 the pipes have not been used in the actual charge. There is an impression that the regimental piper keeps in front of, or alongside, his men, and actually plays them into the enemy's ranks, and this idea has been largely fostered by the pictures that have appeared of such incidents as that of Dargai. As a matter of fact such a method is totally impracticable. In a regiment in line advancing, the pipe band is formed up in the centre, behind the reserves. When a charge is about to take place, the word of command, " Prepare to Charge," is given, and every soldier knows what this means. When the word, " Prepare to Charge," is given, the front rank comes to the charge, while the rear rank remains at the slope. Meantime the line section, or whatever the party may be, steadily advances. Simultaneously the pipers strike up the charge in marching time, and all ranks anxiously await the command, "Charge." When this comes the pipers and drummers instantly change from marching to double time. With the music and the cheers and shouts of the Highlanders, the charge is pressed home, being generally made at a distance

of from fifty to sixty yards from the enemy, the piper
closely following up his regiment, company, or section,
playing the charge and thus cheering the troops onward.
All then is confusion and wild excitement, and after that
the battle is either lost or won. To rally the regiments the
" assembly " is sounded, preceded by the regimental call, to
distinguish what regiment should respond. After the melee
every battalion forms up at lightning speed on their
markers, and are again under the control of their officers
for the furtherance of any other movement. Such is the
position of a pipe band when a charge is made in line.
There is another way while troops are manœuvring, and
when the pipers may be ordered to rejoin their companies.
Their position then would be behind the centre of their
companies, with the buglers, at various points. It is then
quite possible for the piper or pipers to act precisely in the
same way behind their companies as the combined band
would do behind the battalion if they were in line. Under
extraordinary circumstances, where troops are detached outside of military rule, one cannot easily define where the
piper might be placed—he might be anywhere. We read
that in former wars, such as the Peninsular, where a breach
was made by the troops, pipers sometimes got inside the
breach, and, standing on the ramparts, played their hardest
to encourage the troops ; but under ordinary circumstances
the piper's position is behind his party ; and if he is profes-
sionally unemployed, he occupies himself in attending to
his fallen comrades or performing any other duty that may
be assigned to him. It is hardly possible, considering the
methods of modern warfare, to think of circumstances in
which a piper should lead a charge in front of his company.

Although we must sweep away this cherished idea and consign it to the region of muzzle-loading guns and frontal attacks, this does not in the least reduce the military value of the instrument. There is no music half so good for marching purposes as that of the pipes and drums. It gives the soldiers a quick swinging step, taking them over the ground without a drag. This cannot be said of the brass or fife band. The pipers carry no cumbrous accoutrements, and when their bags are full they can keep up the music for two or three miles; in fact, on one occasion in India the Black Watch pipers played for over four miles. During the Indian Mutiny the marching of the British soldier was a wonder to all who knew the climate, the more so, as much of it had to be done with a hot sun beating down upon the feather bonnets and red coats as their wearers toiled across a country of sand, with camels, elephants, bullocks, and camp followers by the thousand, often marching close upon the column. The swing and go of a Highland regiment is something peculiar to itself, and is due in great measure to the pipes. It is something born of the music, and it has often proved its value in actual warfare, where marching was conjoined with fighting, as, for instance, with the 93rd at Balaclava, where

"That thin red line of Gaelic rock,
   Just tipped with shining steel,
Answered with long and steady stride
   Their own loved pipes' appeal."

CHAPTER IX.

The Piper as a Hero.

"Never in battlefield throbbed heart so brave
    As that which beats beneath the Scottish plaid,
And when the pibroch bids the battle rave
    And level for the charge their arms are laid,
        Where lives the desperate foe that for such onset staid?"

One cowardly piper—At Philiphaugh—At Bothwell Bridge—At
    Cromdale—The Peninsular War—At Waterloo—Reay Country
    pipers—At Candahar—At Lucknow—In America—In Ashanti
    —In the Soudan—In South Africa.

THE pipers of a regiment are exposed to very much the
same dangers as are the soldiers, and in all the
history of British warfare we read of only one
cowardly piper. This was *Raoghull Odhar*, a Highlander,
who, being one day in the exercise of his duty in the battlefield along with his clan, was seized with such terror at the
sight of the enemy, whom he thought too many for his
party, that he left off playing and began to sing a most
dolorous song to a lachrymose air. Some stanzas were
picked up by his comrades, and afterwards when an adult
was seen crying for some trifling cause he was said to be
singing "Dun Ronald's tune." Likewise when a Highlander threatened vengeance for some boisterous mischief he
would say, "I will make you sing Dun Ronald's tune."

Where or when the incident which gave rise to the saying took place we cannot tell, and so the only story of a cowardly piper that we have on record is not very well authenticated.

On the other hand, we have numerous instances of the bravery of pipers. Away back as far as the battle of Philiphaugh we have a duplicate of the Dargai incident, only more so. There is a part of the Ettrick opposite the field of battle called "The Piper's Pule." Tradition says that a piper belonging to Montrose's army planted himself on a knowe overhanging this part of the river, during the course of the engagement, cheered his companions, who were fighting below, with a well-known cavalier tune, the refrain of which was :—

> "Whirry, Whigs, awa' man,
> Whirry, Whigs, awa',
> Ye're but a pack o' brosy mou's,
> Ye'll dae nae gude at a',"

until one of Leslie's men sent a shot across the water which brought the piper tumbling down the brae and laid him snug in the pool which bears his name. Then, again depending on tradition, at the battle of Bothwell Bridge in 1679, the piper to Clavers' own troop stood out on the brink of the Clyde playing "Awa', Whigs, awa," with great glee, but, being struck by a bullet, he rolled down the bank in the agonies of death, and always as he rolled over the bag, so intent was he on the old party tune, that with determined firmness of fingering he made the pipes to yell out two or three notes more of it, till at last he plunged into the river and was carried peaceably down the stream among a great number of Whigs. There is a striking resemblance between the two traditions, and possibly they are but variations of one, but I give them as I find them.

Another piper hero of these early days took part in the battle at the Haughs of Cromdale, an engagement which ended the civil war in Scotland in 1690. On the first day of May in that year the Jacobites were unexpectedly attacked by the Royalists, and were literally driven across Cromdale Hill. In the rout one of the Jacobite pipers was badly wounded, but he managed to climb on the top of a large boulder on the hillside, and on this elevated perch he played tune after tune until he fell off the stone, dead. The stone is known to this day as *Clach-a-phiobair*, or the Piper's Stone.

Coming to times of which we have better historical records, we find similar incidents multiplying. The pibroch sounded at Waterloo where fire was hottest, at Lucknow it was heard above the din of battle; at Alma, when Sir Colin Campbell's voice, clear and sharp as a trumpet, sounded " Forward Forty-second," the notes of the bagpipes rose over Kourgave Hill, as the veteran rode through the river and up the slope. At Arroyo-de-Molinos the pipes wakened and frightened the Frenchmen in the grey dawn of a rainy morning and scattered a whole brigade to the tune of " Hey, Johnnie Cope, are ye waking yet ? " At Puebla Heights, on the morning after Vittoria, they animated the Gordons in the face of immense odds to keep the position for many hours, and at Dargai, in our own day, the pipes played the Gordons up the steep slope, although the piper was too badly wounded to do more than play. Findlater's gallantry has been widely extolled, and there is no desire to detract from the merit of his performance, but a very slight study of the history of the Highland regiments will show anyone that there have been many deeds just as brave, and done, too, by pipers of whom nothing whatever has been heard.

Here are a few good instances of the bravery of pipers in the story of the Peninsular War. At the battle of Assaye, when the Ross-shire Buffs charged, the pipers stood to their posts and kept up their music until they were disabled one after another by the fire of the enemy. At Cuidad Rodrigo, John Mac Lachlan, a piper of the 74th, was among the first to mount the walls. Once there he tuned up and played " The Campbells are coming." John was a cool as well as a brave man, for when, on the ramparts, a shot penetrated the bag of his pipes, he calmly sat down where he was and repaired the damage, and soon he was up again and playing his comrades on to victory. At Vittoria the 92nd stormed the town, the band playing all the time amid a storm of shot and shell. Napier, in the *History of the Peninsular War*, referring to this, says : " The pipers contributed in no small degree to produce the enthusiasm. They headed the charge, striking up a favourite war tune composed centuries before. Their war-like music inspired their comrades with a fury nothing could resist. . . . How gloriously did that regiment come forth again to the charge, their colours flying and their pipes playing as if at review." At Vimiera, George Clark, piper to the 71st, was wounded in the leg by a musket ball as the regiment was advancing. Sitting down, he put his pipes in order, and calling out, " Weel, lads, I am sorry I can gae nae farther wi' you, but deil hae my saul if ye sall want music," he struck up a favourite air with the utmost unconcern, and played until victory was secure. This piper afterwards appeared in a competition in the Edinburgh Theatre-Royal (Findlator's story was but history repeating itself after all), where he was warmly greeted.

Whether he was successful history sayeth not, but that he was a good performer is proved by the fact that he was afterwards piper to the Highland Society of London. Charles Mackay made one of his prettiest poems on this piper's bravery, which, excusing the slip made in speaking of people dancing reels to pibroch music, a slip hardly excusable in Charles Mackay, is worth quoting entire :—

" A Highland piper shot through both his feet,
    Lay on the ground in agonising pain ;
The cry was raised, ' The Highlanders retreat ;
    They run, they fly, they rally not again ! '
The piper heard, and, rising on his arm,
    Clutched to his heart the pipes he loved so well,
And blew a blast—a dirge-like shrill alarm,
    That quickly changed to the all-jubilant swell
Of ' Tullochgorum.' Swift as lightning flash,
    Or fire in stubble, the tumultuous sound
Thrilled through the clansmen's hearts, and with a dash
    Of unreflecting valour, at one bound
They turned upon their hot-pursuing foes,
    And faced them with one wild tempestuous cheer
That almost drowned the music as it rose
    Defiant o'er the field, loud, long, and clear !
Scotland was in it, and the days of old
    When, to the well-remembered pibrochs of their sires,
They danced the exultant reel on hillsides cold,
    Or warmed their hearts with patriotic fires.
The startled enemy, in sudden dread,
Staggered and paused, then, pale with terror, fled ;
The clansmen followed—hurling shout on shout—
In martial madness on the hopeless rout.
'Twas but five minutes from the set of sun,
And ere it sank the victory was won !
Glory and honour, all that men can crave,
Be thine, O piper, bravest of the brave ! "

We have several stories of Waterloo which point the same moral. One piper was shot in the leg before he got properly started with his music, and this so roused his Highland blood that, dashing his pipes to the ground, he drew his broadsword and fought with the fury of a lion until he died from many wounds. ·A pipe-major of the Gordons placed himself on an eminence, amid a shower of shot, and proudly sounded the battle charge, and Piper Kenneth Mac Kay, a native of Tongue, and one of the 79th Cameron Highlanders, specially distinguished himself at Quatre Bras a few days earlier. During the formation of the regiment, while the brigade was threatened by a body of French cavalry, Piper Mac Kay calmly stepped outside the bayonets and played *Cogadh na Sith* with inspiring effect, almost right in front of the enemy. The incident is best told in a poem by Alice C. Mac Donnell, of Keppoch, contributed to the *Celtic Monthly* of June, 1895 :—

> " As roe-deer reared within the forests,
>   At Quatre Bras they bounded o'er,
> Graceful, poised, with scarce an effort,
>   The fifteen feet of bank before.
> Then their famous charge was driven
>   Home to the advancing force ;
> Back upon the bridge they huddled,
>   The troopers of Napoleon's horse.
> Theirs the charge the guns to cover,
>   Theirs to hold that dangerous post ;
> Volley upon volley answered
>   From the hedge this charging host.
> Side by side they fought untiring,
>   Full upon their column drove
> The pressing mass of horsemen, falling
>   Back, in vain for order strove.

When their shot gave out, retreating
  Step by step in steady line,
Till their square reformed and bristled,
  Glistening showed the bayonets' shine.
Wild on high the pipes resounded
  From MacKay, who stepped without ;
' *Cogadh na 'Sith !* ' the soldiers answered,
  With a loud, triumphant shout.
Wild notes playing, streamers flying,
  Defiance to the foe was thrown ;
Exposed, undaunted, marched the hero,
  Playing round the square alone."

There died at Melrose in 1899, a woman of ninety-eight, a daughter of the regiment, who heard the guns at Quatre Bras and saw a piper play the Highland Brigade past to the tune of " Hey, Johnnie Cope," after his legs had been cut off below the knee. This can hardly have been MacKay, but it may well have been one of the same name, for at that time there were more pipers from the Reay Country in the army than from any other district of Scotland. Skye and Tongue produced more pipers and gave more pipers to the army than any other two districts, from which it is argued, quite legitimately, that there must have been a piping college at Tongue as well as at Dunvegan.

From the far east, too, we have instances of the bravery of pipers. There is living in Glasgow at the present day, William Middleton, who was for twenty-one years piper to the Gordon Highlanders. At the battle of Candahar, while playing to his company, his pipes suddenly stopped. He sat down to mend them, and his comrades said he was dead; but " Na, na," said the piper, " I'm worth twa dead men yet," and forthwith he got up, and blew away as hard as ever. He continued playing, and, when the engagement was over, it was found that one bullet had gone through his pipes, another had knocked the brass off his helmet, another gone through his kilt, another knocked a button off his coat, another gone through his water-bottle, another through his haversack, and another had struck the heel of his boot. And he himself escaped unscratched.

At Lucknow, no sooner had the 93rd forced their way through the breach than John Mac Leod, then pipe-major, who was right in the front, began to encourage the men by vigorously playing his pipes. The more hot and deadly the fire became, the more highly strung became the piper's feelings, and the louder squealed the pipes, John standing the while in perfectly exposed positions, in which he must have appeared to the enemy like some unearthly visitant. There he stood for over two hours, while bayonet and rifle did their work. A similar story comes from the American War of Independence. The 42nd Highlanders helped to storm Fort-Washington, and a piper was one of the first to reach the top of the ramparts. Once there he began to play the slogan of his clan, which so roused his comrades that they rushed the heights, carrying everything before them. The brave piper, however, lost his life just as victory was assured. Another piper of the 42nd Highlanders distinguished himself in a more recent war. With the regiment at the Gold Coast there was James Wotherspoon, a native of Falkirk, and a piper. At the battle of Amoaful, in the heat of the action, when brave men were falling on every hand, Wotherspoon cheered them on with martial music, and afterwards assisted to carry Major William Baird, who was mortally wounded, off the field. For this act of devotion, Queen Victoria, at Windsor, presented the piper with the medal for distinguished conduct in the field.

In the Ashanti War there was an instance of bravery
under circumstances more trying than open battle.   When
the Black Watch entered Coomassie, they had to march
through a dense jungle infested by savages.   But they
formed in procession, and, headed by the pipers, and firing
at hidden enemies on either side, they stepped—

> " Into the depth of the forest shade
> Into the gloom of the chasm made,
> Into the ambush of deadly night,
> In midst a dashing glare of light.
> Quick in response a volley burst
> With deadly aim, the foemen curst.
> High o'er the din the pipers blew,
> The hardy Scots marched two by two,
> No halt, no pause, the swinging pace
> Lost not one atom's form or grace. "

And they got into Coomassie, but it must have taken no
ordinary courage to make men play at the head of such a
column, themselves with no weapons of defence.   Firing at
an unseen foe among the kopjes of the Transvaal was child's
play to it.

Recent wars have been equally fruitful in similar incidents.   Piper James Stewart of the Cameron Highlanders,
who was killed at the battle of the Atbara, was found to
have seven bullets in his body.   He gallantly led the charge,
playing " The March of the Cameron Men," and during a
bit of rough and bloody work, he mounted a knoll and
stood playing the tune until he fell mortally wounded.
Piper Mac Lellan, of the Highland Light Infantry, kept
playing his pipes at the battle of Magersfontein, amid a
hail of bullets, encouraging the scattered Highlanders to
re-unite in the attack, and he was mentioned by Lord

Methuen in his despatches for bravery in charge of stretcher bearers. At the same engagement, Pipe-sergeant James Mac Kay of the 91st Highlanders, a native of the Reay Country and one of the official pipers to the Clan Mac Kay Society, standing in absolutely exposed positions, rallied parties of his regiment over and over, earning the admiration of all ranks. At Elandslaagate, a piper of the Gordon Highlanders, Sergeant Kenneth Mac Leod, a native of Lewis, continued playing after he had received several wounds, and only stopped when a bullet smashed his pipes.

The pipe-major of the 2nd Seaforth Highlanders, who also served in South Africa, is a son of the well-known military piper, Ronald Mac Kenzie, now in the service of the Duke of Richmond and Gordon at Gordon Castle, Fochabers. He was through Magersfontein and all the other battles with the Seaforths, and escaped with a scratch on the left leg and the loss of his chanter, which was smashed into bits by a bullet. More instances might be given, but these will suffice. Pipers have done quite as much as soldiers, in proportion to their numbers, to falsify estimates like that of the Soudanese women, who, when they first saw the kilted regiments of Kitchener's expedition, thought they were men who had got into disgrace at home, been deprived of their trousers, and degraded to the level of women.

CHAPTER X.

THE REGIMENTAL PIPER.

" The Esk was swollen sae red and sae deep,
   But shouther to shouther the brave lads keep ;
   Twa thousand swam ower to fell English ground,
   And danced themselves dry to the pibroch sound."
                                        —*Lady Nairne.*

Preserving the pipes—Regimental bands—Pay of army pipers—The
   seven pipers of Falkirk—Duties of regimental pipers—The
   meaning of " Retreat "—A story of Napoleon—In a social
   capacity—An army wedding—A military funeral—At the
   officers' mess—Awkward incidents—" Boberchims."

NOTHING has helped more to preserve the bagpipe as
our national musical instrument than the fact that
it has always been used in connection with the
Highland regiments. On several occasions officers, always
English, it should be noted, have tried to get the bagpipe
superseded by instruments more to their own taste, but
they have always failed. The sentiment in favour of the
pipes was too much for them, and the arguments were too
strong to be slighted by the Crown authorities. In one
case, indeed, a regiment did lose its pipes. The 91st, or
Argyllshire Highlanders, landed at Dover in April, 1850,
and were inspected by Major-General G. Brown, C.B., K.H.,
then Adjutant-General to the Forces. For some reason

which has never been explained he ordered the immediate abolition of the pipes, which the men clung to as the last that was left to remind them of the origin, history, and nationality of the corps. This seemed a harsh and uncalled for proceeding, and that it was so is proved by the fact that the authorities afterwards made ample amends to the regiment.

In the British army there are twenty-two pipe bands, one to each battalion of the following regiments:—

Scots Guards.
Royal Scots.
Royal Scots Fusiliers.
Borderers.
Cameronians.
Royal Highlanders.
Highland Light Infantry.
Seaforth Highlanders.
Gordon Higlanders.
Cameron Highlanders.
Argyll and Sutherland Highlanders.

The number of men allowed to each band as full pipers, that is, the number authorised by the War Office, is six— one sergeant-piper (formerly pipe-major) and five pipers— but each battalion has always ten or twelve men in its pipe band, those above the regulation number being acting pipers. Only the Highland regiments and the Scots Guards are allowed a sergeant in excess of the ordinary strength to perform the duties of sergeant-piper. Members of the band get the same pay as drummers—1d. per day more than ordinary privates—with the opportunity to earn " extras " by playing outside at parties, in public parks, or in any other way. The sergeant-piper and his five comrades are clothed by Government, and a. fund is supported by the officers of each battalion, out of which the cost of the pipes, both for full and acting pipers ; long hose, buckled shoes, etc., and the uniform for the acting pipers is defrayed. Captains of companies, however, supply their pipers with banners. The pipers are all drilled in the same way as other soldiers, their training as pipers only beginning after they have served in the ranks for some time. Tuition is given free of charge by competent sergeant-pipers, and any lad joining a Highland regiment will be taught the pipes properly if he chooses. Pipers are generally Highlanders, and it is a remarkable fact that in the time between the middle of the eighteenth and the beginning of the nineteenth century, Skye alone furnished five hundred pipers for the British Army—an average of ten a year. Regimental pipers are, however, quite often Lowlanders, and it is doubtful if any Highland town can boast of having had five pipers in one regiment, as Falkirk, a Lowland town, can. Robert Galbraith, from Falkirk, joined the 42nd in 1854, and served through the Crimea, the Indian Mutiny, and the fighting which ended at Coomassie. Pipe-major James Honeyman, still alive, came through the Mutiny and Ashanti Wars, leading his regiment into Coomassie. John Honeyman, his brother, was also a piper, and so was their father before them. The fifth 42nd piper was James Wotherspoon, who joined after the Mutiny and followed his colours to the Gold Coast. Besides, two other Falkirk men were pipers in the Black Watch—Alexander Mac Intosh and George W. Alexander—making a record which can hardly be beat by any other town of similar size, Highland or Lowland. When, during the Mutiny, the four Highland regiments marched from Lucknow, their pipers numbered one hundred and forty all told, quite a respectable number of fighting musicians.

The duties of regimental pipers are too numerous to give in detail, but it may be worth while to describe " Reveille " and "Tattoo." "Reveille" is generally sounded at early morn by the bugler on duty, or sometimes by all the buglers followed by the pipers and drummers playing round the camp to rouse the troops. No sooner is "Reveille" sounded then the camp becomes animated with busy men preparing for the routine of the day. The tune is usually "Up and waur them a', Willie," "Hey, Johnnie Cope," or sometimes "Up in the morning's no for me." As "Reveille" begins the day, so "Tattoo" is the signal that another day has gone. The guards turn out and stand under arms, picquets are mounted and sentries posted, all in undress and greatcoats, and gates are closed for the night. Of all ceremonies in which a pipe band is engaged, "Tattoo" is the most attractive to spectators. Drummers and pipers march to the ground in full kilt and feather, and form up in perfect silence, save for the curt word of command. The buglers form up in front of the pipers, and at the order, "Sound off," a shrill blast is sounded by the buglers, who then disappear. Drums are slung and pipes placed in position. At the word of command the tattoo rolls are gone through, then the order, "Quick march," is given, and the band steps off, taking up the usual rolls as in an ordinary march. They march and counter-march the length of the parade ground, and come to the halt in the exact position they started from. Then the music ceases, and the tattoo rolls are beat off as before, after which all are marched back to quarters and dismissed. Old Highland tunes are invariably played for " Tattoo," " My Faithful Fair One," and the " Cock o'

the North " being favourites.   Other tunes, too, have been
dedicated by custom for special occasions—as, for instance,
" Highland Laddie" for the march past, or when troops
advance in review order; " The Crusaders' March," for re-
views and inspections, at mess, tattoo, or parade; "Bannocks
o' Barley Meal," or " Brose and Butter," for breakfast,
dinner, or tea, and sometimes for officers' mess; and " Hey
Johnnie Cope" as the warning for parade.   " The Haughs
o' Cromdale," as is well known, is always played by the
Gordons' pipers when the regiment is at the charge, though,
by some inexplicable slip, it got mixed up with the " Cock
o' the North " at Dargai.

A good deal of misunderstanding sometimes crops up
through the use of the word " retreat " in relation to the
pipes.   A story is told of the great Napoleon which
illustrates this very forcibly.   Having heard from afar the
skirl of the pipes, the Emperor wished to know more of the
music, and so when a Highland piper was captured, he sent
for him that he might hear him play.   " Play a Pibroch,"
said Napoleon, and the piper played a pibroch.   " Play a
March," next asked the Emperor, and a march was played.
Then " Play a Retreat "; but at this the Highlander looked
up in surprise.   " Play a Retreat! I have not learned to
play a Retreat," was the reply, and the pipes remained silent.
The story is improbable on the face of it.   First, because it
is the buglers and not the pipers who sound the retreat;
second, because there is no historical record of Napoleon
having ever captured a piper; third, because the same story
has been told of a drummer boy of the Guards who fell into
the hands of the French; and fourth, because, in any case,
the word " retreat " used in this sense does not mean that
the men are running away from the enemy.   It only means

" retire," or if in barracks it means that the time when the
gates are shut for the night has come.   There is no doubt,
however, that the word is not very well chosen, and that on
account of its significance in other connections, it might
with advantage be dispensed with in favour of a better.

Many stories are told, showing that the regimental pipers
not only keep up the spirits of the men, but are themselves
worthy of their position as a social force.   At the Cape of
Good Hope in 1805 the Seaforths suffered excessively from
the heat.   On one of their marches, although the fatigue
was extreme, during a momentary halt the grenadier company requested the pipers to play for them, and they danced
a Highland reel, to the astonishment of the 59th Regiment,
which was close in the rear.   In the Indian Mutiny, again,
in a time of imminent peril, " as we," writes the author of
The Highland Brigade, " approached a big bungalow our
hearts were cheered by the sound of the bagpipes playing a
foursome reel.   When we were halted and dismissed I went
into the building, and there were four or five sets dancing
with all their might."   The terrors of the Mutiny did not
quench their musical ardour—more likely they intensified it.

In the Gordons and in some other Scottish regiments,
when a marriage occurs in the ranks, the happy bridegroom
is forcibly seized by his comrades and placed on a table elevated on the shoulders of four stout fellows.   On the table
a man ludicrously dressed to represent a woman and per-
sonate the bride has been placed to await him.   Both are
furnished with a bag, one of soot and the other of flour, and
they belabour each other unmercifully, while their uproari-
ous following form up in military order, and march after
them round the camp to the tune of " Woo'd an' Married
an' a'," played by one of the regimental pipers.   The pro-

cession is most grotesque, and is headed by a stalwart comrade acting as drum-major, and absurdly dressed in old blankets, etc., his staff of office being a mop, crowned by a 4lb. loaf, which he majestically brandishes in a style irresistibly comic. The procession ends at the canteen, where the bridegroom, as the price of release from his by no means enviable position, must treat his merry following in suitable style.

At a military funeral the band draws up in two ranks facing each other on the right flank of the procession, with a space of about two paces between the men, and forming a lane wide enough to allow of the passing of a gun carriage or hearse. As the cortege begins to move the firing party first pass through the lane in file, with arms reversed. The band follows, closing up in playing order. Next comes the body, the following party, and civilians and friends. When well clear of the house or hospital, the command "Slow march" is given, when the rolls are taken up in slow time. After the start one half the side drummers keep up the rolls during the first part of the tune, and are relieved in the second part by the other half. The drums, of course, are muffled. Should the cemetery be some distance off, the procession breaks into quick time, in which case the pipers play no more until within a reasonable distance from the ground, when slow time is again taken up, and the band plays till the cortege has passed in. They then cease, and follow up, placing themselves in a convenient position near the grave. On the first volley being fired, the first bar of the "Dead March" is played, on the second two bars, and on the third the whole of the first part once through. This ends the ceremony, and the band marches out, and forms in front of the firing party, stepping off with them at quick march, playing tunes on the way home, as on ordinary parade.

In the case of Volunteer funerals, however, where local sentiment might be roused by such a custom, the band usually marches home in silence.

There are often striking incidents at military funerals which are not pre-arranged. At the battle of Fort-Rohya, in India, in April, 1858, General Hope, of Pinkie, and of the 93rd Highlanders, was killed. At the funeral his body was wrapped in a Highland plaid and accompanied to the grave by the pipers of the 42nd, 78th, 79th, and 93rd, playing the "Flowers of the Forest." This action, it may be added, was the first occasion after the battle of Waterloo on which these four regiments met in active service, and the incident of General Hope's death and funeral made it all the more memorable.

In military circles, when pipers play round the officers' mess, they generally start at some considerable distance outside, usually in an adjoining room or the open air, the object of this being that the strains of the instrument may be heard as coming from a distance. After finishing inside, the performers play to and wind up where they started from. The usual procedure may not in strict detail be the same in all Highland or Scottish regiments, but it is something like the following:—The men assemble at the appointed place under their pipe-major, who, on a given order, arranges his men and starts the tune (a march), everything being pre-arranged. When all is steady he turns to his right or left, the others marching in Indian file into the mess-room, round which they go two or three times, afterwards forming up behind the senior officer's chair, when they change into strathspey and reel. When they stop the pipe-major receives a glass of "mountain dew," with which he drinks the company's health, the toast being usually given in Gaelic.

After this he starts another march round the table and then out. All obstacles, animate or inanimate, must be kept out of the leading piper's path. If not he may sometimes find himself in an awkward case. He may have stairs to go up and come down, corners to turn, doors to pass through which are too low for the drones, projecting pegs and all sorts of things to negotiate. The following are a few instances of the difficulties of pipers in such positions :—

The first is in regards to playing in file, which is generally acknowledged to be the most difficult formation in which pipers can be placed. This will become apparent when notice is taken of the fact that the drones of the player immediately in front drown to a considerable degree the sound of the player's chanter. It is therefore only by listening carefully to the different parts of the tune, and watching the marching swing of the pipers in front, as well as keeping the regular step, that one can decide whether the performers are adept players or not, and, as efficient pipers know, such performances require long practice and confidence. Then it sometimes happens that a central piper wanders into the wrong part, thus knocking the pipers in front and behind completely out. There at once ensues a stampede, so to say, no one being able to detect who the erring piper is. This is one of the occasions when the pipe-major looks ferocious, for, being in front, he is powerless to rectify matters, and is compelled to march on and listen to the row. The discordant notes will, of course, continue unless the defaulters and others who are " put out " have confidence enough to stop and catch up the tune at its proper place. Failing this, the pipe-major's only alternative is to form up his men behind the senior officer's chair as quickly as possible, and at once strike into the next tune in his programme. Blunders of this sort, it is only right to state, are usually committed by nervous men or beginners, but seldom through carelessness. Again, when pipers are performing this duty, waiters who, in the exercise of their own functions, are eager to serve their guests, often bump against or unintentionally obstruct the pipe-major. In some cases the chanter is knocked out of his hand, thus causing a temporary derangement as the pipers swing round in their course. Pipers are sometimes called upon to go into queer places. For instance, let us take the huts at Aldershot and elsewhere. Here the pipers start from the outside or from the kitchen, and wend their way round corners and through very narrow and low doors, which necessitate their marching in a crouching position in order to prevent the big drone coming in contact with the top of the door. As they enter the mess-room, they are invariably obstructed by the inevitable draught-screen, which some one has neglected to draw aside at the proper time. "Through an obstruction of this kind," writes a pipe-major of one of the Highland regiments, "an accident happened to myself on the first occasion that I, as a pipe-major, went round the table to play a pibroch in my regiment. I started in an adjoining room, and as I entered the mess-room door, immediately behind the draught-screen, the latch caught the ribbons of the outside drone and pulled the pipes off my shoulder. This caused me to make a few 'boberechims,' and I stopped. This being my maiden tune as pipe-major in my new regiment, a sudden suspicion seemed to seize the officers, who promptly sent out the mess sergeant to see and report what state I was in. After my explanation, which was regarded as satisfactory, I restarted my tune, for the playing of which the officers indicated their approval."

CHAPTER XI.

The Piper as a Man of Peace.

" Dear to the Lowland reaper,
    And plaided mountaineer—
To the cottage and the castle
    The Scottish pipes are dear—
Sweet sounds the ancient pibroch
    O'er mountain, loch, and glade ;
But the sweetest of all music
    The pipes at Lucknow played."

—*Whittier.*

Clan pipers—Chief's retinue—At weddings—Pipers prohibited—
In sorrow—At funerals—Queen Victoria's funeral—To lighten
labour—The harvest dance—The shepherd's pipe—In church
architecture—In church services—As a call to church—Ministers and the pipes—Falling into disrepute—" As proud as a
piper "—Jealousy of the old masters—" As fou as a piper "—
An Irish piper.

THE pipers of old were hereditary pipers, and lived
from generation to generation in the family of the
chief who ruled their clan. They were trained
from childhood to the use of the pipes, and grew
up as retainers of the family, whose services no chief
would dare to dispense with. They were often sent
by their employers to the great masters of Highland
music for instruction, and when they were old they

acted as mediums through which all that was best in Celtic lore and music was passed down to future generations. The piper was, in the days of his splendour, a living exhibition of his clan's glory and greatness. Every chief had a piper. " It's a poor estate," said the piper of Glengarry, in 1801, to a lady who asked him why he did not work some in his leisure time, " that cannot keep the laird and piper without working." Not only was the piper not expected to work ; he had lands for his support, and was of superior rank to the other members of his chief's retinue or " tail." He accompanied his chief everywhere, and with the harper —when there were harpers—had a right to appear at all public meetings. The " tail " of a chief of the old time was rather an interesting company. Its composition, according to Sir Walter Scott, was as follows :—

The henchman, or right hand man.

The *filidh* or bard.

The *bleadaire* or orator, whose duty it was to make harangues to the great folks his chief visited.

The *gille-mor* or armourer, who carried his sword, target, and gun.

The *gille-casfhliuch*, who carried the chief on his back over the brooks.

The *gille-comshreang*, who led his chief's horse in difficult paths.

The *gille-truisernis*, who carried his knapsack.

The *piobair* or piper.

The *gille-piobair* or piper's man, who carried the pipes ; with probably a dozen lads besides, who were always ready to do the bidding of their chief.

The chief of the fifteenth and sixteenth centuries had a retinue twice as large as that of the chief of the degenerate eighteenth century. Besides those named, he had his gentlemen of the house, his harper, his *seneschal*, his treasurer, his standard-bearer, his jester, his body guard, his quartermaster, his cup-bearer, and his forester, all with clearly defined duties and rights. The offices of piper, standard-bearer, harper, cup-bearer, and treasurer descended from father to son. These " tails " were indeed so formidable that they were at last prohibited from appearing in Edinburgh.

In 1809, out of all the big retinue, only the piper remained. He remains still, not exactly as a clan piper— where there are no clans there cannot be clan pipers—but as an appendage to families having a Highland lineage, and to many that have but the remotest connection with the Highlands. His duties are still pretty much what they were. He has not now a *gille*, for the piper of those days is not too proud to carry his pipes himself, but the description written in the early years of the century is still partly applicable to pipers at houses where the Highland traditions are reverenced :—

"In a morning when the chief is dressing, he walks backwards and forwards close under the window without doors, playing on his bagpipe, with a most upright attitude and majestic stride. It is a proverb in Scotland, namely, the stately stride of the piper. When required he plays at meals, and in the evening to divert the guests with music when the chief has company with him. His gilley holds the pipe till he begins, and the moment he has done with the instrument he disdainfully throws it down upon the ground, as being only the passive means of conveying his skill to the ear, and not a proper weight for him to carry or bear at other times. But for a contrary reason his gilley snatches it up, which is that the pipe may not suffer indignity from its neglect."

The last half of the paragraph is not applicable, and never was. One might as well expect a professional violinist to throw down his instrument on the stage after playing a solo, leaving the fragments for a super to pick up. Pipers respect the bagpipe as much as other musicians respect their own peculiar instruments, and they were never so "daft" as to indulge in the antics described by this writer. But then, the writer was an Englishman, and may therefore be excused.

DANCING TO PIPE MUSIC
(Highland Dress with Belted Plaid.)

The piper was a professional gentleman, a skilled musician, who went to college, and had a seat at the table with his chief. As a favoured retainer, he enjoyed certain perquisites. When, for instance, an animal was slaughtered for the family of the chief, a certain part of the

carcase was allotted to the piper. When the civil wars
broke up the clan system, the chiefs ceased to keep hereditary pipers, and the race soon became extinct. Afterwards,
when a man considered he had enough of this world's goods
to warrant the expenditure, and felt that he would like to
hark back a little to the ways of the fathers, he got the
best piper he could, just as he got any other servant. In
this way the system of family pipers is perpetuated, and
will be so as long as the Sovereign and others of high rank
set the example.

The pipes took an important part in the enjoyments of
Highlanders. They were always to the front at weddings or
where the people were making merry. An old time poet
puts it plainly, if rather quaintly, when he says :—

> " A braithel where the broth was fat,
>   In ancient times a token sure,
>   The bridegroom was na reckoned poor ;
>   A vast o' fouk a' roun about
>   Came to the feast then dined thereout,
>   Twa pair o' pipers playing gade
>   About the table as they fed."

Our present day equivalent for this verse is much better
rhyme, if farther from the truth :—

> " At the wedding of Shon Mac Lean,
>   'Twas wet and windy weather,
>   Yet through the wind and rain
>   Cam twenty pipers together !
>   Erach and Dugald Dhu,
>   Sandy of Isla, too,
>   Each with his bonnet of blue,
>   And every piper was fou,
>   Twenty pipers together."

The pipers, however, could not have been very "fou," at least until after the wedding, for,

> " The twenty pipers at break of day
> In twenty different bog-holes lay,
> Serenely sleeping on their way
>   From the wedding of Shon Mac Lean."

Had they been totally incapable they could hardly have got to twenty different "bog-holes." It is difficult to

HIGHLAND FAMILY PARTY RETURNING FROM A FAIR AFTER
A DANCE—*Sketched from Nature. 1829.*

define exactly the meaning of the phrases, "as drunk as a piper" and "as fou as a piper," but they seem to have generally meant half seas over, not helplessly inebriated. The piper, being an important social personage, could hardly escape the reproach of being addicted to liquor, although there is nothing to show that his class were in this respect any worse than the average of the people of their day.

That the piper was a principal character at weddings in old times is certain. The wedding morn was ushered in by the music of the pipers, who followed the bridegroom and his friends on a round of early calls intended to warn the guests of their engagements. These joined the party, and before the circuit, which sometimes occupied several hours, had ended, some hundreds perhaps had gathered. The bride made a similar tour round her friends, and thus the complete company was collected. After the wedding a procession was formed, and with flags flying and pipers playing, and all kinds of demonstrations of joy, passed through the neighbourhood. Festivities were generally prolonged to a late hour, the pipers never ceasing their playing. The company danced either outside to the music of the pipes or inside to that of the fiddle. The Irish bagpipe was long used at festivities in Erin, and at a wedding the hat was sent round three times, the first twice for the priest and the third time for the piper. The piper did not always, however, lead to peace and goodwill at weddings, for at one time the ecclesiastical ordinances of Scotland interposed to prohibit the presence of above " fifteine persons on both sydes " at marriage feasts, among whom there were to be " no pypers." These ordinances were frequently made, and in connection with one it is on record that " still their chief delight at marriages was bagpipes, and home they go with loud bagpipes and dance upon the green."

The bagpipe joined in the sorrow as well as the mirth of the people. The coronach, a wailing recitation which recapitulated the good deeds of the deceased, came most immediately after death, and corresponded to the old ecclesiastical dirge and the Irish " keen " of the present day. The laments on the pipes were performed after the coronach, and accompanied the progress of the obsequies, a number of pipers attending the funeral of any eminent person. The coronach and the lament existed contemporaneously for some time, but gradually the coronach died out. The use of the pipes continued for many years later, more especially in the Lochaber district and also in Aberdeenshire. At a funeral in Skye of a notable chief the procession was two miles in length, six men walking abreast. Seven pipers were in attendance, and, placed at different positions in the procession, played the lament all the way from the residence of the deceased to the cemetery, and " upwards of three hundred imperial gallons of whisky were provided for the occasion, with every other necessary refreshment." In these days a funeral was a funeral.

There was a burial in Inverness in the seventeenth century where few besides Highlanders in their usual garb were present, and all the way before them a piper played, having his drones hung with streamers of crape. In 1737 at the funeral of an eminent performer in Ireland his cortege was preceded by " eight couple of pipers " playing a funeral dirge, and it is alleged that when Lord Lovat was condemned for participating in the rebellion of 1745, he desired that his body might be carried to Scotland for burial, saying " he had once made it a part of his will that all the pipers between Johnnie Groat's House and Edinburgh should be invited to play at his funeral." Rob Roy's funeral in 1736 was the last for many years at which a piper occupied an official position, although we read that in 1820 the pipes were played at the funeral of Sir John Murray Macgregor, of Lanrick, and that in Edinburgh in 1835 a Highland corps attended the funeral of a sergeant, the piper playing " Lochaber no more." In later years, however, the custom has been revived, and the piper now frequently accompanies military funerals or the funerals of those connected with the Highlands. When the then Sirdar entered Khartoum after the Battle of Omdurman, one of the first things he did was to hold a formal funeral service on the spot where General Gordon was murdered, the pipers playing a dirge and the Soudanese band playing the hero's favourite hymn, " Abide with me." In old times, if the poet Dunbar may be believed, the bagpipe was preferred to other forms of honouring the dead :—

> " I will na preistis for me sing,
>   Na yit na bellis for me ring,
>   Bot a bag pipe to play a spryng."

In connection with funerals it only remains to be added that at the magnificent ceremonial in February last (1901), when the body of Queen Victoria was conveyed from Osborne to Windsor, Her Majesty's two Highland pipers had an honourable place in the procession. When the cortege left Osborne they played the dirge of the Black Watch, and later on they changed into " The Flowers of the Forest," a tune that has been played over many a soldier's grave. It was appropriate that the association of the Queen with the 42nd Royal Highlanders should be kept up to the last. In 1854, when the regiment was in Chobham Camp, Her Majesty and the Prince Consort visited them weekly, and the Queen was so pleased with the Highlanders that when she decided to have a piper, she chose Pipe-major Ross of the 42nd, who remained in her service until his death about ten years ago. Mr. James C. Campbell, the present royal pipe-major, was taken from the same regiment.

The bagpipe was also used to lighten labour. While the

inhabitants of Skye were engaged in making roads in 1786, each party of workers had a piper, and in the North of Scotland men engaged in work requiring strength and unity of purpose, such as launching a large boat, had a piper to help them pull or lift together. In the harvest time a piper was often employed to animate the reapers, keeping them working in time to the music, like a file of soldiers, he himself following behind the slowest worker. This custom is alluded to in Hamilton's elegy on Habbie Simpson, the piper of Kilbarchan :—

> " Or wha will cause our shearers shear ?
> Wha will bend up the brags of weir ? "

The dance of the kirn or harvest home was always danced with peculiar glee by the reapers of the farm where the harvest was first finished. On these occasions they danced on an eminence in full view of as many other reapers as possible, to the music of the Lowland bagpipe, commencing the dance with loud shouts of triumph and tossing their hooks in the air. The dance was retained for a time by Highlanders visiting the South of Scotland as harvesters, but it has now been more than a century in disuetude. In a poem of great antiquity, called *Cockilby's Sow*, which describes such a dance, we are told that—

> " Davy Doyte of the dale,
> Was thair mad menstrale,
> He blew on a pype he
> Maid of a borit bourtre. "

Also that—

> " Clarus the lang clype
> Playit on a bag pype. "

In a manuscript of the seventeenth century, a song descriptive of shepherd life says—

> " The life of a shepherd is void of all care,
> With his bag and his bottle he maketh good fare ;
> He hath yon green meadow to walk in at will-a,
> With a pair of fine bagpipes upon a green hill-a ;
> Tringdilla, tringdilla, tring down-adown dilla,
> With a pair of fine bagpipes upon a green hill-a. "

It may sound irreverent to connect the bagpipe with religious ordinances, though why one form of musical instrument should be deemed sacred and another profane is a hard question. To the modern Highlander a blast from the pipes on Sunday would be considered enough to bring a curse on the whole land, but our forefathers were not all so strict. They worked references to the pipes into the architecture of many of their churches, particularly in England and on the Continent. In St. James's Church, Norwich, there used to be a window on which a piper was shown with a bagpipe with one drone; under a stall in Ripon Cathedral there is carved in oak a representation of two hogs dancing to a third playing on a bagpipe ; in Beverley Minster, a group of pigs is carved in wood, all dancing round a trough to the music of one of their number, who plays a bagpipe having two drones and one chanter ; among the numerous carvings in Westminster Abbey, there is a woodland scene representing a group of monkeys along with a bear, the latter playing the bagpipe; and in St. John's Church, Cirencester, a monkey is depicted playing on the bagpipe. Then at Rosslyn and in Melrose Abbey, we have the pieces of architecture mentioned in a previous chapter.* Perhaps the

---

* See pages 37 and 45.

most curious of these semi-ecclesiastical carvings is a representation of an ass playing on a bagpipe, which is graven on an ancient tombstone in the Cathedral Church of Hamburg. The animal walks on its hind legs, holding the instrument between its forelegs, and carved on the stone are the words—

" The vicissitudes of the world compel me,
    Poor ass, to learn the bagpipe."

Pipers, apparently, were not rich then more than they are now.

It is difficult to understand why sculptors should have connected sacred architecture with animals in the way they did. Artists, like poets, have a license, but this hardly accounts for their associating the pig, which never was venerated in any way, with sacred things. The carvings, however, while hardly respectful to the instrument, associate it, if only in a sarcastic way, with ecclesiastical affairs, and show that the foolish prejudice which considers the pipes profane did not always exist. It is possible that the connection between the pipes and churches was confined to ecclesiastical carvings, but as to that we cannot now speak definitely. The early reformers in their reforming zeal practised vandalism, and in rooting out the religion they wished to supersede, they left us but fragments of an architecture we would now have been glad to preserve. The references to the bagpipe in churches are so fragmentary it is impossible to draw any very reliable inference.

The pipes have, however, been associated with religious services on a good many occasions. The Italian shepherds, when visiting Rome to celebrate the Nativity, carry their pipes with them, and play to images of the Virgin Mary and the infant Messiah, which are placed at the corners of the streets. The pipes were used in the services of the Catholic Church in Edinburgh in 1536. In 1556 there was a procession in Edinburgh in honour of St. Giles, the patron saint of the town. The procession was led by the Queen Regent and was attended by bagpipers. When James I. came to Scotland in 1617, he did not take the organ from Holyrood chapel, when he was clearing out every other symptom of idolatry, because "there is some affinity between it and the bagpipes." "I know a priest," says an old English writer, "who, when any of his friends should be marryed, would take his back-pype and so fetch them to church, playing sweetlye afore them, and then he would lay his instrument handsomely upon the aultare till he had marryed them, and sayd masse, which thyng being done, he would gentylle bring them home agayne with back-pype."

Then we have Dunbar, in his *Testament of Mr. Andro Kennedy*, throwing some light on the manners and customs of the Carrick district of Ayrshire, when he makes a brother churchman, with whom he held poetic jousts, desire that no priest may sing over his grave :—

> " Bot a bag pipe to play a spryng,
> 　*Et unum ail wosp ante me,*
> In stayd of baneris for to bring,
> 　*Quatuor lagenus ceruisie.*
> Within the graif to set sic thing,
> 　*In modum crucis juxta me,*
> To fle the fendis than hardely sing,
> 　*De terra plasmasti me.*" *

---

* Scottish Text Society's version.

So the poet knew the sound of the "bag pipe," and thought it an instrument fit to "fle the fendis." Here some lowlanders would, no doubt, be willing to agree with him.

We have at least one instance, and that from the far north, of the pipes being used to call people to church. In that corner of Caithness in which John o' Groat's House is situated there lived, more than two hundred years ago, a parish minister named Rev. Andrew Houston, or Hogston. Mr. Houston somehow could not get his people to attend church, and at last he decided to invoke the aid of the pipes. Accordingly, each Sabbath morning, a short time previous to the hour of service, a piper began at one of the more outlying portions of the parish and played his way to the church. The plan worked well, for the people, attracted by the novelty, followed the music Sabbath after Sabbath, and thus the minister gathered together a good congregation. This Mr. Houston was the first Protestant minister of the parish, and there is a tradition to the effect that not only did he use the pipes for the purpose mentioned, but that after the close of the service he allowed his congregation to have a game at shinty before going home. There is a large headstone to his memory in the kirkyard of his parish. It bears a Latin inscription and the date 1620.

In our own day the most notable instance of the pipes in church was at the first commemoration service held in York Minster in memory of the Duke of Clarence and Avondale. The 1st Royal Scots were stationed in York at the time, and three pipers, under the leadership of Pipe-Major Matheson—a Golspie man—played selections of Highland music inside the Cathedral. The King's Own Scottish Borderers relieved the Royal Scots, their pipers playing " The

Flowers of the Forest." Afterwards the pipers of the Black Watch played.

The late Rev. Dr. George Mackay, of the Free Church, Inverness, was a man of a humorous disposition, and after referring one Sunday in an adverse manner to a proposal to introduce instrumental music into the church, said that if they (the congregation) were obliged to fall back upon a " human instrument " to aid them in the service of praise, they would have nothing to do with the organ—it was an instrument of foreign manufacture—they would use the bagpipe. What was more appropriate than that Highland people should use a Highland instrument? Some time later, when the question of instrumental music was being discussed at Inverness Free Church Presbytery, the Doctor, with a twinkle in his eye, turned to an elder who was a member of Presbytery, and who in his younger days was known to play the pipes occasionally, and asked him, " Could you let us have ' French ' on the bagpipe? " The elder, however, was an austere individual, and, with an attempt at a smile, he replied, " Yes, and ' Balerma ' too, doctor ; but when I want to sing God's praises, I use my own pipe."

This antipathy towards their national music, showed itself very frequently among the " unco guid " of the Highlands. Two ministers in the north of Scotland were going along a country road in a gig towards a town where the following day was to be Communion Sunday. While on their way they heard the sound of pipe music in a field near a roadside cottage. They stopped the gig, and after listening intently to the notes of a pibroch, one of the good men jumped out, walked up to the piper, told him he was quite wrong with the tune, and said that if he (the piper) would lend him his pipes he would show him how the pibroch should be played.   The piper, with some astonishment, consented, when the minister struck up the tune, and went through it in such a masterly manner that the piper was fairly overcome with delight, and thanked his reverend tutor.   During the time the performance was going on the other minister sat in the carriage, quite horrified to see and hear what his fellow-traveller was about.   When the piper . minister returned to proceed on the journey, the other began a sermon on the wickedness of his conduct.   The former replied that on hearing the piper perform he thought it his duty to correct him, as otherwise the false notes would be running in his head during the sermon, but now that he had played the tune he would think no more about it, and be able to preach a good sermon on the morrow.

In this connection it is only fair to ministers to add that they were generally not nearly so prejudiced as their people, especially their elders, were.   Elders nearly always professed more religious knowledge than ministers, and were always less tolerant of what did not agree with their own opinions.   In one Highland parish not quite a hundred years ago, a few people set themselves up as judges of what was right and wrong, and let the exercise of their powers become such that a young man learning to play the pipes laid himself open to exclusion from church privileges. Happily we are long past that stage now.

There is no denying, however, that at one time the race fell into disrepute.   In *Cockilby's Sow*, a poem already referred to,* the bagpipe is mentioned as appropriated to swine herds, and in 1641 a sarcastic writer tells us, "The

---

* See page 155.

troopers rode from citie to court and from court to country
with their trumpets before them, which made the people run
out to see them, as fast as if it had been the bagge-pype
playing before the Beares."

Rather a nasty allusion that to the bagpipe and the
bears. It reminds us of the dancing bear, or the organ and
the monkey of our own day. Whatever the piper might
think of himself, people seemed disposed to think the worst
of him, and innumerable petty offences were laid to his
charge. In 1570 three St. Andrews pipers were admonished
to keep the Sabbath day holy, to attend sermon, and to abstain from playing on the streets after supper or during the
night. Playing and dancing on Sunday came so often under
clerical censure as to show very plainly the general use of
the instrument on the one hand, and on the other its adop-
tion in connection with dancing, particularly in the neighbourhood of Edinburgh.

In 1574 a great complaint was made by a burgess of
Stirling to the Privy Council of an assault " by ane namit
Edmond Broun, ane Highland piper," when bit to the effu-
sion of blood " by the said pyperis dog." In 1591 and 1593
George Bennet, piper in the Water of Leith, and James
Brakenrig, agreed to abstain from playing on the bagpipes
on Sunday ; in 1595 and 1596 Thomas Cairns, following the
same vocation there, fell under displeasure for playing and
dancing on Sunday ; and William Aiken pledged himself
never to profane the Sabbath day again with the pipes. In
1598 " Duncan Ure and Johnne Forbes, pyper," were sentenced to imprisonment, and to be fed on bread and water,
on confessing that they had sat up all night " playing at the
dys quhill iiij hours in the morning," when they quarrelled.
In 1606 Richard Watsone, piper in the Water of Leith, was

threatened with censure, and in 1624 James Clark was "fined of xxsh. for having an pyper playing in his house in tyme of sermon, vpoun the Lord his Sabbath." "William Wallace, pyper," was sentenced by the kirk session of St. Cuthbert's " to stand for one day upon the pillar, and thereafter to remove furth of the parochine, ay an quhill he be ane renewit man of his manneris, and to get lief of presbyterie to retourne, after they sie amendiment in his lyf and conversatioun," and in Galloway there is still the "great well of Larg," of which it is said a piper stole the offering, but when he was drinking ale, which he intended to pay for with the stolen money, the gout seized on him, of which he could not be cured but at that well and after he had restored the money.

At length the immoralities of the humble musicians became a bye-word, so much so that a slanderous biographer of Archbishop Sharpe thought he had blackened his character enough when he said, " As for his father, he was a piper." There was nothing to be said after that. So late as 1860, a traveller in Caithness-shire who visited Brawl Castle, one of the county seats, wrote, more let us hope in joke than in earnest—" John Gunn, their piper, played extremely well, but it was sometimes necessary to station him in a distant room, as the skirl was a little too harsh to be enjoyed at close quarters, particularly when John made too free with whisky, without which, however, it was not easy to get John to play at all."

Gambling, ebriety, nocturnal revels, and gross immoralities, says the author of *Musical Memoirs of Scotland,* accompanied this subordinate species of music, to the manifest annoyance of the more tranquil part of the community, and even then (1849) where frequent in towns, licentiousness was seldom far removed from it. In 1661 the minister of a Scottish parish has left it on record, " he found two women of his congregation ' full ' on a week day, and dancing with pipers playing to them." Truly a severe indictment.

From these things it is refreshing to turn to the story of William Mac Donald of Badenoch, who played so well, even when rivals had given him too much drink, that he always got a prize at competitions. His son was piper to the Prince of Wales, but owing to religious scruples he resigned his situation and burned his pipes. He evidently did not think there was anything sacred about the instrument.

The evil that men do lives after them. So these stories derogatory to pipers have been preserved while many equally good and reflecting credit on their characters as public men have no doubt been buried with their bones. They always had a " guid conceit o' themselves," and were apt to think they were better than average humanity, so much so that " as proud as a piper" passed into a proverb. When the late Duke of Edinburgh required a piper he asked the advice of the Prince of Wales's piper as to how he should get one. The Prince's piper asked the Duke what kind of a piper he wanted, whereupon the Duke said " Oh, just a piper like yourself, Donald." " Oh, it's easy to get a piper," said Donald, " but it's no' easy to get a piper like me." Then there was Mac Donel, the famous Irish piper, who lived in great style, keeping servants and horses. One day he was sent for to play to a large company during dinner, and a table and chair were placed for him on the landing outside the door, a bottle of claret and a glass on the table and a servant waiting behind the chair. Mac Donel appeared, took a rapid survey of the preparations, filled his glass, stepped to the dining room door, looked full in the midst of

the gathering, said " Mr. Grant your health, and company,"
drank off the dram, threw half-a-crown on the table with
the remark to the servant, " There, my lad, is two shillings
for my bottle of wine and a sixpence for yourself," then ran
out, mounted his horse and galloped off, followed by his
groom. An almost similar story is told of *Ian Dall*, the
Gairloch piper, but in his case the language used was hardly
so choice. It was of the kind which is best represented
thus * * * *

Not only were the old masters proud, they were also
jealous. When the colleges for training pipers were in Skye,
the Mac Crimmons had some private " tips " on pipe music
which they did not give away to their pupils. A girl
friend, however, learned how some of the secret notes were
produced, and in private she taught her sweetheart. When
her nearest relatives learned what she had done, they instantly cut off her fingers that she might show no more how
they practised their tunes. Ross, a grand old Breadalbane
piper, in a mad fit of jealousy, thrust the right hand of his
boy brother into the fire, and held it there till it became a
charred lump, to prevent the boy becoming a better piper
than himself, which seemed likely. Neil Munro's story of
Red Hand is but a variation of the same theme. Giorsal,
jealous of her stepson Tearlach's piping being better than
that of her husband, cuts off Tearlach's hand while he sleeps.
It is beautifully told, but that is the whole story.

And they have always been a happy lot who could enjoy
themselves to the utmost with pipe and music and song and
dance, and also perhaps with some of the national beverage
of Scotland, which is still rather unfairly coupled with the
tartan and the pipes. When the Princess of Thule came
back to the Lewis, John the Piper was told—" Put down

your pipes, and tek off your bonnet, and we will have a good
dram together this night! And it is Sheila herself will
pour out the whisky for you, John, and she is a good Highland girl, and she knows the piper was neffer born that
could be hurt by whisky. And the whisky was never made
that could hurt a piper." This, too, passed into a proverb
—" As fou as a piper "—but however true it may have been
in one generation it has nowadays no more than a figura-
tive meaning. Pipers now are as much in the public eye
as ever they were, but they are matter-of-fact people, who
have their livings to make and their characters to uphold.
They are therefore neither over proud, over jealous, nor over
jolly. They have fitted themselves into nineteenth century
circumstances, and do not care how much the public eye is
upon them.

The piper as a man of peace has been and still is closely
concerned with every side of the social life of the Highland
people, but his name is not writ nearly so large on history's
page as is that of the piper as a man of war. In *Whistlebinkie* we have verses by Alex. A. Ritchie, which illustrate
the attachment of the Irish piper to his pipes, and which,
for lack of a better opening, may be inserted here. They
are too good to leave out altogether :—

> " Ould Murphy the Piper lay on his deathbed,
>   To his only son Tim, the last words he said,
>   ' My eyes they grow dim, and my bosom grows could,
>   But ye'll get all I have, Tim, when I slip my hould,
>   Ye'll get all I have, boy, when I slip my hould.

> " ' There's three cows and three pigs, and three acres of land,
>   And this house shall be yours, Tim, as long as 'twill stand ;
>   All my fortune is threescore bright guineas of gould,
>   An ye'll get all I have, Tim, when I slip my hould,
>   Ye'll get all I have, Tim, when I slip my hould.

" ' Go fetch me my pipes, Tim, till I play my last tune,
 For death is coming, he'll be here very soon ;
 Those pipes I have played on, ne'er let them be sould,
 If you sell all I have, Tim, when I slip my hould,
 If you sell all I have, Tim, when I slip my hould.'

" Then ould Murphy the Piper, wid the last breath he drew,
 He played on his pipes like an Irishman true,
 He played up the anthem of Green Erin so bould—
 Then calmly he lay down and so slipt his hould !
 Then gently he lay down and slipt his last hould."

CHAPTER XII.

THE BURGH PIPERS OF SCOTLAND.

> ." The piper cam to our toun,
>   To our toun, to our toun ;
>   The piper cam to our toun,
>   And he play'd bonnilie ;
>   He play'd a spring the laird to please,
>   A spring brent new frae yont the seas,
>   And then he ga'e his bags a squeeze,
>   And play'd anither key.
>   And wasna he a roguey, a roguey, a roguey ;
>   And wasna he a roguey, the piper o' Dundee."
>   —*Old Scots Song.*

Royal pipers—In France—At the English court—The Edinburgh
Piper—Dumbarton—Biggar—Wigtown — Glenluce — Dumfries
—Linlithgow—Aberdeen—Perth—Keith—Dalkeith — Dundee
—Peebles—A weird story—Falkirk—" Gallowshiels " pipers'
combat—The Hasties of Jedburgh — Habbie Simson of Kil-
barchan— Bridgeton—Neil Blane of Lanark — The Piper of
Northumberland.

ALTHOUGH as a clan musician the piper was to a
large extent a public character, he was quite as
public in one or two other capacities. There were
semi-royal pipers, and there were burgh pipers. We have
not much record of the former, that is, until our own day,
when the piper is one of the principal personages in the

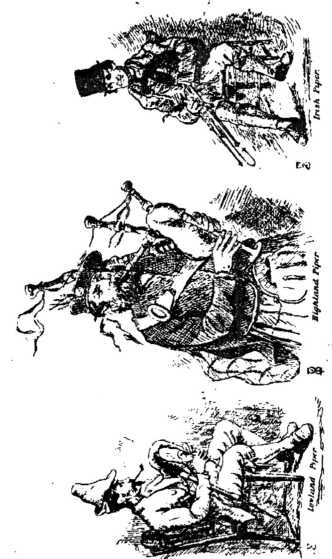

Lowland Piper.

Highland Piper.

Irish Piper.

(From Drawings by J. Sands. By permission of Messrs. J. & R. Glen, Edinburgh.)

Royal retinue—but we have plenty of the latter.   In 1505,
we read, " pipers on drones " shared of the royal bounty of
James IV. ; and we have various references to pipers in
connection with Court ceremonials.   In France the piper
was an appendage of the royal household in the seventeenth
century, and in Ben Jonson's *Irish Masque*, performed at
the Court of England in 1613, six men and six boys danced
to the bagpipe.   But there is nothing to show that the
piper in olden days formed part of the regular following of
Scottish sovereigns.   Pipers were kept by English noble-
men, but their instrument was not the Highland.   It was
as burgh pipers that they were best known in a public
capacity, in the Lowlands of Scotland at any rate.   Each
burgh had one or two, and the office, like that of clan piper,
was in many cases hereditary.   The pipers were supported
out of the public funds along with other minstrels.   Here
is Rev. James Mac Kenzie's description of the relation of
the piper to a burgh, given in his *History of Scotland :—*

"The folk of the old town are fond of music.   We have minstrels
who hold a life appointment in the service of the burgh ; their instruments are bagpipes, to be sure.   Evening and morning and at
other times needful the pipers march through the town to refresh
the lieges with 'Broken Bones at Luncarty,' 'Port Lennox,'
'Jockie and Sandy,' 'St. Johnstone's Hunt's up,' and the like inspiriting strains.   The law of the burgh requires that the pipers
'sall have their daily wages and meat of the neighbours of this guid
toon circulary, conform to the auld loveable use.'   Some of the
burghers are so lamentably void of taste that they count the music
dear and grudge the piper his 'reasonable diet circularly.'   Some
even refuse to entertain the piper when it comes to their turn, and
get fined for their pains."

In 1487 Edinburgh had three public pipers, and the Town
Council then ordained that they should get their food day

about from persons of substance, or that such persons should pay them money equivalent to threepence per piper. In 1660, after the magistrates had permitted "John Johnstone, piper, to accompany the town's drummer throw the town morning and evening," they gave him a salary and perquisites, but next year, rather capriciously, when he applied for a free house during his term of office, they resolved that he was not required, and dispensed with his services. About 1505 we have records of public pipers in Dumbarton, Biggar, Wigton, Glenluce, Dumfries, and elsewhere, and in 1707 we read the piper of Linlithgow was convicted of immorality and excommunicated.

Aberdeen had its piper, and in 1630 the magistrates prohibited him playing in the streets. The language of their prohibition was anything but complimentary. Thus:— " The Magistrates discharge the common piper of all going through the toun at nycht, or in the morning, in tyme coming, with his pype—it being an incivill forme to be usit within sic a famous burghe, and being often found fault with, als weill be sundrie nichtbouris of the toune as by strangeris."

The Aberdonians were canny people then as now, but it is wonderful how their spelling degenerated in the course of one sentence.

Perth had a piper as late as 1831. The piper of the Fair City was in the habit of playing through the streets at five o'clock in the morning and at seven at night. The death of the then town piper about the beginning of the century was much regretted, " the music having an effect in the morning inexpressibly soothing and delightful." The custom of early and late piping was also retained for a long time in Keith.

Old Geordie Syme, the town piper of Dalkeith, was a famous piper in his day. The exact period when he flourished cannot now be ascertained, and little is known of him, even in tradition. The piper of Dalkeith was a retainer of the house of Buccleuch, and there was a small salary attached to the office, for which in Geordie's time he had to attend the family on all particular occasions and make the round of the town twice daily—at five a.m. and eight p.m. Besides his salary, he had a suit of clothes allowed him regularly. This consisted of a long yellow coat lined with red, red plush breeches, white stockings, and buckles in his shoes. Geordie was much taken notice of by the gentry of his time. It is not known when he died. His successor in office was Jamie Reid, who lived long to enjoy the emoluments of the position and about whom there are some interesting local traditions. Jamie was succeeded by Robert Lorimer, and at his death his son was installed in his office, which he held as late as 1837, probably much later. The practice of playing through the town was discontinued about 1821, the custom being considered by the inhabitants a useless relic of bygone days. A long sarcastic poem, printed and circulated about that time, is believed to have helped greatly to finally abolish the practice.

Dundee got a burgh piper after the Reformation, and his mission was to call the people to their work in the mornings. " Dressed in the town's livery and colours, he played through the burgh every day in the morning at four hours and every nicht at aucht hours, a service for which every householder was bound to pay him twelve pennies yearly."

Pipers were, and perhaps are, a dignified race, but few of them were so boastful as the piper of Peebles, who, tradition says, tried to blow his pipes from Peebles to Lauder, a distance of eighteen miles, in a certain number of blasts. He failed in the attempt, but succeeded in blowing himself out of breath. The spot where he fell down dead is on the boundary of the parish of Heriot, in Midlothian, and is still called " The Piper's Grave." This cannot, however, have been the Peebles piper who was written of in 1793 by William Anderson of Kirriemuir in a long poem which appeared in *Provincial Poets*. After describing in the quaint way of eighteenth century writers, the country life of these days,

> " Fan wives wi' rocks an' spindles span,
> An' brawest lasses us'd nae lawn—
> Fan stiffen waana sought, nor blue
> To mutches—fan the sarks were few,
> Some had but ane, some had twa,
> An' money mae had nane ava,
> Fan lasses wi' their rocks set out
> To ane anither night about,"

the author proceeds to tell how a laird near Kinghorn got over head and ears in debt, and was at his wit's end to find a way out of his troubles. At last one evening, as he was wandering alone in the fields, very much dejected, he was accosted by a fine-looking stranger on a black horse, who sympathised with him in his difficulties, and, seeming to know what they were without being told, offered him £10,000 on his simple note of hand.

> " Ye's get it on your single bond,
> As I frae Scotland maun abscond
> To France, or in a woody swing
> For lies a neighbour tald the King—
> An' said I meant to tak' his life,
> To let a gallant get his wife,"

The laird, with little hesitation, accepted the offer, and, according to appointment, the stranger called with the money " on the chap o' twal " the following night—

> " As muckle goud, and rather mair,
>   Than wad out-weigh twal pecks o' bear."

He had not time to wait till it was counted, but, assuring the laird that it was all right, he presented the bond for signature. This, however, read that after fifteen years the laird should be the stranger's servant. But the laird wouldn't have this :—

> " As upright folk abhor mischief—
>   As honest men despise a thief—
>   As dogs detest a grunting sow,
>   So laigh the laird disdained to bow ! "

And, bursting out with :—

> " Hence, Satan ! to your black abode,
>   In name of my Almighty God ! "

he sent the " stranger " right out somewhere through the roof, leaving the money on the table. The supernatural powers of Scottish mythology never could stand the name of the Deity.

But the laird had not heard the last of his great enemy. He prospered and grew richer and richer until, sixteen years after, when, at a feast, he was called out to speak with a visitor on horseback. A minute after there was a loud report, the " stranger " lay dead on the ground, and at the laird's feet lay a pistol. The laird was lodged in Edinburgh prison on a charge of murder, but on the doctors examining the body it was found to have been dead ten days before " it " visited the laird, and that there was no mark where a bullet could have entered. This created a great uproar, and the mystery seemed incapable of explanation, until at last some Peebles folk came to the capital, and swore that the body was that of their piper :—

> " I saw him yerdit, I can swear—
> Frae his lang hame how came he there ? "

It was the Peebles piper, better dressed than ever he had been in life, and he had died in his bed at home. They even identified his " sark " and the pistol. The laird was liberated, but he in his heart knew quite well the real explanation of the mystery :—

> " The laird saw syne it had been Nick
> Contriv'd an' carried on the trick,
> He pu'd the piper frae the moold
> That was in Peebles on him shool'd ;
> An' brought him to the braithel, where
> He left him dead wi' sic a rair,
> That folk wad sworn they saw him shot
> That very instant on the spot.
> Auld Horny thought to gar him howd
> Upo' the gallows, for the gowd
> He gat lang syne, an' wadna set
> His signature to show the debt.
> But in his drift the Devil fail'd—
> The second time the laird prevail'd—
> Liv'd lang at hame, in wealth an' ease,
> An' dy'd at last of nae disease,
> But mere auld age—Renown'd his race
> Unto this day possess his place."

Why the poet should make the Evil One bring the body of a piper from Peebles to Kinghorn to serve his evil ends is a bit strange ; and also how the Devil had but the two plans for encompassing the ruin of the laird. However, the poet's license, especially when coupled with the supernatural, no doubt accounts for a great deal.

Peebles seems to have had more than its share of pipers. James Ritchie, who flourished at the beginning of the eighteenth century, as piper to the Corporation of the town, was told one day by his wife that the flood in the Tweed had carried away their family cow, the fruit of years of piping. "Weel, weel," said the piper, with manly calm, "deil ma care after a'. It cam' wi' the win', let it gang wi' the water." Which is all the record we have of James.

Pipers were, perhaps still are, a philosophic race, and their music was always their first thought. The town piper of Falkirk was sentenced to death for horse-stealing, and on the night before his execution he obtained, as a special indulgence, the company of some of his brother pipers. As the liquor was abundant and their instruments in tune, the fun and music grew fast and furious. The execution was to be at eight o'clock, and the poor piper was recalled to a sense of his situation by the morning light dawning on his window. Suddenly silencing his pipes, he exclaimed, "Oh, but this wearifu' hanging rings in my lug like a new tune," and went out to his fate.

The piper of "Gallowshiels" is known to posterity principally by a poem entitled *The Maid of Gallowshiels*, in which the piper of the town is celebrated. The author was Hamilton of Bangour, and the poem tells of a contest between the piper and the fiddler for the love of the Maid of Gallowshiels. In the first book the fiddler challenges the piper to a trial of musical skill, and proposes that the maid herself shall be the umpire :—

" ' Sole in her breast the fav'rite youth shall reign
  Whose hand shall wake the sweetest warbled strain,
  And if to me the ill-fated piper yield,
  As sure I trust this well-contested field,
  High in the sacred dome his pipes I'll raise,
  The trophy of my fame in after days ;
  That all may know as they the pipes survey
  The fiddler's deed and this the signal day.
  But if the Fates, his wishes to fulfil,
  Shall give the triumph to his happier skill,
  My fiddle his, to him be praises paid,
  And join with those the long-contested maid.'
  All Gallowshiels the daring challenge heard,
  Full blank they stood, and for their piper fear'd ;
  Fearless alone, he rose in open view,
  And in the midst his sounding bagpipe threw."

Then the poem tells the history of the competitions, the piper deducing his origin from Colin of Gallowshiels, who bore the identical bagpipe at the battle of Harlaw with which he himself was resolved to maintain the glory of the piper race. The second book commences with the following exquisite description of the instrument :—

" Now in his artful hand the bagpipe held,
  Elate the piper wide surveys the field ;
  O'er all he throws his quick, discerning eyes,
  And views their hopes and fears alternate rise.
  Old Glenderule, in Gallowshiels long fam'd
  For works of skill, the perfect wonder fram'd ;
  His shining steel first lop'd with dex'trous toil,
  From a tall spreading elm, the branchy spoil.
  The clouded wood he next divides in twain,
  And smooths them equal to an oval plane.
  Six leather folds in still connected rows,
  To either plank conformed, the sides compose ;
  The wimble perforates the base with care,

A destined passage op'ning to the air ;
But once inclos'd within the narrow space,
The opposing valve forbids the backward race.
Fast to the swelling bag, two reeds combin'd
Receive the blasts of the melodious wind.
Round from the turning loom, with skill divine,
Embossed, the joints in silver circles shine ;
In secret prison pent, the accents lie
Until his arm the lab'ring artist ply ;
Then, duteous, they forsake their dark abode,
Fellows no more, and wing a separate road.
These upwards thro' the narrow channel glide,
In ways unseen, a solemn murmuring tide ;
Those through the narrow path their journey bend
Of sweeter sort, and to the earth descend.
O'er the small pipe, at equal distance, lie
Eight shining holes, o'er which his fingers fly.
From side to side the aerial spirit bounds ;
The flying fingers form the passing sounds,
That, issuing gently through the polished door,
Mix with the common air and charm no more."

The piper confounded his opponent with the dexterity of his performance, and the fiddler gave up the contest. The maid, however, with the proverbial fickleness of womankind, gave the preference to the loser, and went away with him, leaving the piper lamenting his misfortunes.

Sir Walter Scott took a considerable interest in the Border pipers, and in his introduction to *Border Minstrelsy* says:—

"It is certain that till a very late date, the pipers, of whom there was one attached to each Border town of note, and whose office was often hereditary, were the great depository of oral, and particularly poetical tradition. About springtime, and after harvest it was the custom of these musicians to make a progress through a particular district of the country. The music and tale repaid their lodging and they were usually gratified with a donation of seed corn. This order of minstrels is alluded to in the comic song of 'Maggie Lauder,' who thus addresses a piper—

> 'Live ye upo' the Border ? '

By means of these men, much traditional poetry was preserved which must otherwise have perished."

In another place he says :—

"These town pipers, an institution of great antiquity upon the Borders, were certainly the last remains of the minstrel race. Robin Hastie, town piper of Jedburgh, perhaps the last of the order, died nine or ten years ago [this was written about 1802]; his family was supposed to have held the office for about three centuries. Old age had rendered Robin a wretched performer, but he knew several old songs and tunes which have probably died with him. The town pipers received a livery and salary from the community to which they belonged, and in some burghs they had a small allotment of land called 'the Piper's Croft.'"

One of the statutes passed by the Town Council of Jedburgh was to the following effect :—

"The swasher (town drummer) and piper to go duly round at four in the morning and eight at night under the penalty of forfeiting their wages, and eight days' imprisonment."

That the drummer and piper attended to their duties is shown by an extract from *The Autobiography of a Scottish Borderer.* The writer of the extract was a Jedburgh lady, who died in 1846, and very probably either saw or heard of a procession such as she describes :—

"The bells rung a merry peal and parties paraded the streets, preceded by the town piper, with favours in their hats."

And, continuing, in a bit of glowing dialogue :—

" ' Walk in, gentlemen, and partake of the cup of joy in my puir dwalling,' quoth Kitty Rutherford as they came down the Burn Wynd, ' the bairns that are unborn will rise up and call ye blessed for this day's wark. Cum in, Watty Boyd, cum in, Rob Hastie, to the kitchen,' " etc.

Watty Boyd and Rob Hastie were respectively town drummer and town piper of Jedburgh.

The " Piper's House " in Jedburgh was No. 1 Duck Row, at the foot of the Canongate, and the fact that it was always known by this name goes to show that it was the house in which the town pipers resided. The Robin Hastie referred to by Sir Walter Scott is supposed to have occupied the house, which was altered in 1896 in order to meet modern requirements.

The instrument with which, according to tradition, one of the Jedburgh pipers, John Hastie by name, played at Flodden, existed till very lately, perhaps still exists, in the keeping of some antiquarian. That burgh pipers were, on the Borders, where they rivalled in fame those of the Highlands, greatly respected, is shown by the *Elegy on John Hasty*, an excellent dirge which elucidates much of the manners of the Border pipers. The name of the author is unknown, but as the piece was out of print before 1730, the piper must have been dead before that time :—

> " O death ! thou wreck of young and auld,
> How alie, and O how dreadfu' bald !
> Thou came unlooked for, nor anes tald
>   What was the crime ;
> But Hastie at the mouth turned cald
>   Just at his prime.

" We mourn the loss o' mensefu' John,
   Yet greet in vain since he is gone ;
A blyther lad ne'er buir a drone,
          Nor touched a lill ;
Nor pipe inspir'd wi' sweeter tone,
          Or better skill.

" Not Orpheus auld, with lyric sound,
   Wha in a ring gard stanes dance round,
Was ever half so much renown'd
          For jig and solo—
Now he lies dum aneath the ground
          An' we maun follow.

" At brydels, whan his face we saw,
   Lads, lasses, bridegroom, bride and a'
Smiling, cry'd, Johnie come awa',
          A welcome guest ;
The enchanting chanter out he'd draw—
          His pleas'd us best.

" The spring that ilk ane lik'd he kend ;
   Auld wives at sixty years wad stend ;
New pith his pipes their limbs did lend,
          Bewitching reed !
'Las that his winsome sell sou'd bend
          Sae soon his head.

" When bagpipes newfangled lugs had tir'd,
   They'd sneer ; then he, like ane inspir'd,
We's fiddle their faggin' spirits fir'd,
          Or e'er they wist ;
Gi' every taste what they desir'd,
          He never mist.

" Then with new keenness wad they caper,
 He slicly smudg'd to see them vaper ;
 And, if some glakit girl shou'd snapper,
        He'd gi' a wink,
 Fie lads, quoth he, had aff, ne'er stap her,
        She wants a drink.

" If a young swankie, wi' his joe,
 In some dark nook play'd bogle-bo,
 John shook his head, and said, why no ;
        Can flesh and blood
 Stand pipe and dance and never show
        Their metal good.

" Not country squire, nor lord, nor laird,
 But for John Hasty had regard ;
 With minstrels mean he ne'er wad herd ;
        Nor fash his head ;
 Now he's received his last reward—
        Poor man he's dead.

" He hated a' your sneaking gates,
 To play for bear, for pease, or ates ;
 His saul aspir'd to higher fates,
        O mensefu' John !
 Our tears come rapping down in spates,
        Since thou art gcne.

" Whan other pipers steal'd away,
 He gently down his join wad lay :
 Nor hardly wad tak' hire for play,
        Sic was his mense !
 We rair aloud the ruefu' day
        That took him hence.

" John, whan he play'd ne'er threw his face,
 Like a' the girning piper race ;
 But set it aff wi' sic a grace,
   That pleas'd us a' ;
 Now dull and drierie is our case
   Since John's awa'.

" Ilk tune, mair serious or mair gay,
 To humour he had sic a way ;
 He'd look precise, and smile and play,
   As suited best ;
 But Death has laid him in the clay—
   Well may he rest.

" A fiddle spring he'd let us hear,
 I think they ca'd it " Nidge-nod-near,"
 He'd gi' a punk, and look sae queer,
   Without a joke,
 You'd swore he spoke words plain and clear,
   At ilka stroke.

" It did ane good to hear his tale,
 O'er a punch bowl, or pint o' ale ;
 Nae company e'er green'd to skaill,
   If John was by ;
 Alas ! that sic a man was frail,
   And born to die.

" But we his mem'ry dear shall mind,
 While billows rair, or blaws the wind ;
 To tak' him hence Death was no kind—
   O dismal feed !
 We'll never sic anither find,
   Since Johnie's dead.

" Minstrels of merit, ilk ane come,
  Sough mournfu' notes o'er Johnie's tomb ;
Through fields of air applaud him home—
        I hope he's weel ;
  His worth, nae doubt, has sav'd him from
        The muckle de'il.

EPITAPH.

" Here lies dear John, whase pipe and drone,
  And fiddle aft has made us glad ;
Whase cheerfu' face our feasts did grace—
  A sweet and merry lad."

The Border pipers were supposed by their countrymen to
excel in musical skill and graceful execution those of the
Highlands, and they commanded a higher degree of respect
than wandering musicians. They traversed the country at
particular seasons, chiefly in spring, for the purpose of collecting seed corn—John Hastie apparently was too dignified
for this, as witness the reference to playing "for bear, for
pease, or ates"—and they were the last remains of the minstrelsy of the Borders. "Like a' the girning piper race"
shows that the pipe then commonly used in Jedburgh was
the Lowland, as that inflated with the mouth prevented
"girning." Either John played the latter, or he had such
command of his features that he did not allow his music to
deprive him of his pleasant looks.

The village of Kilbarchan, too, had its piper. He
was a notable person in his day, and also proved himself
worthy of the attention of the poet. It was the habit in
Kilbarchan for the piper to play a march called "The
Maiden Trace" before a bride as previous to her marriage
she walked with her maidens three times round the church.

"Trixie," in the following epitaph, which was first printed in 1706, refers to a then popular song :—

> " The Epitaph of Habbie Simson
>   Who on his drone bore bony flags
> He made his cheeks as red as Crimson
>   And babbed when, he blew the Bags.

> " Kilbarchan now may say, alas !
> For she hath lost her Game and Grace
> Both Trixie and the Maiden Trace
>   But what remead ?
> For no man can supply his place
>   Hab Simson's dead.

> " Now who shall play, the day it daws ?
> Or hunt up, when the Cock he craws ?
> Or who can for the Kirk—town—cause,
>   Stand us in stead ?
> On Bagpipes (now) no Body blaws
>   Fen Habbie's dead.

> " Or wha will cause our Shearers shear ?
> Wha will bend up the Braga of Weir
> Bring in the Bells or good play meir
>   In time of need ?
> Hab Simson could, what needs you speer ?
>   But (now) he's dead.

> " So kindly to his Neighbours neast,
> At Beltan and Saint Barchan's feast
> He blew and then held up his Breast
>   As he were weid
> But now we need not him arrest
>   For Habbie's dead.

M

" At Fairs he play'd before the Spear-men
All gaily graithed in their Gear Men,
Steell Bonnets, Jacks, and Swords so clear then
　　　　　　　Like any Bead,
Now wha shall play before such Weir-men
　　　　　Fen Habbie's dead ?

" At Clarkplays when he wont to come ;
His Pipe played trimly to the Drum
Like Bikes of Bees he gart it Bum
　　　　　　　And tun'd his Reed.
Now all our Pipers may sing dumb
　　　　　　Fen Habbie's dead.

" And at Horse Races many a day,
Before the Black, the Brown, the Gray
He gart his Pipe when he did play,
　　　　　　　Baith Skirl and Skreed,
Now all such Pastimes quite away,
　　　　　　Fen Habbie's dead.

" He counted was a weil'd Wight-man
And fiercely at Foot-ball he ran ;
At every Game the Gree he wan
　　　　　　　For Pith and Speed
The like of Habbie was na than,
　　　　　　But now he's dead.

" And than besides his valiant Acts
At Bridals he wan many Placks,
He bobbed ay behind Fo'ks backs,
　　　　　　　And shook his Head ;
Now we want many merry Cracks,
　　　　　　Fen Habbie's dead.

" He was Convoyer of the Bride
  With Kittock hinging at his side ;
  About the Kirk he thought a Pride
        The Ring to lead.
  But now we may gae but a Guide,
        Fen Habbie's dead.

" So well's he keeped his decorum
  And all the Stots of Whip-meg-morum,
  He slew a Man, and wae's me for him,
        And bure the Fead !
  But yet the Man wan hame before him,
        And was not dead !

" Ay whan he play'd, the Lasses Leugh,
  To see him Teethless Auld and teugh
  He wan his Pipes beside Borcheugh
        Withoutten dread ;
  Which after wan him Gear enough,
        But now he's dead.

" Ay whan he play'd the Gaitlings gedder'd,
  And whan he spake the Carl bledder'd ;
  On Sabbath days his Cap was fedder'd,
        A seemly Weid.
  In the Kirk-yeard his Mare stood tedder'd
        Where he lies dead.

" Alas ! for him my Heart is sair,
  For of his Springs I gat a skair,
  At every Play, Race, Feast, and Fair
        But Guile or Greed
  We need not look for Pyping mair,
        Fen Habbie's dead.

Besides those mentioned, there were other notable performers, who might, by a slight stretch of language, be called burgh pipers. There was for instance the Piper of Bridgeton, William Gunn, who published a book of pipe music. He died in 1876 at the age of seventy-eight years. He was well known in the east-end of Glasgow, and was engaged by the inhabitants of Bridgeton to play through their streets in the early morning, and thus usher in the new day. This was, of course, before Bridgeton was absorbed by the big city, and when it had some social existence of its own. Gunn was piper to the Glasgow Gaelic Club for a time, and kept a school for pipers. The register of this school, which was kept with great care, would be an interesting document if it could be got, for among his pupils were many who became well-known pipers. Then there was also Neil Blane, the worthy town piper of Lanark, so well described by Scott in *Old Mortality*. Neil, when introduced to the reader, is "mounted on his white Galloway, armed with his dirk and broadsword, and bearing a chanter, streaming with as many ribbons as would deck out six country belles for a fair or preaching." He could not very well have ribbons streaming from his "chanter," but let that pass. It is one of these liberties that Scott sometimes takes in matters of detail. Neil was town-piper of——(why is the town not named directly ?), and had all the emoluments of his office—the Piper's Croft, a field of an acre in extent, five merks and a new livery coat of the town's colours yearly, some hopes of a dollar upon the day of the election of magistrates, and the privilege of paying at all the respectable houses in the neighbourhood a visit at spring-time to rejoice their hearts with his music, and to beg from each a modicum of seed corn. Besides, he kept the principal change-house in the burgh, was a good-humoured, shrewd, selfish sort of fellow, indifferent alike to the disputes about Church and State, and anxious only to secure the goodwill of customers. His advice to " Jenny " as to how the change-house should be conducted makes amusing reading, and illustrates the character very forcibly.

Neil, however, must have been a creature of the novelist's imagination, for there is no trace of him in the burgh records or in local traditions.

" The Piper of Northumberland" was hardly a Scotsman, but he was so closely associated with the Borderland that a reference to his exploits may not be out of place. His name was James Allan, and there is an old booklet which tells at considerable length of " his parentage, education, extraordinary adventures, and exploits, his numerous enlistings, and wonderful escapes : with a brief narrative of his last confinement and death in Durham Jail, which happened in 1810." Jemmy Allan, " the celebrated Northumberland Piper," was a true-born gipsy, born of gipsy parents in the west of Northumberland in 1734. His father was a piper, and he also developed an inclination for the pipes. Besides, he was a first-class athlete, as hardy as the ordinary gipsy, handsome, daring, cunning, resourceful, untruthful, dishonest, and everything that could be called derogatory to the moral character of a man. He attained to great fame as a piper, being installed among the privileged class of minstrels, and allowed to join the " Faa " gang, over which " Will Faa " held sovereignty for many years. At length his fame reached the Duchess of Northumberland, into whose good graces, by a rather mean subterfuge, Jemmy ingratiated himself, and afterwards ranked as one of her musicians. But his habits of dissipation were too much for polite society, and he was dismissed. During his after wanderings he married several times, had " amours " many, enlisted and deserted immediately afterwards times without number, always taking care to secure the bounty money, swindled at cards and billiards wherever he went, charmed village society with his music until the people were off their guard, and finished up by cheating one and all, " borrowed " horses for getting across the country conveniently, had as many marvellous escapes as could be crammed into the lifetime of one man, tried most of the English towns, and made them too hot to live in, took a turn of the Scottish Border towns, with the same result, and finally got imprisoned for life for horse-stealing. He died in the House of Correction in Durham in 1810, just before the arrival of a pardon, which had been obtained by the exercise of some strong influence. The following verses, which, somehow, have the ring of *Habbie Simson's Epitaph*, conclude the book :—

> " All ye whom Music's charms inspire
> Who skilful minstrels do admire,
> All ye whom bagpipe lilts can fire
>   'Tween Wear and Tweed,
> Come, strike with me, the mournful lyre,
>   For ALLAN'S dead.

> " No more where Coquet's stream doth glide
> Shall we view JEMMY in his pride,
> With bagpipe buckled to his side,
>   And nymphs and swains
> In groups collect, at even-tide,
>   To hear his strains.

" When elbow moved, and bellows blew,
  On green or floor the dancers flew,
  In many turns ran through and through
  With cap'ring canter,
  And aye their nimble feet beat true
  To his sweet chanter."

Among Border pipers, it may be added, the perfection of the art was supposed to consist of being able to sing, dance, and play—the Lowland pipe, of course—at the same time, and when the race became extinct there was lost with them many ancient melodies.

Of the burgh pipers of Scotland there is not one left. The nearest approach to a burgh piper is perhaps the town's officer of Leith, who on the occasion of the opening of a new bandstand in 1899 was presented with a set of pipes.

CHAPTER XIII.

From the Seat of the Scorner.

"Then bagpipes of the loudest drones,
  With snuffling broken-winded tones,
  Whose blasts of air, in pocket shut
  Sound filthier than from the gut.
  And make a viler noise than swine,
  In windy weather when they whine."
                                        —*Hudibras.*

Poking fun at the pipes—English caricature—Mixed metaphor—
Churchism and pipes—Fifteenth century satire—A biographical
sneer—Thackeray—Bitter English writers—Testimony of a Jew
—Home sarcasm—The bards—Joanna Baillie—A Frenchman's
opinion—William Black—Ignorance breaking its shins—Imported sportsmen—The duty of Highlanders.

THERE is a curious tendency, except in truly Highland circles, to poke fun at the pipes. This tendency is very noticeable in the domain of English comic journalism, the more or less comic papers hailing from the metropolis finding in Scottish people and Scottish customs an inexhaustible field of humour. They never tire of joking about the strictness of our religious beliefs, our supposed slowness at perceiving a joke, our relations with visitors from the south, our alleged parsimony, our national dress, and our national music ; and they never fail to depict us as on every occasion wearing the kilt, carrying the pipes, and hiding away a bottle of whisky. Sydney Smith once declared that one might as well try to get music out of an iron foundry as out of the pipes, and Leigh Hunt's idea of martyrdom was to be tied to a post within a hundred yards of a stout-lunged piper. Some cynics have said that the walls of Jericho fell

"THE SPIRIT OF THE PIPES"*

at the blast of the bagpipe, and it has even been contended that the important part played by the instrument in many glorious victories achieved by our armies was simply due to the fact that the enemy had only two courses open—either to flee or to remain and lose all desire for existence. However, as all these things amuse our southern neighbours and do not injure us, we do not complain.

Our national music has always lent itself to the caricature of the alleged humourist south of the Border. Thus a writer of perhaps two centuries ago :—

"North-west of a line from Greenock by Perth to Inverness is the land of the Gael—of the semi-barbarous instrument the bagpipe, of wild pibroch tunes, or rude melodies, very little known and still less admired, and of a species of song which has rarely been considered worth the trouble of translation."

English writers who attend northern gatherings feel themselves in duty bound to be partly amused and partly terrified

* Above the door of Dunderave, a ruined castle near Inveraray, there used to be a figure playing upon its nose. This suggested to J. F. Campbell, of Islay, the above design of "The Spirit of the Pipes."

at the din of the pipes, and they often express the greatest wonder that our civilised ears can find pleasure in it. In the same way they used to look on our religion with contempt, and ridicule it on every opportunity. "Suffer Presbytery and bagpipes to flourish beyond Berwick" exclaims one in his wrath. The two seemed to be equally despicable. Butler, in putting this contempt into rhyme, works himself into a fine frenzy of mixed metaphor ;—

> " Whate'er men speak by this new light,
> Still they are sure to be i' the right ;
> 'Tis a dark lanthorn of the spirit,
> Which none can see but those who hear it.
>
> This light inspires and shines upon
> The house of saint like bagpipe drone."

How men can speak by light, how this light can be a lanthorn, how men can hear light, or how a bagpipe drone can shine upon a house, he does not stop to explain, but proceeds :—

> " See Phœbus or some friendly muse
> Unto small poets songs infuse,
> Which they at second hand rehearse,
> Through reed or bagpipe, verse for verse."

Needham, another Englishman, writing in 1648, after calling a typical Presbyterian such names as " a sainted Salamander that lives in the flames of zeal," " an apocryphal piece of university mummery," " a holy picklock," " a gunpowder politician," " a divine squib-crack," " a pious pulpit-cuffer," and " a deadly spit-fire," winds up with—

> " The Scotch bagpipes, the pulpit drums,
> And priests sound high and big,
> Once more a Cause and Covenant comes
> To show 's a Scottish jig."

And yet another seems to think the Separatists, a Scottish religious sect of the 17th century, would have been better at the bagpipe than at singing. They had, he thought, "need of somewhat as a bagpipe, or something never used by Antichrist, to tune them ; singing in their own conventicles like hogs against raine."

A satirical writer of 1659, when he wished to be specially cynical, proposed that two illustrious persons should be married, and that " the banquetting house should be prepared forthwith, with a pair of bagpipes and a North Country jig to entertain the nobles that shall attend the nuptials." There was apparently nothing to be said after that.

In a political satire of the same year, Sir Archibald Johnstone, a prominent person of that time, is thus addressed :—" Pure Sir Archibald Johnstone, wea is me for thee, for thou hadst thought to be a muckle laddy, but now the peeper of Kilbarchan will laugh thee to scorne." He could get no lower than to be laughed at by the piper.

A sneering biographer of Archbishop Sharpe, speaking of the prelate's grandfather's pipes, says :—" If the pipe and bags be yet in the prelate's possession, it is like he may have use for them, to gift them to some landwart church, to save the expense of a pair of organs, which may be well enough for our rude people, who can sing to the one as well as to the other ; and if instrumental music be *juris divini*, as the prelates assert, it cannot be thought that any people should be so phanatick as to admit the organs in divine service and refuse the pipes."

The Earl of Northampton, a contemporary of Shakespeare, concludes a treatise against alleged prophecy with the remark that " oracles are most like baggepypes and showmen, that sound no longer than they are puffed up with winde and played upon with cunning."

Thackeray, in *The Irish Sketch Book*, says, " Anything more lugubrious than the drone of the pipe, or the jig danced to it, or the countenances of the dancers and musicians, I never saw. Round each set of dancers the people formed a ring, in which the figurantes and coryphees went through their operations."

Thomas Kirke, the Englishman who wrote *A Modern Account of Scotland*, in 1679, said—" Musick they (the Highlanders) have, but not the harmony of the sphears, but loud terrene noises, like the bellowing of beasts ; the loud bagpipe is their delight ; stringed instruments are too soft to penetrate the organs of their ears, that are only pleased with sounds of substance."

Dr. Mac Culloch, already quoted,* who travelled Scotland in 1824, calls the bagpipe as vile a contrivance as can be imagined, and describes in graphic language all its alleged defects, and the sad result of listening to its music :—

" It is harsh, imperfect, and untunable. It is not wonderful if the responsive vibrations of the piper's tympanum are not very accurate, nor the musical organ of his brain peculiarly sensitive to sweet sounds after the daily induration which they must have undergone from such outrageous and unceasing inroads on their sensibility. The auricular wave is probably hardened as effectually as if it had been immersed in a tan pit. So much the better for them,

---

* See Page 80.

but it is not easy to describe the subsidence of feeling the general deliquium, as physicians have it, which such worthless auditors as we are experience when an act of this music closes. It cannot be much unlike what the Mickmak or Dog-ribbed Indian feels, when his teeth have all been drawn. . . . As a vocal accompaniment this instrument is plainly inappropriate, unless it were to accompany a concert of tigers and cats. Nevertheless it is used for reels, and with bad enough success, if the ears are to be consulted. As a moving force, however, it answers its purpose very effectively. There are very few dancing airs that lie within its compass. . . . Six inches of Neil Gow's horse hair would have beaten all the bagpipes that ever were blown. . . . The variations were considerably more abominable than the ground, musically speaking, but they are the best tests of the artist's merit, as all that merit lies in difficult and rapid execution. Any man can blow the charge, but when it comes to action it is he who has the strongest fingers and the worst taste who will carry the day. Yet there are rules for all this cutting of notes as it is called. The term is not ill-chosen, as the ground is literally cut into tatters by a re-iteration of the most clumsy, common-place and tasteless flourishes, offensive in themselves, but still more so by their excess, since every note is so encumbered that whatever air might have existed is totally swallowed up in the general confusion."

Mac Culloch, however, admits in another place, the merits of the bagpipe as an out-door instrument, and an instrument of war especially.

Carr, another Englishman, who wrote in 1809, had not a good word to say of the pipes :—

" Whilst refinement is rapidly spreading over Scotland, it is to be lamented that anyone should prevent the barbarous music of the country from yielding to instruments more agreeable to the ear. The bagpipe is among the few remaining barbarisms in Scotland. . . . It is a sorry instrument, capable of little more than making an intolerable noise. Every person of taste and feeling must regret the decline of the harp and be shocked at its having been succeeded by the bag-pipe. . . . I shall never forget a playing competition in Edinburgh at which I was present. As soon as the prize judges were seated the folding doors opened. A Highland piper entered in full tartan array, and began to press from the bag of his pipes, which were decorated with long pieces of riband, sounds so loud and horrible that to my imagination they were comparable only to those of the eternally tormented. In this manner he strutted up and down with the most stately march, and occasionally enraptured his audience, who expressed the influence of his instrument by loud and continued plaudits. For my part, so wretched is the instrument to my ears that I could not discover any difference in regard to expression between 'The Gathering of the Mac Donalds' and 'Abercrombie's Lament," each sound being to me equally depressive, discordant, and horrible. . ·. . I believe that it might have been three hours that common politeness compelled me to endure the distraction of this trial of skill, and I left the room with nearly the same sensations with which I should have quitted a belfry on a royal birthday. . . . One of these barbarous musicians, attempting in a fit of enthusiasm to pipe over eighteen miles of ground, blew the breath out of his body. It would have been well if he had been the last of his race."

In conclusion he addresses " Lines to the Caledonian Harp," and in passing gives a final kick to the bagpipe—

" No Highland echo knows thee now ;
A savage has usurped thy place,
Once filled by thee with every grace—
Th' inflated pipe, with swinish drone,
Calls forth applauses once thine own."

We have also the testimony of a Jew, who was compelled, by the heavy hand of misfortune, to wander in the Highlands, and in 1828 formed his impressions into a book which he called *The Jew Exile.* He praises the people for their hospitality, but alas! for their music. When leaving the village of Strathglass he says he was, in compliment, preceded by a young piper in real Highland style :—

"My young Highlander played me on the road five miles, and I would gladly have sunk the portable screech-owl appendage. A man had better have a poll-parrot chained to his ear or be doomed to listen to a concert of files and saw teeth in a saw manufactory, than be obliged to listen to such music. If, 'Sir Harry,' has any musical instrument, it will be the great Highland bagpipe. What a hideous yell it makes ! . . . that grunting, howling, yelling, screaming, screaking pig of a bag or portable screech-owl. It seems to hook its tedrum threthrum crotchets and quavers upon your nerves, and tears them to tatters, like the 'devil machine' in a cotton manufactory. I would speak with the same deference of the music of a country, as I would of its superstitions; but what can a man do when his very soul is twisted out of its socket. . . . To think that this squealing pig in a poke should be the great lever of a people's passions. It would not let a man die quietly, but would almost wake the dead."

Even in the Highlands there seems to have been a tendency to joke at the expense of the pipes. A well-known proverb is said to have originated in this wise. The fox being hungry, found a bagpipe, and proceeded to eat the bag. There was still a remnant of breath in it, and when the fox bit it the drone gave a squeal. The fox was surprised, but not frightened, for he only said—"There's meat and music here," and went on with his meal. His remark has gone down to posterity as a proverb.

The bards, whom the pipes supplanted when they supplanted the harp, did not welcome the instrument, and satirised it in many of their poems. Duncan Ban Mac Intyre, the bard of Glenorchy, in the poem *Aoir Uisdein Phiobair*, abused it with sledge-hammer power; but his abuse was coarse, and contained little genuine humour. John Mac Codrum, the Hebridean bard, did better in *Di-Moladh Piob Dhomh'uill Bhain*, one of the most laughable things he wrote. The history of Donald Bain's bagpipe he traced in an imaginative way through all its vicissitudes, from the days of Tubal Cain, through the disaster of the Deluge, and its damaging treatment by incompetent pipers. He compared the strains to some of the most discordant sounds in nature, spoke of it as a trump whose horrid music might rouse every Judas that ever lived, and used a multiplicity of illustrations to show its want of melody.

This spirit of cynicism was not confined altogether to the Gaelic bards. In *The Family Legend*, written by the distinguished poetess Joanna Baillie, there is introduced a short argument between the Duke of Argyll's piper and "Dugald," another of the characters. The piper has been playing in a small ante-room leading to the Duke's apartment, when Dugald enters :—

> *Dugald.*—Now pray thee, piper, cease ! That stunning din,
>   Might do good service by the ears to set
>   Two angry clans ; but for a morning's rouse,
>   Here at an old man's door, it does, good sooth,
>   Exceed all reasonable use. The Earl
>   Has passed a sleepless night ; I pray thee now
>   Give o'er and spare thy pains.
>
> *Piper.*—And spare my pains, says't thou—I'll do mine office
>   As long as breath within my body is.
>
> *Dugald.*—Then mercy on us all ! If wind thou mean'st,
>   There is within that sturdy trunk of thine,
>   Old as it is, a still exhaustless store.
>   A Lapland witch's bag could scarcely match it.
>   Thou could'st, I doubt not, belly out the sails
>   Of a three-masted vessel with thy mouth ;
>   But be thy mercy equal to thy might,
>   I pray thee now give o'er, in faith the Earl
>   Has passed a sleepless night.

Piper.—Think'st thou I'm a Lowland day-hired minstrel,
To stop or play at bidding. Is Argyll
The lord and chieftain of our ancient clan,
More certainly than I to him as such,
The high hereditary piper am ?
A sleepless night, forsooth ! He's slept full oft
On the hard heath, with fifty harnessed steeds
Champing their fodder round him—soundly too.
I'll do mine office, loun, chafe as thou wilt.

And so on for a few more stanzas, till Argyll himself
appears and puts an end to the discussion. But, after all,
it is mostly non-Scotsmen who sneer at the pipes. They
often understand as little of Scottish sentiment or Scottish
music as did the Frenchman, who, after hearing "Tam o'
Shanter" recited, said it was "a story of how the devil came
out of an old church and stole the tail from the horse of a
farmer called Tam because he had played the pipes in the
churchyard. I have heard," he added, "play your pipes
Scottish, and I would like well that some person would
steal away all the pipes in Scotland." Even our own
William Black, the most inoffensive and delightful of latter-
day writers, cannot resist the temptation to joke at the
expense of the bagpipes. "Sermons," he says, "are like
Scottish bagpipes. They sound very well when one doesn't
hear them." William Black, however, rarely if ever
sneers, and this is very mild indeed, compared with what
some other writers have thrown at the instrument.

The subject of Scottish national music is one against
which ignorance is always breaking its shins. In a recent
English novel, for instance, a Highlander is represented as
sitting by the roadside singing a Jacobite song and accompanying himself on the bagpipe, while one of the most
reputable of London afternoon papers gravely remarked

N

when referring to the letting of Inveraray Castle, after the
death of the eighth Duke of Argyll—"Ichabod is the
watchword for the Highlands and Islands, and the pibroch
may skirl the lament with better cause than if half the
clan had fallen before the claymores of an alien tartan."
These are extreme cases, no doubt, but they are only two
out of many. It is, of course, vain to expect Scottish feelings from non-Scottish people, and the over-running of our
land by imported sportsmen does not improve matters a
bit—

> "Cockneys, Frenchmen, swells, and tourists,
>   Motley-garbed and garish crew ;
> Belted pouches, knickerbockers,
>   Siken hose and patent shoe."

Although these people may cease their scoffing and make
themselves as Highland as anyone can be whom nature has
not made Highland, their affection for the music and their
professions of goodwill are not likely to help to preserve it.
It is for real Highlanders to keep alive their own music and
show scorners that it is not going to die the death, but live
while there are Highlands and a Highland people. If, on
the other hand, they are playing the lament for a perishing
race and a dying language, it is not much wonder if neighbours chime in with an emphatic Amen. Better far is the
spirit of Alexander Fisher, a Glasgow poet, who wrote for
Whistlebinkie :—

> "You'll may spoke o' ta fittle, you'll may prag o' ta flute,
> An' ta clafer o' pynas, pass trums, clairnet an' lute.
> Put ta far pestest music you'll may heard, or will fan,
> Is ta kreat Hielan' pagpipe, ta kran Hielan' pagpipe, ta prite o' ta
>   lan'.

O ! tere is no one can knew all her feelin', her thought,
Whan ta soon o' ta pibroch will langsyne to her prought,
Au' her mint whirl rount apout wi' ta pleasure once fan,
When she hears ta kreat pagpipes, ta kran, etc.

  .   .   .   .

Whan ta clans all pe kather't, an' all rety for fought,
To ta soon o' ta fittle, woult tey march tid ye'll thought ?
No not a foot woult tey went, not a claymore pe drawn,
Till tey heard ta kreat pagpipe, to kran, etc.

Whan ta funeral is passin' slow, slow, through ta klen,
Ta hearts all soft wi' ouskie what prings tears from ta men !
'Tis ta Coronach's loot wail soonin' solemn an' kran,
From to kreat Hielan' pagpipe, ta kran Hielan', etc.

Whan ta wattin tauks place, O ! what ahoy, frolic an' fun,
An' ta peoples all meetit, an' ta proose has been run,
Tere's no music for dancin', has yet ever been fan,
Like ta kreat Hielan' pagpipe, ta kran Hielan', etc.

O, tat she hat worts to tolt all here lofe an' telight
She has in ta pagpipes, twoult teuk long, long years to write,
Put she'll shust teuk a trap pefore her task sh'll pegan,
So here's ta pagpipe, ta kran Hielan' pagpipe, ta prite o' ta lan'."

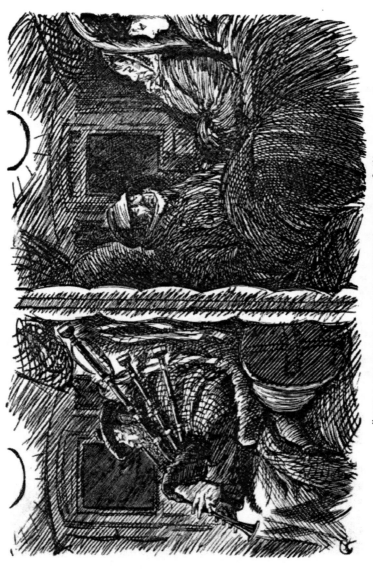

"WHILE BREATHING CHANTERS PROUDLY SWELL."—*Scott.*

Mr. McSkirligug (beguiling the time with some cheerful pibrochs on his national instrument).

Mr. Southdown (travelling north with his Family by the Night Mail). "Dear, dear, dear! What a Shame they don't Grease the Wheels of these Carriages! I can't get a Wink of Sleep! (*Mrs. S. groans in sympathy.*) I declare I'll Complain to the Directors.

BY CHARLES KEENE, Jan. 21, 1871.

(Reproduced from *Punch*, by special permission of the Proprietors.)

CHAPTER XIV.

THE HUMOUR OF THE PIPES.

" Wha wadna be in love
   Wi' bonnie Maggie Lauder ?
A piper met her gaun to Fife
   And spiered what was't they ca'd her ;
Richt scornfully she answered him,
   ' Begone, you hallan shaker :
Jog on your gate, you bladder skate,
   My name is Maggie Lauder.' "
                            —*Old Scots Song.*

Punch's joke—King Charles's heads—An amusing competition—A
Highlander's Irishism—Wedding experiences—A piper's fall—A
resourceful piper—A Cameron piper and his officer—" Lochaber
no more "—An elephant's objection—Embarked in a tub—
Glasgow street scene—Bad player's strategy—What the wind
did—A new kind of tripe—A Pasha and a piper—A Gordon
nervous—A jealous piper—Dougal Mac Dougal's downfall.

APART from the wilfully sarcastic humour exemplified
in the previous chapter, there clings round the pipes
a host of innocently laughable stories. *Punch*, the
recognised pioneer of comic journalism, and always the ablest
of that class of papers, has in its day had a number of jokes
about the pipes, and, to do the writers and artists justice,
they have always been enjoyable, even to the perfervid Scot,
and not of the kind which does more to show the ignorance

of the inventors than create a laugh.   *Punch's* humour is
broad, but hardly ever offensive, and the picture by Charles
Keene, reproduced on another page, may be taken as a
fair sample.   The drawing, which appeared on January 21st,
1871, shows the best art of the caricaturist wedded to the
broadest and yet the most enjoyable humour.   Charles
Keene, by the way, was himself a performer on the pipes,
which he studied thoroughly.   On one occasion he was some
distance from home seeing a sick friend, and, writing
afterwards to London, he said : " My only solace was skirling
away for an hour on the lonely beach, and I generally chose
the most melancholy pibroch I could think of."   So he can
hardly be accused of endeavouring to joke at the expense of
the instrument.

   After *Punch* I must be permitted to work off several
stories which have been King Charles's Heads unto me
since I began to compile this volume.   They persisted in
cropping up, now in some book which I was consulting, then
in a newspaper, and next in conversation with acquaintances.
I know all their variations so well now that I recognise
them a long way off, and generally manage to avoid them.
Four are particularly determined in keeping themselves to
the front :—

   A wandered Celt found himself laid up in an hospital in
America with a disease which fairly puzzled the physicians.
They did not know what to do with their patient, for he
seemed to be sinking into the grave for no reason whatever.
They held a consultation, and decided as a last resource to
try music, preferably bagpipe music, as the patient was a
Scotsman.   So every night for a fortnight a piper played
in the lobbies of the hospital, and gradually the Celt began
to revive.   At the fortnight's end he was well enough to be

discharged, but—and this was the worst feature of the case
—*all the other patients had died.*

Once, I remember, that story hailed from the Crimea and
referred to a dying soldier of Sir Colin Campbell's, who was
cured by the pipes in one hour. The music was, however,
the death of forty-one of his comrades. The exact number
killed varies from time to time, but that is a small matter.
The incident is always the same. The last occasion on
which it crossed my path was in the spring of 1900, when it
appeared in the "London Letter" of a Glasgow evening
paper, to which it had been telegraphed the same morning
from the "City Notes" of one of the leading London
dailies, each of the journalists concerned treating it as a
great discovery in the field of humour. And I had been
doing all I could to keep out of its way for about a year
previously.

The next also shows the wonderful powers of pipe music.
Music, apparently, hath charms to soothe the savage *beast*.
A Scotsman, a piper of course, lost his way on an American
prairie, and was overtaken by a bear. To appease the
brute Sandy threw it his modest lunch, the only food he had
to keep him alive until he found shelter. But Bruin was
not satisfied, and threatened to dine off Sandy himself,
whereupon the piper thought he would play a farewell
lament before quitting the world. So he struck up "Lochaber no more." No sooner, however, did the big drone give
its first squeal than the bear stood stock still, then turned
and fled precipitously. Then Sandy exclaimed—

" If she had known she was so fond of ta music, she could
have had ta pipes before ta supper."

On its last round that story had reached Siberia, and the
Celt, who was hungry, was pursued by a pack of wolves,

who " fled with hideous howls " when the slogan of the clan was heard.

The next illustrates the Highlander's propensity towards whisky drinking, and it rarely varies to any great extent. A Highland laird, being unable to maintain a permanent piper, employed a local musician occasionally when he had a party. Donald was once overlooked as to his usual dram before commencing to play, and in revenge he gave very bad music, which caused the laird to remonstrate with him and ask the cause. " It's the bag," said Donald ; " she pe ferry, ferry hard." " And what will soften it ? " asked his employer. " Och, just whusky." Accordingly the butler was sent for a tumblerful of the specific, which Donald quickly drank. " You rascal," said the laird, " did you not say it was for the bagpipes ? " " Och, yess, yess," said Donald ; " but she will pe a ferry peculiar pipes this. *She aye likes it blawed in.*"

The piper's story associated with " Boyne Water " is the fourth. The name and the regiment vary, but the story is always the same :—

Sandy Mac-something or other—the surname has not come down to posterity—was an old piper in the 92nd, and when his detachment was located in Ireland an order was given that " Boyne Water " was not to be played. The colonel probably did not wish to hurt the feelings of any of his neighbours. " Boyne Water," however, was Sandy's favourite tune, and to the surprise of the colonel, the first time the company marched out after the prohibitory order had been issued, Sandy struck up the forbidden air. " What do you mean ? " cried the officer. " Do you not know that you are not allowed to play ' Boyne Water ? ' " " It'll no pe ' Boyne Water ' at all," replied Sandy. " It'll pe quite another tune, but to the same air." But Sandy had to stop playing it all the same.

An amusing description is given by a writer who travelled in the Highlands about seventy years ago, of a competition which he witnessed between two pipers in Tongue. There was a certain John MacDonald who had blown before the Emperor of China, having accompanied an embassy to that country, and a Donald Abroch, who traced his descent from some of the hereditary pipers. Both had gained prizes in public, and they were natural rivals :—

"The drone of Donald's pipes streamed with bonny flags of red and blue, while he made his cheeks as red as crimson, and bobbed around as he blew. Meantime the banner of defiance hoisted on his antagonist's spirit-stirring engine floated on the troubled air in the radiant yellow of the Celestial Empire. As etiquette demanded that each should be heard in turn, the Imperial piper, having the preference, as of divine right, put forth all his energy on the advent of his rival, as the cock crows a louder defiance should some neighbour chanticleer intrude on his hereditary domain. But John was now seventy, nor had his wind much improved by the quantity of monsoon which he had swallowed in the Indian seas. His breeze being blown, Donald, who knew the weak point in his rival's lungs, now raised a blast so loud and dread that it reminded one of the roaring of the lion of Rabbi Johosuah Ben Hananiah, at the sound of whose voice all the people's teeth dropped out of their heads. John turned yellow with despair, as the Imperial ribbons, and thus ended the first act.

"It was not for us to decide between rival pibrochs or rival pipers, but by the aid of some judicious applause and more acceptable whisky a sort of amicable armistice was produced till the next act should begin. It was now necessary that they should play together a duet, composed of different pibrochs in different keys, in which it was the business of each to outscream his neighbour by the united force of lungs and elbows. The north side of the room was in possession of the Emperor's piper, and he of our clan drew up his force on the south ; each strutting and bellowing till, like rival bullfinches, they were ready to burst their lungs and bag, each playing his own tune in harmonious dissonance ; and both as they crossed each other at every turn, looking the defiance they would have breathed had their wind not been otherwise employed. The chanters screamed, the drones grunted, and as the battle raged with increasing fury, Donald's wind seemed ready to burst its cerements, while the steam of the whisky distilling through the bag dropped as from the nozzle of a worm-pipe. Poor John was now nearly blown, but as we were unwilling that he should puff out for our amusement the last of that breath which he had with so much difficulty brought all the way from Pekin, we determined that enough had been done for honour, and put an end to the concert according to the rules of bucolic contest, by allowing equal praise and equal prizes to each swain. That they had both played *fort bein* could not be doubted, still less according to the French pun that they had played *bein fort.*"

Pipers, when playing in public, often get into awkward positions. During the performance of the well-known Julien Army Quadrilles, in connection with which local bands represent England, Scotland, and Ireland—the chief performing band being the orchestra—the pipes were once put into a cellar in the lower part of the building and the door closed. Here, on a given signal, they struck up "The Campbells are coming." Thereupon the doors gradually opened, and the pipers marched up from the lower regions and through the vast hall, which was crowded. On their approach the cheering was so vociferous that it was impossible to hear the sound of the pipes, and it was only by carefully watching the parts of the tune, the step, and the swing of the leading piper (who was endeavouring to reach the platform on which the orchestra was seated) that they were able to play in unison. Having ascended the platform, they placed themselves in a conspicuous position, and when they stopped playing, the well-known imitation fierce battle, for which these quadrilles are famous, began. While rehearsing this performance, it should be added, the door of the lower apartments had been accidentally left open, so that the sounds were distinctly and loudly heard by the bandmaster. who was a German. With lightning rapidity he came tearing downstairs in a furious rage, exclaiming in wild tones—"Mein Got, fat is this. You may be as well up on de stage. Why is de door not closed according to my instructions?" Being thus interrogated, the pipe-major appealed to piper Dougal MacDonald, who was the last to enter, and who should have closed the door.

"Why did you not shut the door when you came in, Dougal?" he asked.

Dougal's reply, which was characteristic of the man, was—

"Ach man! What did I know? The door wasn't shut when I opened it."

After this matters went on all right and to the satisfaction of the bandmaster.

On another occasion, when taking part in these quadrilles, the same band had to cross a plank arrangement erected above the heads of the audience before they could get to the platform. To get there under such circumstances required tact, in addition to a good nerve.

To relate another awkward experience :—A piper was on one occasion ordered to play at a wedding near Glasgow, at which his colonel was one of the guests. The object was to take the company by surprise. The piper therefore went there secretly. He had three and a half miles to walk, as the 'bus which plied to and fro at that time (twenty years ago) was full of ladies. The day being exceptionally wet, he got drenched. The first incident took place shortly after leaving the barracks in the Gallowgate, where a fairly well dressed but drunken woman unceremoniously slipped her arm inside his and said—" I am going where you are going." She vowed she knew him and all the pipers, as well as all the officers, and the colonel in particular—in fact, she knew the whole regiment. While making these declarations she clung tenaciously to the piper, and nothing would shake her off. A motley crowd gathered round them, and, to make matters worse, no policeman was in sight. A gentleman, however, opportunely came to the rescue, and extricated the piper from his predicament by inviting him into a shop and letting him out by a side door into another street. In due course the piper arrived at the mansion house where he was to play. He first made for the kitchen, in order to be out of the way and to have his clothes and appointments dried and replenished. Here he was accosted by a head official, a woman, who wished to know what he was doing there and what he wanted. The piper replied that he was sent there.

" Who sent you, and what for ? " she asked.

He replied—" Colonel .———."

" And who is he ? " she next asked.

" He is my colonel."

" Well," she replied, snappishly, " I don't know him, and never heard anything about you."

The piper, however, entered the kitchen, and made for the fire. It so happened that the head cook—a stout, portly, good-natured woman—was a native of Tobermory. She took the drenched man in hand, and when she discovered that he could speak Gaelic, they became the best of friends. He got himself so much into her favour that she undertook to dry his coat and polish all his accoutrements. In

course of time he got brightened up and ready for any
call. He had to ignore all the time the repelling looks and
nasty hints of the head official referred to, who would have
nothing to do with him, and whose dignity was evidently
hurt at his presence there without her being consulted.
At two in the morning he was sent for by the mistress of
the house—a fine specimen of the old Scottish lady—who led
him to a door which communicated with the ball-room,
and, without more ado, she gave him the following instructions:—

" You'll just blow up your bags and you will play in
there "—pointing to the door—" and John will show you
where to go to."

The piper struck up the " Cock of the North " very suddenly, to the surprise of everyone. When he entered the
room he nearly fell, the floor was so smooth. Next, his big
drone touched the chandeliers, under which were standing
three or four ladies with the usual long trains to their
dresses. He naturally became somewhat embarrassed, for
he had to watch his tune, to watch his feet, to watch the
chandelier, as well as to avoid the ladies' dresses, and at the
same time to watch " John," who ultimately led him into
the recesses of a window, where he played the " Highland
Scottische " and " Reel of Tulloch." This done, it was part
of his programme to play " The Campbells are coming,"
and make his exit by the door through which he entered.
There were, unfortunately for him, too many doors, and, as
" John " had left, he was again perplexed. He, however,
made for, as he thought, the proper door, under the same
difficulties as he experienced on his entrance ; but, instead
of getting out, he was landed in a pantry where there were
two young women busily engaged cutting up sandwiches.

Here he was kept prisoner for about half an hour. Any pipers who have had the same experience will admit that it requires no little confidence and caution to discharge satisfactorily such duties under similar circumstances.

There is a story told of another piper, which does not terminate quite so happily. Piper Hugh Mac L—— was engaged to play at an Irish wedding. Now, Irish people are generally very kind, and on such occasions are possessed of a good supply of " the mercies." The room in which the wedding was held was rather small for dancing purposes, considering the number of guests. They therefore placed a table in the corner of the room, on the top of it a chair, and on the top of that a small flat stool, on which sat the piper. Here he blew with might and main till three o'clock in the morning, when down fell piper, pipes, and all on the floor. There were, luckily, no bones broken. Legs were broken, but they were wooden ones. After this somewhat amusing catastrophe the music ceased for the night.

Pipers were a resourceful race, if the following story is to be considered a typical one. A well-known piper, whose name is withheld because some of his people are still with us, was very often hard put to it for money, and many and various were the means he took to raise the wind. One day, more than usually dead-broke, he found an old mahogany leg of a table lying at the Clydeside, near Glasgow Green. He picked it up, and going to a joiner's shop in the Briggate, he hired a turning lathe for an hour or two. Being an expert maker as well as player, he soon had an imitation set of drones and a chanter turned out of the mahogany. Then he got a piece of old skin and made a bag which would not have kept in small stones, not to speak of wind, and by means of borrowing pence from acquaintances, he raised some green velvet and ribbons. After he had carefully covered and adorned his "pipes,". he bored holes about an inch down the "drones," stained the "virls" black, and gravely offered the lot to a pawnbroker. He, poor man, did not know much about pipes, for he gave the piper £1 on them. Then the dead-broke man repaid all his loans and went off a richer man by some seventeen or eighteen shillings. What the pawnbroker said when he attempted to sell the "pipes" has not come down to posterity.

The best of the bagpipe stories, however, come from the regimental piper. Army pipers were, and perhaps still are, treated a little more leniently than their fellows. A piper of the 79th Cameron Highlanders was brought before the officer in command for being drunk. The officer was a bit of a wag, and on the delinquent being marched in he, looking very severe, said, "Are you the piper that played before Moses?" "Yes, sir," said the piper, taking advantage of the familiarity. The officer was a bit nonplussed, and shouted, "Get out of here, you scoundrel, and never come before me again." A day or so after the piper was again brought up for being drunk, and the officer, annoyed at seeing him back so soon, said, "I don't wish to punish you, but if you continue coming before me I must treat you like any other delinquent." Quoting from the defaulters' sheet, he continued, "Drunk, drunk, drunk; why, sir, you're always drunk. Look here, just put yourself in my position and see what you would do." On the officer vacating the chair the piper, nothing daunted, took his place, and proceeding to scan his own defaulter sheet, said in grave tones, "Drunk, drunk, drunk. Why sir, you're always drunk; I'll give you seven days' cells and twenty-eight days confined to barracks." The officer was too amazed at the piper's impudence to do more than shout at the top of his voice—" Sergeant-major, take this man out of here," and as we have no record of any future infliction of punishment, we may infer that the piper's game of bluff succeeded in getting him off scathless.

Another story of a piper who " took more than was good for him " is associated with " Lochaber no more." It was the duty of a piper of the 93rd Argyll and Sutherland Highlanders to play the officers' mess. Feeling somewhat unsteady, he chose " Lochaber no more " as being an easy tune and suited for hiding his condition. His eccentric performance, however, did not escape the colonel, who was in quarters close by dressing for dinner, and, in passing to the mess room he called out " Piper Mac Donald." " Yes, sir," replied the piper, approaching the colonel with his best salute and under the impression that he was to be complimented for serenading the commanding officer by his rendering of such a beautiful air. " What tune was that you played ? " growled the colonel. " Hic ! ' Lochubu no more,' sir." " Then," said the colonel severely, " you'll be piper no more, sir," and Piper Mac Donald forthwith returned to the ranks.

It is a well-known fact that pipers in Highland regiments are posted to companies, and follow them wherever they go. On one occasion a company of the Gordons were marching from a place called Jullunder to Fort Kangra, situated on one of the lower ranges of the Himalayas. Accompanying them was an elephant, on which were placed sick and exhausted men. After a few days' march they were deprived of music on account of the piper's feet becoming blistered, and he was relegated to the back of the elephant. On the

last day's march, before entering their new station, some
one suggested that in order to brighten them up the piper
might be requested to play on the elephant's back at the
head of the company. To this the officer assented, and
accordingly the piper was handed his pipes. When he
began to tune them up it was evident that the elephant had
no appreciation of such sounds, for he shook his head,
flapped his big ears menacingly, raised his trunk, with which
he embraced the piper round the waist, and violently threw
him and his pipes into a ditch as a mark of his disapproval
of such music.

A camp of exercise some three miles out of Delhi was
visited at night by a terrible storm of rain and wind. Tents
were blown over, and much wreckage and damage done. The
pipe-major and drum-major, who, of course, were both staff-
sergeants, occupied a small tent by themselves, situated in a
hollow. Towards morning, just as daylight appeared, it
was observed from the sergeants' mess that the pipe-major
had got all his valuables — silver, pipes, banner, dirk,
sporran, etc.—placed in a tub in which he himself was
sitting. All round outside his tent, for a considerable distance, was a sea of water, so hard had it rained during the
night. Being very anxious to save his valuables, uniform,
and appointments he embarked in the tub and paddled
shorewards, and while doing so his comrades began to shout
and jeer at him. This roused the pipe-major's temper to
boiling pitch, and caused him to become rather unsteady in
his precarious craft. Veering a little too much to one side,
over it went, and piper and cargo were thrown into the
water, to the evident delight of his comrades.

The playing of the Lords of Session from the hotel to the
Court House in Glasgow was an old custom. After having

o

performed this duty, the captain usually marched the band and escort to Gallowgate Barracks by way of Saltmarket, which was at one time a very rough locality. While playing through the street, the pipe-major of a gallant corps suddenly found himself in a very unpleasant fix. A decrepit, drunken fish-wife pounced upon him, lovingly caught him round the neck, and insisted on hugging and kissing him. To make things worse the band kept marching on through the large crowd, and no amount of struggling and swearing would make this enthusiastic follower relinquish her hold of the pipe-major. At last by a supreme effort he managed to extricate himself from her dirty clutches. It is needless to say that the escort and pipers enjoyed a fine laugh at the pipe-major's predicament.

To show how good may sometimes come of evil, one of our gallant pipers, who had evidently been enjoying himself rather freely the night before, on returning to barracks found himself detailed for the duties of orderly piper, the first of which is to play the men's breakfast pipes. The piper's condition not being what it might have been, and the morning being cold and raw, he was not making a very good tune. This attracted the notice of the orderly officer, who belonged to the piper's company, and forthwith he had the piper brought before him and rebuked for his bad playing. The piper, quick as thought, ingeniously turned matters into quite a different channel by putting all the blame on his chanter. He impudently pointed out to the young officer the lowest hole, which is the largest on the chanter.

" Just look at the size of that hole, sir," said he. " It is far too large, sir, and while I was *birling* with my little finger it went into the hole, sir, and when I was getting it out it caused that nasty screeching, sir."

" Oh," replied the officer, " is that the cause of it? Then you require a new chanter."

" Yes, very badly, sir," replied the piper.

The officer, being a man of means, said, " Very well, I will give you a present of one."

This is obviously a case where the piper gulled the young officer into presenting him with a new chanter, whereas he should have been severely reprimanded for his unfitness to perform his duty.

A novel accident once happened to the pipers of the Cameronians while playing in the Botanic Gardens in Glasgow. At that time they wore a Tam o' Shanter or blue bonnet, slightly cocked to one side. The day was stormy, and the wind came in gusts. Eight of the pipers were marching jauntily along in line when a gust of wind suddenly came and blew off the eight Tam o' Shanters, as if by word of command, starting with the pipe-major, who was on the right. The scramble for bonnets which followed can be more easily imagined than described.

Piper Donald Menzies, of the Breadalbane Fencibles, was one of the resourceful kind. The men were in the habit of receiving money in place of a certain quantity of rations, and on one occasion instead of buying food in the usual way many of them bought whisky. This came to the colonel's ears, and he at once ordered the adjutant to go round at a certain hour and report to him what the men were cooking for dinner. The order got wind and the Fencibles were on the alert. When the adjutant came to where Piper Menzies was doing his cooking he asked " What have you got here, Donald?" " Tripe, sir," said Donald. " Tripe," said the adjutant, " now just let me see," and he lifted the lid off the pot. " Well, Donald," he said, walking away and smiling, " I never saw tripe before with buttons and holes in it." Donald had cut up a pair of white moleskin trousers and put pieces of them into the pot to make believe he was to have a dinner.

Shortly after the occupation of Cairo by the British troops, the late Nubar Pasha took a prodigious fancy to the music of the Black Watch, and had the idea of having a servant taught the use of the bagpipes. Nubar despatched a French friend, who spoke English, to interview a piper on the subject. Donald replied—" Weel, he micht learn or he micht no'. But, let me tell you, it needs wind an' mickle strength to fill the bag o' the pipes an' keep blawin'. Sae if yin o' thae Egyptian chaps took the job on he'd need to be bandaged a' ow're like yin o' thae old mummies, or maybe he'd burst himsel' ! " This conversation was reported to Nubar, who took the remarks seriously. So he gave up the idea of having a piper attached to his household, as the use of the bagpipe was attended with the prospect of such danger to the performer.

Soldiers are not nervous men as a rule, but a pipe-major of the Gordons was. While the regiment was being inspected, he noticed while standing behind the band that the colonel's helmet was reversed. The officer seemed perturbed about something, strutting backward and forward, every now and then digging his sword into the ground. This made the pipe-major, who was anxious to call the colonel's attention to the mistake in connection with his headgear, more nervous than before. At last by a supreme effort he mustered up courage, and stepping out of the ranks he approached the colonel, and after saluting said, " I beg your

pardon, sir, but your helmet is upside down, sir." "What!"
roared the officer, evidently thinking the man had become
insane. The pipe-major became more nervous than ever,
and stammered out, "I beg your pardon, sir, but I mean to
say, sir, that your helmet is outside in, sir." "The devil it
is, sir," roared the colonel, and the pipe-major as a last
resource got out, "Well, I mean to say, sir, that your
hat is backside foremost, sir." The colonel instantly calmed
down, and took the incident in good part, put his "hat"
right and thanked the pipe-major, who did not forget his
nervousness or his mistakes for many days.

Yet another instance of how the piper made free with his
superiors. A Highland officer having in obedience to orders
added a drum to his pipe band, a spirit of jealousy soon
afterwards arose between the piper and the drummer respecting their title to precedence. This gradually increased until
it became personal animosity. At length the subject of the
quarrel was submitted to the officer, who decided in favour
of the drummer, whereupon the piper exclaimed, "Ads
wunds, sir (whatever that may mean), and shall a little
rascal that beats upon a sheep's skin tak' the right hand of
me that am a musician?" A musician, no less!

The last item to be given under this heading is meant to
illustrate the high opinion Highlanders have of the pipes,
but I do not vouch for its authenticity. It is from a book
of *Scottish Life and Character* :—

"Dougal MacDougal, he left his native fastnesses for the great
city of Glasgow, where he joined the police, as many a better man
has done since. But Dougal was not content with being a policeman, he must needs join the police band. By-and-by another native
of the fastnesses came to Glasgow, and meeting Dougal, he said—

' And wad it be true Tougal that her is a member of the polis prass pand ? '

" ' Yus, Alastair, her was.'

" ' And what instrument was she play, Tougal ? '

" ' Ta trombone.'

" Ta trombone !   Her as draws and draws and plaws and plaws ?   Och, Tougal, wad she tempt Providence by leaving ta pipes for that ? ' "

After which we had better adjourn.

CHAPTER XV.

Demoniac Pipes and Pipers.

" A winnock bunker in the east,
   There sat Auld Nick in shape o' beast;
A towzie tyke, black, grim, and large,
   To gi'e them music was his charge ;
He screw'd the pipes and gart them skirl,
   Till roof and rafters a' did dirl."

                                        —*Burns.*

Tam o' Shanter—The Devil's favourite instrument—" Sorcerers "
burned—A bard's satire—Glasgow Cathedral story—A Hebri-
dean Tam o' Shanter—Continental ideas—Reformation zeal—
Ghostly pipers—A " changeling piper "—*The Lost Pibroch*—
The Chisholm " enchanted pipes "—The Black Chanter of Clan
Chattan.

IT was not at all a new idea that of Burns, when he represented the arch-enemy of mankind playing the pipes to
   the revellers in Alloway's " auld haunted kirk." The
ancients had it, and the sylvan divinity Pan, who can be
identified with the Satan of Scottish superstition, is said to
have appeared as a performer on the bagpipe. A flute with
seven reeds was his favourite instrument, and this may be
identified with the bagpipe of tradition. Popular belief in
the seventeenth century labelled the pipes as the Devil's
favourite musical instrument. In 1679 some unhappy

women were burned at Bo'ness for sorcery, and they were accused, among other things, " of meeting Satan and other witches at the cross of Murestane, above Kinneil, where they all danced, and the Devil acted as piper." Satan is also alleged to have acted in the same capacity in the guise of a rough, tawny dog at a dance on the Pentland Hills. Mac Mhurich, the bard of Clan Ranald, composed a Gaelic satire on national music, in which the " coronach of women " and *piob gleadhair*, the pipe of clamour, are called " the two ear sweethearts of the black fiend—a noise fit to rouse the imps," and there is a story connected with Glasgow Cathedral which shows further the prevalence of the idea. The gravestones round the Cathedral lie so close that one cannot walk across the ground without treading on them. This, however, has not always been able to prevent resurrections, as would appear from the legend. Somewhere about the year 1700 a citizen one morning threw the whole town into a state of inexpressible horror and consternation by giving out that in passing at midnight through the kirkyard he saw a neighbour of his own, lately buried, rise out of his grave and dance a jig with the devil, who played the air of " Whistle ower the lave o't " on the bagpipe. The civic dignitaries and ministers were so scandalised at the intelligence that they sent the town drummer through the streets next morning forbidding any to whistle, sing or play the infernal tune in question.

A story curiously like that of Tam o' Shanter, but of a much more pleasant nature, at least for the human participator, comes from the Hebrides—the particular isle is not stated. A gentleman innkeeper, who was taught by Angus Mac Kay, the late Queen's piper, and could play the pipes as well as the violin, was sadly addicted to the drinking habit, and had frequent fits of *delirium tremens,* in which he had extraordinary experiences. Once when he had been indulging with his usual prodigality, the result found him in a large hall, laid out for dancing, and with a band of performers dressed in blue. The chief of the blue imps stood as if in front of the orchestra, grinning, capering, and gesticulating in the most fantastic manner. In the course of time, however, he became more amiable, and, drawing up his tail over his shoulder, he fingered it as if it were the chanter of the pipes, and there poured out a most inspiriting jig, the force of which neither demon nor man could resist, and the performance rivalled that in Alloway's "auld haunted kirk." But, and this is where Tam o' Shanter failed and the innkeeper succeeded, " mine host" remembered the tune after his recovery, and played it, and the last teller of the story says he " heard it played by another party who had learned it from him." But, unfortunately, he was too lazy to make a copy, so the " Lost Jig" went the way of the " Lost Pibroch," and is now unknown to the world.

THE DANCE OF DEATH
From a Woodcut of the Time of Henry VIII.

That the idea of a demoniac piper is not peculiar to Scotland is shown by the sculpture executed by the celebrated German artist, Durer, which represents the Devil playing on the pipes; by an engraving of a pageant at Antwerp in the sixteenth century, where a similar figure occurs, and by various Continental stories and pictures. The pipes were, it should be added, far more often associated with religious matters than with demoniacal. The figure on the "apprentice pillar" in Rosslyn Chapel is that of a. cherub playing on a Highland bagpipe, and, as has been shown in a previous article, there are many indications in ecclesiastical architecture and in ecclesiastical history that the pipes were not altogether banned from associating with the good. After the Reformation, it is true, they were held to be the Devil's instruments, and between 1570 and 1624 pipers were severely persecuted; but the zeal of the reformers, while always praiseworthy, often outran their discretion, and in their condemnation of instrumental music they included all minstrels. They vested supernatural powers in things which we now look upon as ordinary. The miseries of the Civil War were foretold by the appearance of a monster in the River Don, the disappearance of gulls from the lakes near Aberdeen, the loud tucking of drums in Mar, and in a seaman's house at Peterhead, where trumpets and bagpipes and tolling of bells gave additional horror to the sound.

The ghostly piper of Highland mythology was often seen mounted on a big black horse, while multitudes of voices sang round him, sometimes in light clothing and with long white staffs in their hands. In one instance—it comes from Dalry, in Ayrshire—"the sound of voices was terrible, and all struck in at the chorus. The tunes seemed to part and make way for the rider to get out, but, no, they closed again." One such piper frequented the wild passes of Drumouchter, about the highest and most dreary part of the hills now crossed by the Highland Railway. At the hour of gloaming passers-by could hear the melancholy wailing of the pipes, but they never could tell from whence it came. Prince Charles Edward Stuart is alleged to have fought there a band of English cavalry, when on his retreat from Derby in 1745, and though his men won, the piper, if he was Prince Charlie's piper, seems to have considered the incident a matter of perpetual mourning. Other sights and spectres, as of people engaged in mortal combat, are said to have been seen near the place.

In a North Highland story, a " changeling " plays the pipes. A tailor went to a farmhouse to work, and just as he was going in, somebody put into his hands a child of a month old, which a little lady dressed in green seemed to be waiting to receive. The tailor ran home and gave the child to his wife. When he got back to the farmhouse, he found the farmer's child crying and disturbing everybody. It was a fairy changeling which the nurse had taken in, meaning to give the farmer's own child to the fairy in exchange, but nobody knew this but the tailor. When they were all gone out, he began to talk to the child. " Hae ye your pipes?" said the tailor. "They're below my head," said the changeling. " Play me a spring," said the tailor. Out sprang the little man and played the bagpipe round the room. Then there was a noise outside, and the elf said, "It's my folk wanting me," and away he went up the chimney, and then they fetched back the farmer's own child from the tailor's house.

Apart from their connection with supernatural beings or supernatural agencies, the pipes have at various times in the history of Scotland been credited with supernatural power. The " Lost Pibroch " itself is an echo, but a magnificently worded echo, of the old connection between the pipes and the supernatural. In it we have something like a modern literary curiosity, a Highland story written in the true Highland ring and spirit, and yet as splendid an intellectual treat to a non-Highland reader as he can get anywhere in the King's English. It exaggerates the power of the pipes, but it is an exaggeration that is fully in unison with the nature of the people, and it is the gem of all the stories of pipers and the supernatural. "Then here's another for fortune," said *Paruig Dall*, and he went through the woods with his pipes under his oxter, to follow those whom his notes had already set awandering.

The Chisholm preserves, or at least did at one time preserve a relic believed to be of great antiquity. It is a chanter which is supposed to have a peculiar faculty of indicating the death of the chief by spontaneously bursting, and after each fracture it is carefully repaired by a silver fillet, which is an improvement on the original method of mending with a leathern throng. The family piper, when from home at a wedding, heard his chanter crack, and at once started up, saying he must return, for The Chisholm was dead. And he was.

But the most famous of all such articles is "The Black Chanter of Clan Chattan." This is a relic of the fight between the Clan Quhele and the Clan Yha on the North Inch of Perth in 1396. It is made of *lignum vitæ*, and, according to tradition is endued with magical powers. About the end of the battle, so the tradition goes, an aerial minstrel was seen hovering over the heads of the Clan Chattan, who, after playing a few wild notes on his pipes, let them drop to the ground. Being made of glass, they all broke except the chanter, which was made of wood. The Clan Chattan piper secured the chanter, and, though mortally wounded, he continued playing the pibroch of his clan until death silenced him. Some traditions say the original chanter was made of crystal, and, being broken by the fall, that now existing was made in exact fac-simile, others that the cracks now seen were those the chanter received on falling to the ground. In any case, the possession of this particular chanter was ever after looked on as ensuring success, not only to the Mac Phersons, but to any one to whom it happened to be lent. The Grants of Strathspey once received an insult, through the cowardice of some unworthy members of their clan, and in their dejection they borrowed the Black Chanter, the war notes of which roused their drooping energies and stimulated them to such vigour that it became a proverb from that time, " No one ever saw the back of a Grant." The Grants of Glenmoriston afterwards received it, and they restored it to the Mac Phersons about 1855. It is still carefully preserved at Cluny Castle, and some entertain the belief that on its preservation depends the property of the house of Cluny.

The Black Chanter seems to have kept its magic power, for, during all the troubles of the '45, Cluny Mac Pherson accompanied Prince Charlie in his victories and helped him much by his own and his followers' bravery. But when the final blow was given to the fortunes of Charles Edward at Drummossie Moor, the Mac Phersons were not there, and it is said that before the battle an old witch told the Duke of Cumberland that if he waited until the green banner and the Black Chanter came up he would be defeated. The battle was over before Cluny arrived, for he was met by the fugitives when on his way from Badenoch to join the Prince. The Mac Intoshes, who claim that their chief is the chief of the Clan Mac Pherson, were at Culloden and in the thickest of the fight, but they had not the Black Chanter, and so they, too, shared in the defeat. It is certainly curious that no battle at which the Mac Phersons were present with the

green banner of the clan, the Black Chanter, and the chief
at their head, was lost.   We do not, of course, believe in this
phase of the supernatural nowadays, and it has been
irreverently asserted that this particular chanter will not play,
that a piper of Cluny's who was in the service of the chief
for seven years testified to this, and that it is nothing more
nor less than a chanter that has been spoiled in the making.
We do not contend that it really had supernatural powers
—the probability is all the other way—but when the clan
believed it had, that, by inspiring them with confidence,
perhaps served the same purpose.   Many clans and peoples
find inspiration in that which to the sceptical and hyper-
critical is but a fetish, and though we may smile at old-
time stories of the supernatural, we should remember that
those things were not smiling matter to the people of those
days, and that the people who live as long after us as we live
after those who believed in fairies and other uncanny things
are almost sure to find much more to laugh at in our practice
and beliefs than we find in the practice and beliefs of our
ancestors.   Meantime, let us close with a piece as grand as
ever was written in any language, dedicated to Culloden
and the Black Chanter of Chattan by Mrs. Ogilvie—remembering that the past deserves our respect, not only
for the brave people it produced, but also for the legacy
of enjoyable song and poetry and tradition it has handed
down to us—

" Black Chanter of Chattan now hushed and exhausted,
　　Thy music was lost with the power of the Gael ;
　The dread inspiration Mac Pherson had boasted
　　For ever expired in Drummossie's sad wail.

" On old St. Johnstone's dark meadow of slaughter
    Thy cadences buried the piper's last breath ;
The vanquished escaped amid Tay's rolling water,
    The conqueror's pibroch was silenced by death.

" That piper is nameless, and lost in like manner
    The tribes are forgotten of mighty Clan Quhele ;
While Chattan that bears the hill-cat on his banner,
    No time can extinguish, no ruin assail.

" From the hand of a cloud-cleaving bard thou wert given
    To lips that embraced thee till nerveless and dead ;
Since then never idly Mac Pherson hath striven,
    Nor trust in his fortune been shaken by dread.

" O mouth-piece of conquest ! who heard thee and trembled ?
    Who followed thy call, and despaired of the fight ?
Availed not that foemen before thee dissembled,
    For quenched was their ardour and nerveless their might.

" The blast of thy pibroch, the plaint of thy streamer,
    Lent hope to each spirit and strength to each arm ;
While the Saxon confronting was scared like the dreamer
    Whose sleep is of peril, of grief, and alarm.

" Led on by thy promise, what chieftain e'er sallied
    Nor proved in the venture how just was thy vaunt ?
At the spell of thy summons exultingly rallied
    The faltering pulse of dispirited Grant.

" Forerunner of victory ! Why didst thou tarry ?
    Thy voice on Drummossie an empire had changed ;
We then had not seen our last efforts miscarry,
    The Stuart had triumphed, the Gael been avenged.

" Ah, fatal Drummossie—sad field of the flying !
　　The Gathering sank in the hopeless Lament ;
　What pibroch could stanch the wide wounds of the dying ?
　　What magic rekindle the fire that was spent ?

" Proud music, by shame or dishonour ne'er daunted,
　　By murmur of orphan, by widowed despair,
　The fall of thy country thy spell disenchanted,
　　With the last of the Stuarts it vanished in air !

" Yet rouse thee from slumber, Black Chanter of Chattan,
　　Send forth a strong blast of defiance once more ;
　On the flesh of thy children the vulture doth fatten,
　　And sodden with blood are the sands of Lahore.

" As fierce as the tiger that prowls in their forest,
　　Those sons of the Orient leap to the plain ;
　But the blade striketh vainly wherever thou wanest,
　　Black Chanter of Chattan bestir thee again ! "

CHAPTER XVI.

PIPERS AND FAIRIES.

" The green hill cleaves, and forth with a bound
    Comes elf and elfin steed ;
 . The moon dives down in a golden cloud,
    The stars grow dim with dread ;
 But a light is running along the earth,
    So of heaven's they have no need.
 O'er moor and moss with a shout they pass,
    And the word is spur and speed—
 But the fire maun burn, and I maun quake,
    And the hour is gone that will never come back."

—*Allan Cunningham.*

In fairies' hillocks—Stories with a common origin—Sutherlandshire version—Away for a year—Harris piper and the fairies—Seven years away—Fairies helping pipers—Helping the Mac Crimmons—A boy piper—How the music went from Islay to Skye—Faust-like bargains—A Caithness story—A fairy piper.

PIPERS with a leaning towards the uncanny dealt largely with fairies, and in West Highland mythology piping is said to have been heard in fairies' hillocks. " I know two sisters," says a boy in a story of Skye—" one of them is a little deaf—and they heard a sound in a hill, and they followed the sound, and did they not sit and listen to the piping till they were seven times tired ? There is no question about that." We do not

P

believe in those things now. Our forefathers did, however, and there seems to have been an idea that pipers were special favourites of the little harmless green-coated ones. It is, indeed, their association with fairies that provides the most interesting of all the stories about pipers. There are ever so many stories of their adventures in the fairies' mounds and caves, and, like other classes of Celtic tales, they all run in one groove though they are located as far distant as Scotland is long. Like the story of *Faust*, where a man sells his soul for a period of worldly pleasure, so the story of the piper who goes to the fairies for a while, and sometimes comes back again, permeates all the literature of its class. It turns up all over Scotland, it has been heard often in Ireland, and even in the Scilly Isles it is known. It does not require much ingenuity to show that those legends have all been derived from one original story. The same remark, however, applies to the legendary lore of the entire Celtic race—Scottish, Irish and Continental. Divested of " trimmings " added by the passing of ages and the difference in circumstances, Celtic stories are found to have so much in common as to create strong presumptive evidence that the race must some time or other have lived together, a united people, a mighty scattering taking place afterwards, during which the Celts spread themselves over the world, carrying their folk-lore with them. That is one theory regarding the race, and this singular fact about its traditions is one of the strongest arguments in its favour.

Perhaps the most concise version of the fairy story comes from Sutherlandshire. A man whose wife had just been delivered of her first-born set off with a friend to the village of Lairg to have the child's birth entered in the session books, and to buy a cask of whisky for the christening. As they returned, weary with the day's walk, they sat down to rest at the foot of the hill of Durcha, on the estate of Rose-hall, near a large hole, from which they were ere long astonished to hear the sounds of piping and dancing. The father, feeling very curious, entered the cavern, went in a few steps, and disappeared. The other man waited for a while, but had to go home without his friend. After a week or two had passed, and the christening was over, and still there was no sign of the father's return, the friend was accused of murder. He denied the charge again and again, and repeated the tale of how the child's father had disappeared into the cavern. At last he asked for a year and a day in which to clear himself of the charge. He repaired often at dusk to the fatal spot and called for his friend, and prayed, but the time allowed him was all spent except one day, and nothing had happened. In the gloaming of that day, as he sat by the hillside, he saw what seemed to be his friend's shadow pass into the opening. He followed it, and, passing inside, heard tunes on the pipes, and saw the missing man tripping merrily with the fairies. He caught him by the sleeve and pulled him out. "Bless me, Sandy!" cried the father, " why could you not let me finish my reel." " Bless me ! " replied Sandy, " have you not had enough of reeling this last twelvemonth ? " " Last twelvemonth ! " cried the other in amazement, nor would he believe the truth concerning himself till he found his wife sitting by the door with a year-old child in her arms. The time passed quickly in the company of the good people.

Here, again, is perhaps the best of the long stories of pipers and fairies. It is from the *Celtic Magazine*, so ably conducted by the late Alexander Mac Kenzie :—

" Jamie Gow, a celebrated piper of many, many years ago, lived at Niskisher, in Harris. He had a croft, but neglected it for the pipes, which brought him his livelihood. His home was five miles from a famous fairy knoll, in which thousands of fairies were. Till Jamie's time no one ever found the entrance. It was said that if a piper played a certain tune three times round the base of· the knoll, going against the sun, he would discover the door, but this no hero of the chanter had previously attempted.

" Among a number of drouthy neighbours one day a debate got up as to the nature of the inside of the knoll. Jamie Gow declared that he would for a gallon of brandy play round the knoll in the proper way, and if he found the door he would enter and play the fairies a tune better than anything they had ever danced to. A score of voices cried " done," and the bargain was made. About noon on the following day Jamie, after partaking of something to keep his courage up, proceeded to *Tom-na-Sithichean,* the Fairy Knoll. He was accompanied by scores of people, some cheering, some discouraging him. On reaching the knoll he emptied other two " coggies," took up his position, and began to play. As soon as the first skirl of his pipes was heard all the people fled to the top of an adjoining hill to wait the result. With a slow but steady step Jamie marched round the *Tom.* Twice he completed his journey without mishap, and he had almost finished the third round. But when within two or three paces of the end he was seen to stand for a moment and then disappear. There was an opening in the side of the hill, which admitted him to a long dark passage, so rugged and uneven as to make it most inconvenient for a piper to keep march--ing and playing a particular tune, as Jamie was. The air, too, was chilly and disagreeable, drops of water continually trickling down the cold damp sides of the passage. Jamie, however, marched on fearlessly, and strange to say the farther he went the lighter grew his step and the livelier his tune. By and by the long passage became illuminated with a faint light, by which he saw that the roof and sides were very thickly covered with short and starry pendants, which shone white and radiant, like marble. Forward still, till he reached a door which opened of its own accord and led into a chamber of indescribable splendour. The floor seemed of solid silver, the walls of pure gold, and the furniture most costly. Around the table sat hundreds of lovely women and smiling men, all perfect in form and clothed in spotless green, brilliant and rich beyond description. They had apparently finished a sumptuous dinner, and were now quaffing the purple juice of the grape out of diamond-mounted cups of exquisite beauty.

"At the sight of such splendour, the piper for a moment was amazed, the drones fell powerless on his arm, for he stood with open mouth, ceasing to blow his bag. Noticing this, one of the green gentlemen rose from his seat, and, smiling coyly, handed him a cup of wine to drink, which Jamie loved too dearly to refuse. So, taking the proffered cup, with thanks, he said—' I am a piper to my trade. I have travelled and played from one end of the island to the other, but such a pretty place and such lovely people I never saw.' And he quaffed the cup at one draught.

"The gentleman in green then asked if he would favour the company with a tune called ' The Fairy Dance,' at which they knew he excelled all other performers. Nothing pleased Jamie better than a little puffing—this, probably, the inhabitants of the knoll knew— and he replied lustily, ' And, by my faith, I will, and I will play it as true as ever any piper played a tune.' In a moment the vast assembly was on its feet, swinging from side to side in a long country dance. Nothing that Jamie had ever seen compared to the graceful manner in which both ladies and gentlemen performed their evolutions, and this encouraged him to blow with might and main and stamp hastily with both feet, as if inspired, like the other performers.

"Meanwhile the people who had accompanied Jamie surrounded the knoll in search of him. They saw the spot where he disappeared, and some asserted that they saw the door itself, but when they came near the place there was no door. They continued the search for weeks, looking and listening in the hope of hearing the well-known notes of his chanter, but without success. Years passed, and Jamie did not return. The story of his disappearance at the knoll had spread far and wide, and his fate was the subject of conversation at many gatherings throughout the Western Isles. But though he was sadly missed at the balls and weddings, no one missed or pined for Jamie like his widowed mother and his sweetheart, *Mairi Nighean Gilleam,* to whom he was to have been married shortly after he left on his rash journey round the knoll.

"For several years Jamie continued to play 'The Fairy Dance,' and the dancers seemed as fresh as when he began. At long last the piper, wearied almost out of breath, cried 'May God bless you, friends! my breath is almost gone.' The mention of the Great Name produced a revolution. In a moment all lights were out, the beautifully clad assemblage and the gorgeous hall immediately disappeared, and Jamie found himself standing on the top of Tomnahurich, at Inverness. Until he inquired at a cottage in the vicinity he was entirely ignorant of his surroundings, but as soon as he found out where he was he made direct for Harris, reaching there after a journey of six weeks.

"Jamie was seven years with the fairies. When he got back to Harris he found his cottage deserted, for his mother had died a year before. No one in the place recognised him, he was so changed. His beard reached to his girdle, his cheeks were bulged out to a prodigious size by the continual blowing of his pipes, and his mouth was twice its original proportions. *Mairi Nighean Uilleam* knew him by his voice, and a few weeks after they became man and wife. Jamie never again visited *Tom-na-Sithichean.*"

I should think not. He had had quite enough of the fairies. They, however, seem to have had a soft side to pipers, at least we often read of them helping the musicians with their music. The first story which illustrates this comes from one of the Inner Hebrides, and is given in J. F. Campbell's *Tales of the West Highlands,* the actual words of the narrator being used. It was told in a houseful of people, all of whom seemed to believe it :—

"There was a piper in this island and he had three sons. The two eldest learned the pipes, and they were coming on famously, but the youngest could not learn at all. At last, one day, he was going about in the evening very sorrowfully, when he saw *bruth,* a fairy hillock, laid open. (There was one close to the house, which was exactly like the rest of its class. It was afterwards levelled and human bones were found in it.) He went up to the door and stuck his knife into it, because he had heard from old people that if he did that the *slaugh* could not shut the door. Well, the fairies were very angry, and asked him what he wanted, but he was not a bit afraid. He told them he could not play the pipes a bit, and asked them to help him. They gave him *feadan dubh*, a black chanter, but he said : ' That's no use to me for I don't know how to play it.'

" Then they came about him and showed him how to move his fingers ; that he was to lift that one and lay down that, and when he had been with them a while he thanked them and took out his knife and went away, and the *bruth* closed after him.

" Now, that man became one of the most famous pipers, and his people were alive until very lately. I am sure you all know that."

Chorus—" Oh yes, yes indeed. It is certain that there were such people whether they are now or not."

If all tales be true, the fairies had something to do with the eminent genius of the Mac Crimmons themselves. Once upon a time, to use the proper phrase, there was a great gathering of the clans at Dunvegan Castle. Mac Leod was entertaining the chiefs, and each chief was accompanied by his piper. The chiefs were great and the pipers were great, and somehow it was agreed that there should be a trial of skill among the musicians present—twelve in all. Mac Leod himself directed the proceedings, and one by one the great instrumentalists stepped into the hall and made the rafters dirl with their well-known strains. But Mac Leod became anxious as he noticed that there was no sign of his own piper, the old piper who had served him so long. He sent a boy to search, and the boy returned with the sad news— the piper was hopelessly drunk. The brow of Mac Leod grew dark with anger, for he was not to be humbled in his own household and in the presence of his guests. The tenth piper was tuning up—there was but another, and then his disgrace would be public property. In the desperation of despair Mac Leod seized the boy by the hand and whispered : "You are the twelfth piper, remember your chief's words." The boy, Mac Crimmon by name, left the hall, while the feasting and fun went on as merrily as ever, and lay down on the hillside and bemoaned his fate. But his good fairy was not far away. She came right out of the ground, as pretty a little fairy as ever helped poor mortal in desperate plight. She knew his trouble, and did not waste words, but gave the distracted boy a curiously-shaped whistle, and bade him play on it. The youngster would do anything to oblige the kind lady, so he blew on the whistle, and lo! the hills and the rocks re-echoed with the finest music ever heard in Skye. The good fairy disappeared, and the boy ran back to the castle, where the eleventh piper was playing the last notes of his pibroch. The chiefs and the pipers laughed to see the boy step it out into the centre of the assembled company, but their scorn was turned to admiration as compositions played in faultless and brilliant manner poured from the boy's "pipes." Thenceforth Mac Crimmon was prince of pipers, and we do not read that ever the good fairy came back to claim any recompense for what she had done ; neither have we any explanation of why she gave him a whistle (? a chanter) and not a set of pipes right off.

Another story of the Mac Crimmons, but one that has not many points of resemblance to the other, is told by Lord Archibald Campbell in *Records of Argyll.* It is from the lips of Hector Mac Lean, of Islay, and tells of how, when Mac Donald of the Isles resided in the palace on Finlagan Isle, in Loch Finlagan, he had a ploughman who, from his large stature, was called the Big Ploughman. This ploughman was out one day at his work, and he had a boy with him driving the horses, as was the custom in those times. The Big Ploughman was seized with hunger, and he said to the boy :

" My good fellow, were it to be got in the ordinary way, or magically, I would take food in the meantime, were I to have it."

After he had said these words, he and the boy took another turn with the team, till they came to the side of Knockshainta. There was an old grey-haired man by the side of the hill, who had a table covered with all manner of eatables. He asked them to come and partake of what was on the table. The ploughman went, but the boy was frightened, and would not go. After the ploughman had eaten enough, the old man gave him a chanter to play. When he put his fingers to it, he, who had never played before, played as well as any piper that ever was in the island of Islay. A day or two after, Mac Donald heard, in his palace on Island Finlagan, the Big Ploughman playing the Black Chanter. He inquired who it was, and they told him it was the Big Ploughman. When he heard how well the ploughman played there was nothing for it but to get for him the bagpipe of the three drones, and he was Mac Donald's piper as long as he lived.

Mac Donald went on a trip to the Isle of Skye. He took with him from thence a young man of the name of Mac Crimmon, who was fond of music, and was doing a little at it. He went to the Big Ploughman to learn more music from him than he had already. Mac Crimmon and the ploughman's daughter began courting and in consequence of the fancy that the girl took to Mac Crimmon—believing that he would marry her—she took the Black Chanter unknown to her father out of the chest, and gave it to Mac Crimmon to try it. When Mac Crimmon tried it he could play as well as the Big Ploughman himself. The girl asked the chanter back, but he entreated her to let him have it for a few days until he should practise a little further on it. A short time after Mac Donald of the Isles went off to Skye, and Mac Crimmon went with him. He did not return the chanter, neither did he come back to marry the Big Ploughman's daughter. The people of Islay say it was in this way that the music went from Islay to the Isle of Skye.

"The Powers" were not always so unselfishly inclined as the stories already given make them appear. They often drove a Faust-like bargain with the piper. They did with Peter Waters, a Caithness lad, who, when driving home his cattle one day over the common in the parish of Olrig, stopped to quench his thirst at a spring which flowed from the side of a well-known fairies' hillock called Sysa. Peter was tired, the spot was quiet, and the air invited him to slumber. So he slept till near sunset, when he was awakened by a gentle shake of the shoulder. Starting up, he saw a most beautiful lady, dressed in green, with golden ringlets, blue eyes, and the sweetest countenance in the world, standing beside him. Peter was shy, and his first impulse was to run away, but the lady looked at him and he couldn't.

"Don't be afraid of me, Peter," she said, with one of her most captivating smiles, and with a voice soft and clear as a silver bell. "I feel a great interest in you, and I am come to make a man of you."

"I am much obliged to you, indeed," stammered Peter. "The greatest nobleman in the land might be proud of your fair hand, but I have no desire to enter into the silken cord; and, besides, I would require to be better acquainted with you before I took such a step. People commonly court a little before they marry."

The lady laughed.

"You mistake me altogether," said she. "Though you appear a very nice young man, I make no offer of my hand. What I mean is that I will put you in the way of rising in the world and making your fortune. Here are two things —a Book and a pipe. Make your choice of the one or the other. If you take the Book you will become the most popular preacher in the north, and if you take the pipe you will be the best piper in Scotland. I shall give you five minutes to consider," and she took from her bosom a golden time-piece about the size of a sovereign.

The book was a splendidly bound Bible, richly embossed with gold, and with a golden clasp; the pipe a beautiful instrument, with a green silk bag of gold and silver tissue, and superbly finished with a number of silver keys. Peter gazed in admiration on the articles, and was greatly puzzled. It would be a grand thing, he thought, to be a popular preacher, to have a manse and glebe, and be fit company for the laird and his lady. But he was an enthusiast for music, and he should like above all things to be able to play the bagpipe. So he said—

"Since you are so kind, I think I will choose the pipe; but as I have never fingered a chanter in my life, I fear it will be a long time before I learn to play such a difficult instrument."

"No fear of that," said the lady. "Blow up, and you'll find that the pipe of its own accord will discourse the most eloquent music."

Peter did as he was desired, and lo ! he played "Maggie Lauder" in splendid style—so splendidly that the cattle near by began capering about in the most extraordinary manner.

"This is perfectly wonderful," he said. "There must surely be some glamour about this instrument."

He thanked the lady, and was about to take his departure, when she stopped him with—

"Stop a minute. There is a condition attached to the gift. This day seven years, at the very same hour in the evening, you must meet me by moonlight at the Well of Sysa. Swear by its enchanted spring that you will do so."

Peter was elated over his new acquisition, and rashly swore as she desired. Then he went home to his father's farm, the "Windy Ha'." With an air of triumph he produced his pipes, which excited much curiosity, and were greatly admired. But when he told how he came by them, the old people were fearful.

"It's no canny, Peter," said his father, shaking his head, "and I would advise you to have nothing to do with it."

"The Best protect us!" exclaimed his mother, "my bairn is lost. He must have got it from none other than the Queen of the Fairies."

"Nonsense," said Peter; "it was not the Queen of the Fairies, but a real lady—and a kind and beautiful lady she was—that gave me the pipes."

"But of what use can they be to you," said his father, "when you canna play them?"

"I'll let you see that," Peter replied, and, putting the wind pipe to his mouth, he played the "Fairy Dance" in a style that electrified the household. The whole family, including the grandmother, ninety years of age, started to their feet, and danced heartily, overturning stools and scattering the fire, which was in the middle of the floor, with their fantastic movements. The piper played as if he would never stop.

At length his father, panting for breath and with the perspiration running down his cheeks, cried out, "For mercy's sake, Peter, gie ower, or you'll be the death o' me and yer mither, as well as poor old grannie."

"I think," said Peter, laying aside his pipes, "I think you'll no longer say that I cannot play," and from that time his fame as a piper spread rapidly, and he was sent for to perform at weddings and merrymakings all over the country, till he realised a small fortune. But the seven years soon rolled away, and the afternoon arrived when he must keep his appointment with the donor of the pipes. Rover, the house dog, attempted to follow him, and when he was sent back he gazed after his master as far as he could see him, and then howled long and piteously. The evening was just such another as that seven years before, and the hillock of Sysa seemed, in the yellow radiance of the setting sun, to glow with unearthly splendour. Peter went, but he never returned, and the general belief was that he was carried away to Fairyland. At any rate, he was never again seen at Windy Ha'.

Not only did the fairies take an interest in pipers, but they played the pipes themselves. In one case where, after a deal of trouble, a young man, Charlie Mac Lean by name, got nearly to the Fairies' Palace in search of his beautiful young wife, who had been stolen to nurse the young prince of the fairies, he was met by a withered "atomy" of a man, finely dressed, with a cocked hat on his head and a magnificent set of pipes under his arm.

"A happy May eve to you, Charlie Mac Lean," said the little man, coming up with a dignified bow.

"The same to you, sir, and many," Charlie replied. "May I ask where this road leads?"

"Why, you goose, don't you know? It leads to the Fairies' Palace. Don't you be trying your tricks on travellers, my fine fellow. However, come on. I'll lead the way, no matter who plays the pipes."

With that he tuned up his pipes and marched along, Charlie following. "What tune do you like?" said he, turning round suddenly.

"Oh! *Cailleach Liath Rarsair,*" answered Charlie, scarcely knowing what he said.

"It's a capital tune," said the "atomy," and immediately striking it up, he played with such life and spirit that Charlie felt able to fight the whole fairy court for his wife.

"Now," said the little piper, as he finished the tune, "I haven't time to play more, else I'd give you the prettiest pibroch ever was battered through a chanter. I must be going. Look up, there is the palace before your eyes. One you know bade me tell you to stand in the porch till the company comes out to the green. Your wife will be among them. A word to a sensible man is enough. You have the purse of dust in your pocket: (Charlie had got this from a 'wise man' before setting out on the journey); use it, I say, use it, whenever you see your wife." With that he struck up "Charlie is my darling," and marched back the way he had come.

Charlie got his wife all right, by following the advice of the "wise man" and the "atomy," but that part of the story has nought to do with pipers.

UAMH AN OIR: THE CAVE OF GOLD

CHAPTER XVII.

PIPERS IN ENCHANTED CAVES.

" The Banshee's wild voice sings the death dirge before me,
The pall of the dead for a mantle hangs o'er me ;
But my heart shall not flag and my nerve shall not shiver,
Though devoted I go—to return again never ! "

—*Scott.*

Allied to fairy stories—Venturesome pipers—The Skye cave—The
Mull version—The Argyllshire—The Ghostly piper of Dun-
derave—" Wandering Willie's Tale "—A Sutherlandshire cave
—A Caithness story—Underground passages.

THE story of a piper endeavouring to explore a
mysterious cave is so closely allied to the class dealt
with in last chapter, that all might quite fairly have
been included under one heading. The only difference often
is that in the one case the piper enters a cave opening out
to the sea, whereas in the other he enters a knoll, which
may be any distance inland. There are always fairies in
the knoll, but in the majority of cases there are none in the
cave. Their place is taken by wild beasts, who take the
life of the venturesome explorer. The piper generally has
a dog with him when he enters the cave, and the dog
always returns, though the last that is heard of his master
is the sad wail of his pipes playing a lament for his own
terrible fate.

" Oh, that I had three hands—two for the pipes and one
for the sword," is recorded as the tune played by a piper
who entered a cavern and could not get out again.   The
incident is located in several places—in Skye, in Mull, and
at a cave eight miles up the river Nevis, in Inverness-shire.
The Mull cave reached, it was believed, right across the
island, and it was inhabited by wolves and other wild
animals.   The Skye cave was called *Uamh an Oir*, the Cave
of Gold, and·was situated about four miles from Dunvegan,
the other end opening out at Monkstad on Loch Snizort.
It, too, had wild animals for inhabitants.   The inside of
the cave in most cases consisted of many confusing offshoots
leading in different directions, the want of knowledge of
which prevented the people of the neighbouring districts
from exploring it.   However, on one occasion a piper (the
Skye version makes him a Mac Crimmon) accompanied by a
member of the Clan Mac Leod (also the Skye version) made
bold to enter the cave.   A crowd gathered outside to wait
for the result.   The piper, who of course had his pipes, went
first, playing his best.   After a considerable time had elapsed,
the waiting people began to feel anxious as to their safety.
But by and by Mac Leod returned.   He could give no
account of Mac Crimmon except that he had lost him in the
labyrinths of the cave.   He considered himself extremely
fortunate in finding his way out.   Their torches had been
extinguished by the dim and foul atmosphere.   Just when
Mac Leod was telling his story the wailing notes of Mac
Crimmon's pipes were heard issuing from the cave.   All
listened, and as they listened the pipes spoke, and the notes
that came out of the darkness represented :—

> " I will return, I will return, I will return no more ;
>   Mac Leod may return, but Mac Crimmon shall never."

And also :—

" The she wolf, the she wolf, the she wolf follows me ;
  Oh for three hands ; two for the pipes and one for the sword."

And so on the wailing notes continued, the piper bewailing
his fate in that he could not stop his playing for an instant,
because if he did this the wolf would attack him. So long as
he played he was safe. Ultimately he began to speak of
how long his strength would last, sometimes coming near to
the mouth of the cave, but anon wandering away again into
its recesses till the music was scarcely audible. This went
on all that day and night, but in the early morning the
listeners heard the music cease, and they knew that exhaus-
tion had overtaken the piper, and that the wolf had
conquered.

This is the story as I had it from an old lady still living
in Glenquoich, Inverness-shire. Another version has it
that this Mac Crimmon had twelve other men with him,
that none of them ever returned, having been met by an
uile bheisd or monster, and devoured. The last despairing
notes of the piper were heard by a person sitting at *Tobar
Tulach* in the neighbourhood, who listened to the lament
as it came up from the bottom of a well.

The Mull story is told of two of a wedding party who
entered the cave and never came out, and also of twelve
men of the Clan Mac Kinnon, who, headed by a piper,
attempted to explore the cave. In the latter case another
party walked along the top keeping pace with the music
below. When the party who travelled in the cave arrived
at the end, the fact was to be signalled to those outside by
a certain bar of music, and they were to mark the spot to
indicate the termination of the cave. After the explorers

had travelled some distance they encountered a fairy woman, who attacked the band and slew them one by one. She was, however, so charmed with the music of the pipes that she offered no injury to the person who played them. The poor piper made the best of his way back to the mouth of the cave followed by the fairy, she meanwhile informing him that if he ceased playing before he saw the light of day he too would be killed. He staggered along in the dark, bravely playing out his life breath, but at last, in spite of his struggles, the music ceased. The charm was then broken and the piper shared the fate of his comrades. Those outside knew that something had happened and with drawn swords rushed into the cave. They found the dead piper and his comrades. The last notes he played, says the tradition, were :—

> " Alas ! that I had not three hands—
> Two for the pipes and one for the sword."

This identifies the story as just a variation of the others, though how it comes to be located in so many different places it is difficult to explain. In connection with the Mac Kinnon exploring adventure, it may be added, the tradition further tells of how a dog accompanied the party, and emerged from the cave at some other place, but bereft of his hair. He had been in a death struggle with some monster inside and had escaped.

The dog, the same dog presumably, went into an Argyll-shire cave with a piper. There are many large caves on the Kintyre coast, one of the biggest being at Keill. This cave was long the resort of smugglers, and was said to possess a subterranean passage extending six miles from the mouth of the cave to the hill of Kilellan. It was haunted, and whosoever would penetrate beyond a certain distance would never again be heard of (a very convenient tradition for smugglers). A piper, however, made up his mind to explore its inmost recesses, and, accompanied by his dog, a little terrier, he set out on the expedition, while his friends watched and listened at the cavern's mouth. The piper went in boldly, blowing his pipes till the cave resounded. His friends heard his music becoming gradually fainter and fainter until all at once, when, as they supposed, he had passed the fatal boundary, his pipes were heard to give an unearthly and tremendous skirl, while an eildrich laugh re-echoed through the cave. The terrier shortly after came running out, but without his skin. In process of time he obtained a fresh skin, but he never tried to bark after that adventure. As for the piper, his fate was purely a matter of conjecture, but he is supposed to have stumbled in the subterranean passage, for about five miles from the cavern's mouth there was a farm house, and underneath its hearth-stone the piper was, in after years, often heard playing his favourite tune, and occasionally stopping to ejaculate—

> " I doubt, I doubt
> I'll ne'er get out."

Then there is the tale of the ghostly piper of Dunderave. At certain times his music was heard issuing from a cavern which faced the sea, and into the recesses of which the waves swept. On winter nights the sounds that came from that cavern were wild and unaccountable, and often the fishermen in the vicinity were startled by fierce, blood-curdling yells, especially in the early morning. When the tide went out the children of the village, unaware of its terrible mystery, strayed near the yawning cavern, and

occasionally sad hearts were made by the disappearance of
the little ones who wandered too far in. The legend of
Dunderave was that the seventh son of the seventh
son of a Mac Gregor, who would play the gathering
of his clan in the cavern, would scatter for ever the evil
spirits who frequented it. A piper, who thought he had
the necessary qualifications, was got, and he had the courage
to play in the cavern of Dunderave. Whether he played
the gathering of his clan satisfactorily or not could never
be known, but certainly he never came out of the cave, the
mouth of which fell in after him, blocking up the cavern
for ever. No more children were lost, but ever after there
could be heard by anyone standing over the cavern, the
faint music of Mac Gregor's pipes.

Wandering Willie's tale in *Redgauntlet* is much too long
to quote entire. In it Steenie the Piper, who has paid his
rent to the dead Sir Robert Redgauntlet, is threatened
with eviction by the next laird because he has not a receipt,
and when riding home through the darkness in great per-
plexity of mind, is accosted by a stranger, who guides him
to an unearthly place, where he finds Sir Robert and many
people whom he knew were dead gathered round the festal
board. He demands his receipt from Sir Robert, but the
laird, or rather " the something that was like him," asks
him to play up " Weel Hoddled, Luckie," a tune he had
learned from a warlock, that heard it when they were worshipping Satan at their meetings, and which he never
played willingly. Now he grew cauld at the name of it,
and said, for excuse, he hadna his pipes wi' him :—

" ' Mac Callum, ye limb of Beelzebub,' said the fearfu' Sir Robert,
' bring Steenie pipes that I am keeping for him.'

" Mac Callum brought a pair of pipes that might have served the piper of Donald of the Isles. But he gave my gudesire a nudge as he offered them ; and, looking secretly and closely, Steenie saw that the chanter was of steel, and heated to a white heat, so he had fair warning not to trust his fingers with it. So he excused himself again, and said he was faint and frightened and had not wind aneugh to fill the bag.

"'Then ye maun eat and drink, Steenie,' said the figure, 'for we do little else here, and its ill speaking between a fu' man and a fasting.'

"But Steenie was not to be cajoled or threatened into any more transactions with the ghostly crew than he could help, so he spoke up like a man, and said he came neither to eat or drink or make minstrelsy, but simply for his receipt, which in a rage 'the appearance' gave him. Then, when Sir Robert stipulated that the piper should return after a twelvemonth to pay homage, Steenie's tongue loosened yet more, and he exclaimed :—

"'I refer mysel' to God's pleasure and not to yours.'"

Whereupon, as in all other tales of the kind, at the mention of the sacred Name, "all was dark around him, and he sunk on the earth with such a sudden shock that he lost both breath and sense." When he came round he was lying in the kailyard of Redgauntlet, and he would have thought the whole experience but a dream, only he had the receipt in his hand fairly written and signed by the auld laird, and dated " From my appointed place, this twenty-fifth day of November," the previous day, in fact. This he carried to the new laird, who accepted it as evidence of the rent having been paid, but made Steenie swear never to divulge his adventure.

Away up in the north, too, we come across stories connected with caves into which pipers went. At Durness, in Sutherlandshire, a piper went into a cave and never returned. According to the version current in the locality, the Devil himself got hold of the venturesome explorer and kept him.

From Caithness we get something better. A piper, in a spirit of braggadocia, as is often the case in these stories, entered a cave near Dunnet Head. Jock was " a stout, long-winded chap,"

> " Who was a piper to his trade,
>   And by his trusty chanter earned his bread,"

and the fairies had often heard him play and wished to get him to take the place of their own piper, who had died. Though they were immortal themselves, they had not a piper of their own race, and when they got one from among mankind they could not make him immortal. Jock lived near a famous cave called Puddingoe, the inmost recesses of which no man had ever explored, and one day he laid a wager that he would play up Puddingoe and see how far it went.

> " ' For,' added Jock, ' though Nick's a roguish elf,
>   I canna think he'd harm a hair o' me,
> For he is just a piper like myself,
>   And dearly loves, I'm told, a funny spree—
> Nae doot then he would treat me as a brither,
> And we would play a merry jig together."

Then he " quaffed a cog of prime home-brewed " and hied him to the cave, and entered, screwing up his drones and beginning a lively march that startled the wild pigeons from their ledges and echoed among the recesses of the walls. Farther and farther he went, past the dripping sides of cold, damp stone and through the dark, chilly air till at last, strange to say, the darkness was dispelled and the cave became illuminated with a light like that of the moon. Jock was, he reckoned, about two miles underground when all at once he came to a door, which opened of its own accord and admitted him into a chamber of exceeding beauty. The floor was inlaid with silver, the walls seemed burnished gold, and a jovial party of ladies and gentlemen banquetted at a splendidly spread table. The piper stood amazed for a moment, until one of the company handed him a glass of wine.

> " ' I am a piper to my trade,' cried Jock,
>   Am I upon the earth, or where am I ?
> I never saw before such beauteous folk,
>   Or such a chamber with my naked eye ;
> Here's a' yir healths,' and saying this he quaffed
> The brimming cup and smacked his lips and laughed."

Then, of course, the fairies asked him to play, which Jock did, and the party danced, and danced, and danced, until Jock cried—

> "Lord save's, ohon !
> Have mercy on my soul, my breath is gone."

This had the inevitable result. The lights went out with a fiery hissing sound, the party vanished, as well as the gorgeous hall, and when Jock again came to himself he found that he was on the top of an elf-haunted knowe in the vicinity. He had been a year and a day away from home, his friends had given him up as dead, and his features were so changed that they did not recognise him when he returned. With the long spell of blowing his mouth was distended, which also helped to disguise him. But he made himself known, and was duly received by his friends and his sweetheart, and he married shortly after. But, as J. T. Calder, the historian of Caithness, who tells the legend in rhyme, says—

> " Never after was he seen to enter
>   The enchanted cave in quest of fresh adventure."

A slight variation of the cave stories are the stories of underground passages. There is, for instance, the passage that is supposed to exist between Edinburgh Castle and Holyrood Palace. The piper went in at the Castle end, intending to play all the way to Holyrood. His pipes were heard as far as the Tron Church, but then the music ceased. It did not start again, and the piper was never more heard of.

A similar legend is referred to by Hugh Mac Donald in his ramble, *Rutherglen and Cathkin.* It is to the effect that Glasgow Cathedral was built by the " wee pechs (Picts) who had their domicile in Rutherglen." Instead, however, of making their journeys overland, they dug an underground passage, through which they came and went. Even in Mac Donald's youth, those who doubted this story were silenced and awed by the solemn assurance that a Highland piper, to put down the sceptics, had volunteered to explore the dark road. He was accompanied by his dog, and he entered playing a cheery tune, as if confident of a successful result. But " he was never seen or heard tell o' again." Only the sound of his pipes was heard as he passed underneath Dalmarnock, playing in a mournful key, which suggested the words, " I doot, I doot, I'll ne'er get oot." Another version tells, however, that his poor dog returned, but without its skin. According to a Glasgow ballad, it was a dominie who ventured to explore the secret path. He encountered the Deil and other " friends," who blew him up through the waters of the Clyde, and the point at which he emerged is known to this day as " The Dominie's Hole."

CHAPTER XVIII.

THE HEREDITARY PIPERS.

" 'Tis wonderful,
That an invisible instinct should frame them,
To loyalty unlearned ; honour untaught ;
Civility not seen from others ; valour
That wildly grows in them, but yields a crop
As if it had been sowed."
—*Shakespeare.*

Hereditary in two senses—When they ceased—The Mac Crimmons
—A traditional genealogy—A Mac Gregor tradition—The Mac
Crimmon College—Dr. Johnson—College broken up—An Irish
college—Its system—A Mac Crimmon's escapades—Respect for
the Mac Crimmons—The Rout of Moy—The last of the race—
How they excelled—The Mac Arthurs—The Mac Intyres—The
Mac Kays—The Rankins—The Campbells—The Mac Gregors.

THE hereditary pipers were hereditary in at least two
senses. They were hereditary because son followed
father, generation after generation, in the service of
one chief, no one disputing their claim to the succession.
But they were also hereditary in the sense that their talents
were not self-acquired. They came of a race of pipers, and
piping to them was hereditary. Seven generations of pipers
for ancestors and seven years of personal training were considered necessary to produce the true hereditary piper. It
is this to which Neil Munro alludes when he says—" To the

make of a piper go seven years of his own learning and seven generations before."

The hereditary pipers were second only to the chiefs of the various clans, and their fame has come down through the years with wonderful persistence. The chiefs were proud of their pipers and treated them as gentlemen. The pipers, on their part, were proud of their chiefs, and would do anything for them. Hereditary pipers existed until the passing of the Heritable Jurisdiction Abolition Act of 1747, which, by abolishing clanship, made the possession of a retinue by a chief an offence against the civil law. The chiefs then deprived their pipers of the lands they had formerly held by virtue of their office, and by that act degraded them to the level of ordinary musicians. And, with the absence of a sure position, the enthusiasm for pipe music dwindled, succeeding generations failed to attain to the high level of their forebears, and the hereditary pipers were merged in the general race of Highland musicians.

The greatest of the hereditary pipers were

THE MAC CRIMMONS,

pipers to Mac Leod of Dunvegan. There is nothing to show how or where the race originated. Some traditions state that the first Mac Crimmon came from Cremona in Italy, and was named Donald. He settled in Glenelg, and had a son named *Iain Odhar*, who, about 1600, became the first piper to the family of Mac Leod. This traditional genealogical tree, supplied originally by a man who had seen the wife of him who, according to the tradition, was the last of the Mac Crimmon pipers to Mac Leod of Mac Leod, shows that a direct descent from this *Iain Odhar* was :—

SUPPOSED TO REPRESENT A MACCRIMMON PLAYING A SALUTE
(From *MacIan's Clans.*)

Malcolm, married with issue :—

1. John, who succeeded him as piper.
2. Donald (Roy), D.S.P.
3. Rachel, who married in Glendale.
4. A daughter who died unmarried.

John (*Dubh*) married first a Mac Askill, with issue :—

1. Donald, D.S.P., a Captain in the Army.
2. Peter, D.S.P., a Captain in the Army, and considered one of the strongest men of his day. Emigrated to Cape Coast Castle.
3. Malcolm, married in Ardrossan, with several sons.
4. Elizabeth, married a cooper of the name of Mac Kinnon, in Islay. Had two daughters—(*a*) Mary Ann, married Malcolm Mac Leod, Shipmaster, Lochmaddy, with issue ; (*b*) Effie, married Chisholm, Tacksman, of Gairnish, South Uist, with issue.
5. Janet, married a Ferguson. in America, with issue, an only daughter, who resided in Greenock.
6. Flora, who married Mac Donald, Tacksman, of Pein-a-Daorir, South Uist, factor for South Uist.
7. Marion, married, with issue.
8. Catherine, married with issue.

John, married secondly Ann Campbell, with issue :—

9. Duncan, married a Mac Queen, with issue—(*a*) John, who went to New Zealand ; (*b*) Donald, who married a Mac Leod, went to America, and had a family.
10. Peter, married Ann Mac Donald from Trotternish, with issue, one daughter. Married secondly Margaret Morrison, by whom he had three daughters.
11. John, died unmarried, but left an illegitimate son named John, who married a daughter of Neil Mac Sween, mason, Roag.
12. Euphemia, married Malcolm Nicholson, with issue—(*a*) Hector, died without issue ; (*b*) John, married with issue ; (*c*) Murdo, who married a daughter of James

Wood ; (*d*) .John, married Janet, daughter of John *Bàn* Mac Leod, Lusta, with issue ; (*e*) Donald, married a Mac Nab, with issue ; (*f*) Catherine, unmarried ; (*g*) Ann, married Murdo Mac Innes, Roag, without issue ; (*h*) Marion, married Norman Mac Askill, tenant, Ullinish, with issue ; (*i*) Effie, married Samuel Thorburn, Holmisdale, with issue.

According to this genealogy, which however does not profess to be complete, the line of hereditary Mac Crimmon pipers was very short indeed, consisting of only *Iain Odhar*, Malcolm, John, and John *(Dubh)*. That this is not the complete line is undoubted, for we have historical proof that there were other Mac Crimmons pipers to Mac Leod. As a matter of fact, one of the family living in Alexandria, Dumbartonshire, as late as 1898, writes as follows :—

"My uncle, Donald Mac Crimmon, was the last piper of the Mac Crimmons that was in the Castle, and he died over fifty years ago. My father also, Norman Mac Crimmon, was a pibroch player, and was taught by Captain Mac Leod of Gesto, who is now dead fifty-four years. Both were born at Lowerkill, Glendale. My great grandfather, Donald Donn, was brother to Donald *Bàn*, who composed 'Mac Crimmon's Lament,' and was with the Mac Leod Highlanders near Moy Hall, the residence of Lady Mac Intosh, reconnoitering Prince Charlie."

Some stories—they are only stories—assert that the Mac Crimmons were originally Mac Gregors. The Mac Gregors, it is pointed out, had an academy for the teaching of pipe music in Lochaber many centuries ago, and the Mac Gregor music, such as the "Reel of Tulloch" (that this is a Mac Gregor tune is a matter of debate, however) is the merriest and also the saddest in the Highlands. Rob Roy's deathbed tune is said to have simply been "We Return no More," in other words, "Mac Crimmon's Lament," and his piper was himself a Mac Crimmon, who, under the mournful circumstances, recalled the traditional strain. There is certainly a great deal that is probable in this, but that is the most that can be said about it.

The best, and what, on the face of it, is the most reliable · story of the Mac Crimmons is that given by Angus Mac Kay in his book of pipe music.* It is beyond doubt that high musical talent as well as high moral principle and personal bravery descended from father to son during many generations in the family of the Mac Crimmons. They became so famous that pupils were sent to them from many parts of the Highlands, and one of the best certificates a piper could possess was his having studied under the Mac Crimmons. Finding the number of their pupils increasing daily, they at length opened a regular school or college on the farm of Boreraig, about eight miles south-west of Dunvegan Castle, but separated from it by Loch Follart. Here seven years' study was prescribed for each scholar, regular lessons were given out, and certain periods were fixed on for receiving instruction. The tuition was carried on as systematically as ·in any of our northern schools, and the names of some of the caves and knolls in the vicinity still indicate the places where the scholars used to practise respectively the chanter, the small pipe and the large bagpipe, before playing in the presence of the master. This school was not entirely extinct in 1779, for Dr. Johnson, who was at Dunvegan in that year, alludes to it and says his dinner "was exhilarated by the bagpipes at Armadale and Dunvegan." The school proper was the "ben" end of the dwelling-house, which seems to have been about seventy feet in length and two

---

* See page 109.

storeys in height. In actual practice, however, the room was little used. The "professors" preferred the open hillside, a small hollow near the house, or a cave in the neighbourhood, which came to be known as the Pipers' Cave. Near the Pipers' Cave is another known as the Pigeons' Cave, which is about a mile in length. To it, tradition asserts, the daughters of the Mac Crimmons were wont to slip with a favourite set of pipes, for they too were musically inclined, and so proficient did some of them become, an ancient chronicler tells us, that they were able to superintend the class work in the absence of their fathers.

The speciality of the Mac Crimmons was the pibroch, and many students studied with them for years so as to become proficient in this one branch of pipe music—a branch which is, in the estimation of most pipers, far superior to reels and strathspeys. They held the farm of Boreraig rent free until the time came when all the hereditary pipers were either dispossessed of their lands or asked to pay rent for them. The proud Mac Crimmons declined to pay rent, broke up the college, and from that day ceased to exist as a family for the cultivation of pipe music. Their farm was afterwards let to eighteen different tenants, and drew over £100 a year in rent, so they must have been treated with considerable liberality by their chiefs.

No tradition exists, says Mac Kay, relating to the time when the Mac Crimmons became professional pipers to the Mac Leods, but neither is their trace of any others holding the office. The first of whom there is any account is *Iain Odhar* or Dun-coloured John, who lived about 1600, but it is evident from their compositions that the family must have been established long before that date. They were a minor sept, and they are supposed to have derived their name from the fact that the first performer studied at Cremona. After *Iain Odhar* came his son, *Donull Mór*, or Big Donald, who became a great pibroch player, and getting into the good graces of Mac Leod, got special opportunities for learning. He was sent to a college in Ireland, which is said to have been started there by a celebrated Scottish piper, and he learned all there was to learn.

The system of this Irish school permitted one pupil only to be in the presence of the master at a time, but *Donull Mor*, in his anxiety to learn, hid himself in a corner, where he could hear all the other students—there were twenty-four —at their lessons. He required only to hear a tune once to remember it completely, so he very soon exhausted the repertory of the master. When he came back to Skye, Mac Leod was delighted with the progress he had made. But the piper was not destined to remain at peace long. He had a brother who, because of a squint in one of his eyes, was known as *Padruig Coag*, or Squinting Peter, and this brother quarrelled with a foster brother of his own, a native of Kintail, who afterwards treacherously killed him. Big Donald swore vengeance, and going up to his chief's room threw his pipes on the bed. Mac Leod asking what was wrong, Donald told his story, and demanded that his chief should avenge his clansman. Mac Leod promised to see justice done within a year, and Donald took his leave. The chief, however, had no intention of executing vengeance on the Kintail man ; he only wished to give Donald's anger time to cool. But he did not know his man, for at the end of the year Donald, without giving a hint to anyone, set out in pursuit of his brother's murderer. He found that he was in Kintail, but in hiding, and as the people of the village declined to give him up, the wrath of Donald *Mór* Mac

Crimmon broke all bounds. He set fire to eighteen of their houses, a trick which cost several lives. It was then his turn to go into hiding, which he did in Lord Reay's country. The Lord of Kintail offered a big reward for his arrest, but he was not caught, though he was known to be wandering among the hills. His principal place of concealment was in a shepherd's house, where a bed was specially made for him in the wall. At last Kintail came to know of this haunt of Mac Crimmon's, and sent his son with a dozen men to seize him. Donald *Mór* was in the house when the shepherd's wife saw the party coming, and he betook himself to bed. The woman then made a big fire in the centre of the floor, where fires were always made in those days, and when the avenger of blood came with his men she welcomed them effusively, and, making them sit round the fire, she hung their plaids on a rope between them and Mac Crimmon's bed. Then the fugitive slipped out behind and was free, profiting as other and more notable men have done by a woman's astuteness. When the pursuers had searched the house and found nothing, the shepherd's wife entertained them hospitably and kept them for the night. When they had gone to rest Mac Crimmon came in and, gathering all their arms while they slept soundly, he placed the weapons all over their leader and retired. When morning broke, Mac Kenzie of Kintail immediately realized what had taken place, and was astonished at the generosity of Big Donald. "If Donald *Mór* Mac Crimmon is alive," he said, "it was he that did this, and it was as easy for him to take my life as to do so." When they went outside they saw Mac Crimmon on the other side of a stream, and when his men essayed to ford the stream and seize him, Mac Kenzie threatened to shoot the first who touched the piper, and swore to

R

Mac Crimmon that if he would cross the river he would not be injured. After all the men had been sworn to the same purpose, Mac Crimmon did cross, and in consideration of his nobility in sparing his life during the night, Mac Kenzie took the piper home with him, and by dint of special pleading managed to obtain for him the forgiveness of Lord Kintail. Then Donald *Mór* returned to his allegiance at Dunvegan, where he remained ever after—a great piper. It was after his day that the Mac Crimmons were universally acknowledged to be the best pipers in Scotland, so much so that no piper was considered perfect unless he had studied for some time under them.

Donald *Mór* Mac Crimmon was succeeded by his son Patrick *Mór*. This Patrick had eight sons, seven of whom died within twelve months. On this great bereavement he composed a tune called *Cumha no Cloinne*, or "The Lament for the Children." In 1745 Mac Leod's piper was Donald *Bàn* Mac Crimmon, the composer of "Mac Crimmon's Lament." Mac Leod was opposed to Prince Charlie, and when he was defeated at Inverurie by Lord Louis Gordon, Donald *Bàn* was taken prisoner. On this occasion a striking mark of respect was paid to Mac Crimmon by his brother pipers in Lord Louis Gordon's following. The morning after the battle they did not play as usual, and on inquiry it was found that they were silent because Mac Crimmon was a prisoner. He was immediately set at liberty, but was killed shortly after at "The Rout of Moÿ," a rather tragic incident in Highland Jacobite History. It was before leaving on the expedition in which he met his death that Donald *Bàn* composed "Mac Crimmon's Lament," under the presentiment that he would never see Dunvegan again. On the night of the Rout of Moy, it was said, a second-sight man saw the body of Mac Crimmon shrunken to the proportions of a child, a sure sign of impending death. Donald *Bàn* was said to excel most of his race by the beauty and neatness with which he noted on paper the tunes he played and composed.

How the race became extinct—if it is extinct—cannot be determined. John *Dubh* Mac Crimmon was the last who held the hereditary office, and of him it is related that about 1795 he determined, probably because of the changed circumstances, to emigrate to America, that he actually went as far as Greenock, but that there his love for the misty island became too much for him, and he went back to Skye. But he was not then piper to Mac Leod, and he spent the rest of his life in retirement. When he became too infirm to play the pipes, he would sit outside and run over the notes on his walking stick. He lived to the age of 91, dying in 1822, and was buried with his fathers in the kirkyard at Durinish. *Music of the Highland Clans*, written in 1862, states that the last of this noble race of minstrels was a blind and venerable old gentleman then living at Gourock ; but Logan's *Scottish Gael*, written in 1831, says a Captain Mac Crimmon " died lately in Kent at an advanced age, and the descendant of these celebrated pipers is now a respectable farmer in Kent." The author of *Musical Memoirs of Scotland* (1849) says the Mac Crimmons ended in a woman then keeping school in Skye, who could go through all the intricacies of the pibroch on the family instrument. There is said to have been a piper of the name in Glasgow about 1872, who claimed to be a direct descendant of the Mac Crimmons. He was an old man then, and all trace of him is now lost. If he is dead, which is highly probable, it is almost certain, that although the race as

such is not extinct, there is not now a real Mac Crimmon
piper in existence.

The Mac Crimmons were never excelled or even equalled
as pipers and composers of pipe music.   Their productions
were all peculiarly appropriate to the instrument, and
remain its classics to this day.   They produced no second-
rate pieces, and this was the secret of their success.   But
they did not compose off-hand, as any good piper can compose a strathspey or a quickstep.   They took a long time
to a tune, sometimes several months, but they made it
perfect.   Strathspeys and quicksteps they looked on as
inferior music, and all their attention was devoted to
pibrochs.   They were very studious and practised a great
deal, rising early in the mornings to play by themselves.
They noted their music by that special notation of their
own which has been fully dealt with in Chapter VII.

THE MAC ARTHURS,

pipers to Mac Donald of the Isles, contended strongly with
the Mac Crimmons for the superiority as pibroch players.
One of the Mac Donalds, it is said, chanced to hear a Mac
Crimmon piper, and he was so delighted with the music that
he had a young man of much musical talent sent to Dunvegan as a pupil, with instructions that he was not to be
returned until he could play as well as his master.   This
Mac Arthur peculiarly enough is stated to have played on
Mac Crimmon almost the identical trick which one of the
first of the Mac Crimmons played on his Irish tutor.   Mac
Crimmon had some tunes he did not wish the boy Mac
Arthur to hear, as the latter, being an expert pupil could,
if he once heard them, play them ever after as well as his
master, whose fame would therefore be in danger of being

A MAC ARTHUR PIPER

dimmed. So Mac Crimmon generally found some excuse for sending Mac Arthur away to some distance when he wished to play these tunes. One day his master had a visitor who desired to hear one of the highly-prized melodies, and in order to get the boy Mac Arthur out of the way Mac Crimmon sent him a message to a neighbouring township some miles distant. But the boy, suspecting the plot, lingered about the door until he heard the tunes, and then rushed off on his message. Afterwards in a secluded spot he practised the airs until he became perfect. But Mac Crimmon one day suddenly heard a tune which he thought he alone could play, and angrily approaching the performer, whom he found to be his pupil, he said :—" You young rascal, where have you picked up that piece of music ? " " I picked it up in the back door that day you entertained your friend to it," said Mac Arthur, assuming the utmost indifference ; " and," he continued, " I shall lose no more time than the boat shall take on her voyage to Mull in telling my master that you are not giving me the full benefit of your talents, for which you were amply paid by my benefactor." Old Mac Crimmon felt somewhat alarmed at the cool indifference with which his pupil addressed him, and, knowing what would result from the matter being made known to his influential patron, he very discreetly confessed his guilt, and promised his clever pupil better attention in the future. Pupil and tutor seem to have got on very well after this incident, and when, in the course of a year or two, Mac Arthur quitted the Mac Crimmon College, he was ranked among the foremost pipers of his day.

Mac Donald granted the Mac Arthurs a perpetual gift of the farm of Peingowen, near the castle of Duntulm.

Like the Mac Crimmons, they kept a "college." Their establishment, which was at Ulva near Mull, was divided into four apartments, one for their own use, one for receiving strangers, one for the cattle, and one for the use of the students while practising. Charles Mac Arthur, the best known of the race, received his education from Patrick *Og* Mac Crimmon, staying at Dunvegan Castle for this purpose for eleven years. He taught a nephew, who afterwards settled in Edinburgh, became piper to the Highland Society of Scotland, and was known in the capital as "Professor" Mac Arthur. At a competition in 1783, he performed, we are told, "with great approbation," receiving a splendid set of pipes specially made for him, and a number of the then leading pipers subscribed to a testimonial to his merits. It was also agreed to support a plan of his for a college to instruct those whose services might be useful in Highland regiments, but of this nothing more was heard. The last of the Mac Donalds' hereditary pipers was another nephew of the great Charles Mac Arthur, who died in London. He was piper to the Highland Society of London, and composed many pieces of considerable merit. Like the Mac Crimmons, the Mac Arthurs noted their music by a system of their own, and they made large collections of pibrochs.

The Archibald Mac Arthur, of whom a sketch is given on another page, was a native of Mull, and was acknowledged to be well skilled in bagpipe music, having been taught by a Mac Crimmon. In 1810, the date of the print, he entered for the annual competition at Edinburgh, but failing to carry off the first prize, he refused to accept the second, thereby debarring himself from again appearing on a similar occasion. When the King visited Edinburgh in 1822, this

Mac Arthur followed in the train of his chief, from whom he held a cottage with a small portion of land. That part of the island of Staffa on which this croft was situated was sold, but Mac Arthur, though no longer employed in his former capacity, was allowed by the new proprietor to remain in his old home. Angus Mac Kay, it should be added, tells of a John Mac Arthur, who, in 1806, obtained second place in the Edinburgh competition, but declined to accept the prize. Probably there was but one such incident although name and date are mistaken in one case or the other.

THE MAC INTYRES

were hereditary pipers to Menzies of Menzies. The Menzies' lived in Rannoch, and the first Mac Intyre of whom we hear was Donald *Mór*, who is said to have returned from the Isles about 1638, having apparently been at Skye receiving the finishing touches to his musical education. His son, John Mac Intyre also studied at Dunvegan. Donald *Bán*, his son, succeeded him as piper to the chief, Sir Robert the Menzies, third Bart. When he died his son Robert, who should have succeeded him, was piper to the chief of Clan Ranald, and although, being the eldest son, he inherited the pipes which, according to tradition, were played at Bannockburn, he did not take up his father's office. Ultimately he went to America, leaving the old pipes with the Mac Donalds of Loch Moidart. John Mac Intyre, his only brother, lived in the Menzies country, but cannot have been a piper, for he does not seem to have filled the office either. He died about 1834, and men of other names were afterwards pipers to the Menzies. Descendants of the Mac Intyres were living near Loch Rannoch about the middle of the last century, and some are probably there to this day.

THE MAC KAYS

were pipers to the Mac Kenzies of Gairloch, and one of them at least was accounted second only to the Mac Crimmons. The family came originally from Sutherlandshire, and began with Rorie, or *Ruaraidh* Mac Kay, who about 1592 found it advisable to leave his native place. As a boy he was appointed piper to the laird of Mac Kay, and on one occasion he accompanied his master to Meikle Ferry with John Roy Mac Kenzie of Gairloch, who had been on a visit to the Mac Kay Country. At the ferry the servant of another gentleman, who was also about to cross, tried to retain the boat, and Mac Kay, then a lad of seventeen, in hot-headedness drew his dirk and cut off the servant's hand. Thereupon his master said he could not keep him in his employment. Mac Kenzie at once gave the piper an invitation to come with him, and the matter was arranged on the spot. Rorie ever after was a Gairloch man, but beyond the story of how he came to the district, little of his personal history is known. In his duties as piper he was frequently assisted by his brother, Donald *Mòr* Mac Kay, who, however, returned to the Reay Country before his death. Rorie was piper in succession to four chiefs of Gairloch. He died in 1689 at an extreme old age, leaving one son. Him he sent to Dunvegan to be trained by Patrick *Og* Mac Crimmon, and when he left, after seven years' study, it was acknowledged that he had no equal except his master. This piper, *Am Piobaire Dall, Iain Dall,* or, in plain English, John Mac Kay, was the most famous of the Gairloch pipers. He was an enthusiast in his profession, and

composed twenty-four pibrochs, besides a number of strathspeys and reels. He was well read, though blind, and knew
the histories of Ireland, France, Greece, and· Scandinavia,
while none excelled him in knowledge of Ossianic poetry and
legendary lore. When he became advanced in years he was
superannuated, and passed his time in making excursions
into the Reay country and Skye, visiting at gentlemen's
houses, to which he was always welcome. He died in 1854, *1754 ?*
at the age of ninety-eight, and was succeeded by his son
Angus, who in his turn was succeeded by his son John
Mac Kay. The four members of the family were pipers in
succession to eight chiefs of Kintail, the succession in each
case being from father to son. The Mac Kays, as has been
said, came originally from the Reay Country, the home of
all the Mac Kays, where there seems to have been a college
similar to that kept at Dunvegan by the Mac Crimmons;
at any rate, a peculiarly large number of Mac Kay pipers
came from the district, just as if they had been trained in a
school.

The changing times were too much for the Mac Kays,
as for the other pipers, and in 1805 the representative of
the family, the John Mac Kay last mentioned, went to
America. He died in Pictou in 1835, when over eighty
years of age. The late Mr. Alexander Mac Kenzie, editor
of the *Celtic Magazine*, on a tour through the States in
1880, met one of the family. "More interesting to me,"
he wrote, "than all my other discoveries on this continent
was finding a representative of the famous pipers and poets
of Gairloch in the person of John Mac Kay, who occupies
the most honourable and prominent position in this thriving
town (New Glasgow), that of stipendiary magistrate. His
great-grandfather was the celebrated blind piper of Gair-

loch." Afterwards Mr. Mac Kenzie tells of the circumstances of the family in America. They had, he says, ceased to be pipers, and no one of the race kept up the traditions of their fathers in the strange land.

THE RANKINS

—called in Gaelic *Clann Raing*—were anciently called *Clann Duille*, being descended from one of the progenitors of the Clan Mac Lean called *Cudulligh*, or *Cu-duille*. They were pipers to the Mac Leans of Duart, the High Chief of the Clan, and became pipers to the Mac Leans of Coll after the Duarts lost their lands, when Sir John Mac Lean was chief in the beginning of the eighteenth century. They were hereditary pipers from time immemorial, and the most noteworthy incident associated with them of which we have any authentic record occurred when the great Dr. Johnson visited their island. The piper who played every day while dinner was being served attracted the doctor's attention, and he expressed admiration of his picturesque dress and martial air, and observed that " he brought no disgrace on the family of Rankin." We have few dates connected with the Rankins, but we have on record a letter from a John Mac Lean, on the garrison staff of Fort-William, Bengal, written in January, 1799, which states that thirty years before " Hector Mac Laine was piper to John Mac Lain of Lochbuoy, and was allowed to be the first in Scotland." This " Mac Laine " was probably a Rankin. Like so many of the others, America provided them, too, with an ultimate home, the last hereditary Rankin emigrating to Prince Edward Island.

THE CAMPBELLS

were pipers to the Campbells of Mochaster, in Argyllshire, and they, too, were indebted to Patrick *Og* Mac Crimmon for a good deal of their training. The latest record of them in their official capacity is to be found on a tombstone. in Bellside Churchyard, Lanarkshire, erected by Walter Frederick Campbell of Isla and Shawfield, an M.P. in the year of grace 1831, over his piper, John Campbell.

Besides those mentioned, there were famous, if not actually hereditary, pipers in different parts of the Highlands. A branch of the Mac Gregors established a school in Rannoch, and the Mac Phersons of Cluny and nearly all the other Highland chiefs of any note had excellent pipers, many of whom produced pieces of considerable merit. But the hereditary pipers have all passed away long ago, with the passing of that phase of life which was necessary to their existence. Their names, however, are still names to conjure with, and are likely to be so long as a love for their music remains a prominent trait of Highland character.

CHAPTER XIX.

Some Latter Day Pipers.

"Ours the strains renowned in story,
Of peaceful hall or deadly corrie,
Would you call to field or foray,
Melt to love or rouse to glory?
Sound our mountain melody."

Angus Mac Kay—Queen Victoria's first piper—His book—Donald Mac Kay—John Bane Mac Kenzie—The Queen's offer—The piper's reply—Donald Cameron—His achievements—His theory of pipe music—His system of noting—His last competition—A special reed—"The King of Pipers"—Other latter day pipers.

AFTER the death of the last Mac Crimmon piper in 1822 no one was left to maintain the traditions of the hereditary pipers. But the class was not wholly extinct. The next notable name we come across is one that is not likely to be soon forgotten by those interested in Highland music. There is no name better known to the world of pipers than that of Angus Mac Kay, the compiler of the first really serviceable book of pipe music, but, curiously enough, very little is known of his life. He belonged to a well-known family of pipers, and was connected with the famous Mac Kays of Gairloch. The family home was at Kyleakin, the pretty Skye village opposite the Kyle terminus of the Highland Railway. His father, John Mac Kay, was piper to Mac Leod of Raasay, who sent him to Boreraig, Dun-

ANGUS MAC KAY: FIRST PIPER TO QUEEN VICTORIA
(From a drawing in the possession of Duncan Munro, Kyleakin, Skye)

vegan, to be instructed by John *Dubh* Mac Crimmon. He was afterwards piper to Lord Willoughby de Eresby in Perthshire, and finally settled in Kyleakin, where he trained some of the best-known pipers, including John Bane Mac Kenzie.

Angus was born in Kyleakin about 1813, and was instructed by his father. He was piper to Davidson of Tulloch and also to Campbell of Islay. Afterwards he entered the service of Queen Victoria, in which he remained for many years. He was, by the way, Her Majesty's first piper. He devoted a great deal of his time to collecting and noting the leading pipe tunes, and in 1838 he published his collection as a book. This was, and still is, a unique work, being the first systematic collection. Mac Donald's, which came before it, was crude and could hardly be played from except by expert performers, but Mac Kay's book, which consists of sixty pibrochs, although it contains various errors, is to this day considered by many competent judges the best of its kind ever written. It is the author's lasting monument, and although comparatively little is known of his life, it cannot fail to keep his name in remembrance long after the names of those who were pipers only are forgotten. Mac Kay was a tall, gentlemanly-looking man, with a taste for literature. He died at Dumfries on 21st March, 1859, under sad circumstances. His mind had given way, and when out walking near the Nith, he somehow got into the river, and was drowned before those with whom he resided were aware that he was out of their charge. His nephew, Donald Mac Kay, who was trained at Maryburgh, Ross-shire, by Donald Cameron, became piper to H.R.H. the Prince of Wales, now King Edward VII., and his wife was for a long time in the Royal service at Sandringham.

John Mac Kenzie, familiarly known as John Bane Mac Kenzie, or *Am Piobaire Bàn*, was born near Dingwall about the end of the seventeenth century, and died in 1864, full of years, and with as high honours as piper could expect to get. His first situation as piper was with Mr. Mac Kenzie of Allangrange, about 1820. The following year he entered the service of Mr. Davidson of Tulloch, where he remained for twelve or thirteen years. While at Tulloch John was was often taken by his master to Applecross, where a friend of his, a Captain Mac Kenzie, resided. One of Captain Mac Kenzie's daughters fell in love with the handsome piper, and one night they ran away and got married at Crieff. Shortly afterwards John was appointed piper to the then Marquis of Breadalbane, in whose service he remained for thirty years, when ill-health forced him to retire. He spent the evening of his days in a fine cottage which he bought in the village of Munloahy, Ross-shire, and died in 1864, deeply regretted by all who knew him. He was buried at Strathpeffer, where a fine headstone was erected by his wife, to mark his grave.

John Bane Mac Kenzie was the foremost player of his time, and as an all round exponent of the national instrument it is doubtful if he ever had an equal. In appearance he was the finest possible specimen of a Highlander, of tall, handsome physique, upright in appearance as in character. When in full uniform his tunic was covered with medals and decorations won at competitions, including the gold medal of the Highland Society of London, which he won in 1838, when it was first offered. His knowledge of English was limited, but what he lacked in English he made up in the quaintly humorous nature of his replies and his good knowledge of his native tongue. He composed a number of

JOHN BANE MAC KENZIE

(From a Photograph in the possession of Pipe-Major Ronald Mac Kenzie, Gordon Castle)

tunes, the best known of which is " Mac Kenzie's Farewell to Sutherland." Her late Majesty Queen Victoria having seen John, asked his master if his piper would enter her service. The story of how he declined the Queen's offer is worth telling. When she communicated to Breadalbane her desire to have *Am Piobaire Bàn* as a member of the Royal household, the chief felt taken aback, but not wishing to offend Her Majesty, he approached John on the matter :—

" ' John,' he said, ' the Queen wants a piper.'

" ' Yes, ma Lort.'

" ' He must be thoroughly first-rate at marches, and also at strathspeys and reels, just the same as you are yourself, John.'

" ' Yes, my Lort.'

" ' The Queen also wishes her piper to be a fine specimen of a Highlander, tall and handsome, with a fine face and figure ; in fact, one something like yourself, John.'

" ' Yes, my Lort.'

" ' There is one other indispensable qualification. He must be sober, reliable, and in every way a respectable man, just like yourself, John.'

" ' Yes, my Lort.'

" ' Well, I have now told you all that is required in the man wanted by the Queen. He must be in all respects like yourself, both as man and as piper. Can you recommend any ?'

" ' Inteet, ma Lort, there's no sich a man to be found in aal Scotland.'

" ' And will you go yourself, John ?'

" ' Na, na, my Lort, na, na.' "

This finished the conversation, and John remained with Breadalbane. This story, it may be noted, bears a striking resemblance to one told of the Prince of Wales's piper in a previous chapter.*

---

* See page 164.

Queen Victoria seems to have coveted the best of the Highland pipers, but while no one doubted their loyalty, they did not always agree to serve Her Majesty. Not only did John Bane Mac Kenzie prefer the service of his chief to that of his Queen, but Donald Cameron, a pupil of his, and the piper who, more than any other, was acknowledged to be the true successor of the Mac Crimmons, declined a similar offer, and remained with his Highland master.

Eleven years before the last Mac Crimmon piper died, Donald Cameron was born at " the burn of the music," in Strath-Conan, Ross-shire, and at eight years of age he was playing the pipes. The late Mr. Mac Kenzie of Millbank, an influential Highland gentleman in the district, took a great interest in the youthful musician, and put him under the tuition of Big Donald Mac Lennan, of Moy, father of the well-known John Mac Lennan, piper to the late Earl of Fife. Cameron was next taught by Angus Mac Kay, whose father, John Mac Kay was taught by John *Dubh* Mac Crimmon. His last tutor was John Bane Mac Kenzie. He first competed in Edinburgh in 1838, at seventeen years of age, and won second prize, a claymore marked "Andria Varara," which afterwards came into the possession of the late Major A. C. Mac Kenzie, Maryburgh, Ross-shire.

The prizes won by Cameron during his career as a professional piper were not very numerous, but they were all high, and he soon became ineligible through having won all the possible firsts. In his early days there was generally a rehearsal of intending competitors, and only the best were allowed to compete in public, with the result that the very permission to compete was considered an honour, and the winning of a prize a distinguished honour. Cameron won

DONALD CAMERON
(From a Photograph in the possession of Pipe-Major Mac Dougall Gillies, Glasgow)

at Perth, in 1850, a large silver challenge medal presented
by his employer, the late Colonel Keith W. Stewart Mac
Kenzie of Seaforth ; and he won the Highland Society of
London's challenge gold medal in Inverness in 1859, a feat
which was subsequently performed by his sons, Colin and
Alexander ; and also six sets of pipes at different meetings.
His first service as piper was with Mr. Robert Morison,
Scallisaig, Glenelg. Afterwards he was employed by Sir
James J. R. Mac Kenzie, Bart., of Scatwell and Rosehaugh,
but his principal service was with Colonel Mac Kenzie of
Seaforth, with whom he continued till his death at Mary-
burgh in January, 1868. When the Brahan Company of
Volunteers was formed by Seaforth in 1866, Cameron was
appointed honorary piper, and when he died a detachment
accompanied his remains to the burying-ground of the
High Church, Inverness.

In 1863, Seaforth presented his piper with the title deeds
of one of the best houses in the village of Maryburgh, thus
following to a certain extent the practice of the chiefs when
the piper was a part of the household. Ten years previously he was selected to be piper to Her Majesty Queen
Victoria, an honour which he highly appreciated, but so
strong was his attachment to Seaforth that he preferred to
remain with him. Donald Cameron was very like the Mac
Crimmons. He lived in different times, but had he lived
when they lived he would have been as one of them. In his
theory of pipe music the sounds formed a continuous and
harmonious whole, as distinguished from that of one or two
other well-known pipers, whose playing, even of pibrochs, was
marked by its jerkiness. He was practically an illiterate man,
but, besides being able to read ordinary music, he noted his
tunes in a special manner, on the lines of the *Canntaireachd* of

the Mac Crimmons or the Mac Arthurs.   Each of these systems of notation was different from the others, and the invention of the piper who originally used it, so if Cameron was
illiterate he was certainly also clever.   He was a shrewd old
man, with a fund of stories connected with the Highlands
and leading Highland families.   He was a keen angler and a
great favourite with Seaforth.   When, at a comparatively
early age, he had ceased playing at competitions, he determined once more to try his skill in public..   So he took
advantage of the Northern Meeting, Inverness, where a
competition was to be held for former gold medalists only.
This competition was the first of its kind, and all the best
men were there.   When Donald Cameron began to play a
great hush fell on the crowd, and he played to an audience
that scarcely breathed.   He was, of course, placed first.   On
that matter there was no room for dispute.   The photograph here reproduced was taken immediately after that
competition.

When Cameron was playing in the year 1859 for the
Highland Society of London's gold medal at Inverness, he
had rather an awkward experience.   The tune was " Mac
Intosh's Lament," and he had not got much more than
through the ground or *urlar* when the drones began to slip
off his shoulder.   He made several futile attempts to adjust
them, but down they would come, and down they did come,
until they rested on his arm.   But this made no difference
whatever to the rendering of the tune.   He played just as
if the instrument was on his shoulder in the ordinary way.
An onlooker remarked to Alexander Mac Lennan how
splendidly he played, although under a disadvantage.
" Sandy " replied that " it made no difference to Donald
although he held the bag between his knees."

In personal appearance, as the sketch shows, he was the ideal successor of the hereditary pipers. In 1862 he won a prize of £10 offered by the Club of True Highlanders for the best rendering of pibrochs, and the chronicler of the event refers to him as being " with his grand, massive face and ample grey beard, the very impersonation of an old Highland piper." His favourite music was pibroch, but he was an all-round master of the pipes. Like many old players, he made all his own reeds, and was very particular about them. He had one special reed, which he used only on high occasions, such as a guest night at Brahan Castle. He kept it, when not in use, in an air-tight bottle, and one day a tinker piper called at his house, and, as usual with the class, begged for a reed. Mrs. Cameron thoughtlessly gave him this old-looking reed out of the bottle, and when Donald came home some time after, and was told what had been done, he was sorely put about. Cameron was one of that small number of men who could keep up a continuous sound when playing the practice chanter, a thing very few players can do. He was the composer of some first-class tunes, including " Kessock Ferry," " Brahan Castle," and " Lady Anne MacKenzie's Farewell to Rosehaugh." Of his four sons, three became pipers. Colin, piper to the Duke of Fife, is well known as a teacher of pipe music; Alexander was piper to the Marquis of Huntly; and Keith Cameron, now dead, was piper to the Highland Light Infantry. They all made names for themselves in the musical world, but in no case is their personality so outstanding as that of their father. Although the mantle of the MacCrimmons seemed to fall on him, the changing circumstances of life made it impossible for him to pass it on to another generation, and to find the true representative of the old pipers in the pipers of to-day would task the ingenuity of those best acquainted with the accomplishments of the different men.

John Bane Mac Kenzie and Donald Cameron were the only players who held the title, " King of Pipers." This was played for at the Northern Meeting, Inverness, and was the prize given at a competition between champions, the winner being known as the "champion of champions" or " King of Pipers." After Donald Cameron's day, when he won the prize and the title, the competition lapsed, and though there are now many so-called " champions," there is no " King of Pipers."

Among other latter-day pipers it is almost impossible to pick and choose. There was Donald Mac Phee, a miner lad from Coatbridge, who became pipe-maker, teacher, composer of and writer about pipe music, and died in Glasgow in 1880; William Ross, piper to the Black Watch, and later to Queen Victoria, who compiled a book containing forty pibrochs, and 437 strathspeys, marches, and reels; Donald Mac Phedran, a first-class Glasgow player who had one of the largest known collections of manuscript tunes; Alexander Cameron, a brother of Donald Cameron, who won all the champion gold medals, and was looked on as the Mac Crimmon of his day; Duncan Mac Eachern, an apparently clumsy manipulator of the pipes, but an able player; Donald Galbraith, a native of Islay; Alexander Mac Donald, late piper to the Duke of Fife; the Mac Lennans, especially William Mac Lennan, who as a piper and dancer occupied a unique position; Alexander Mac Donald, Glentruim, a splendid pibroch player, who died a few years ago at Aberlour; Malcolm Mac Pherson, Cluny's piper, and a well-known pibroch player; John Mac Rae, known as *Piobaire Beag*, who was piper to Francis,

Lord Seaforth, and John Bane Mac Kenzie's first tutor;
Duncan Campbell, piper to Sir Charles Forbes, Castle Newe,
Strathdon, a piper who on arriving at a competition always
asked if Donald Cameron was there, as " he did not care for
anyone else ; " Pipe-Major Alexander Mac Lennan, of the
Inverness Militia ; John Mac Lauchlan, a first-rate player
of the " little " music ; and many others who deserve to be
written about. In our own day we have Colin Cameron,
son of Donald, piper to the Duke of Fife and recognised as not only one of the best living pipers, but
a man who takes more than a passing interest in the
literature of his art and of the Highlands generally ;
William Sutherland, Airdrie, now retired, a man who had
not his equal at jigs, was very successful as an all-round
player, and composed numerous tunes ; Pipe-Major Mac
Dougal Gillies, of the 1st H.L.I., a pupil of Alexander
Cameron, son of Seaforth's famous piper, and himself one of
the best known and most successful of living players ; John
Mac Coll of Oban, a pupil of Mac Phee's and holder of
most of the highest possible honours ; Ronald Mac Kenzie,
late of the 78th Highlanders and now piper to the Duke of
Richmond and Gordon ; Angus Mac Rae of Callander ;
Farquhar Mac Rae of Glasgow, and other leading pipers
whose success and popularity deserve notice. But to do
justice to the subject would require a large amount of space
and it would also necessitate comparisons between the
abilities of lately deceased and still living men, which the
present writer is not at all inclined to make. The task of
general biographer would no doubt be pleasant, and there
are materials enough in existence to justify anyone in believing that the result would be well worthy of the effort,
but this is hardly the place for it. It is enough for us, at

present, to know that we still have men fully capable of keeping pipe music up to the high standard set by its old time exponents and that, if we have few who, like Saul of old, are head and shoulders above the crowd, the stature of the crowd itself is of a high average. Perhaps that very fact will make the task of the biographer all the more difficult.

BAND OF THE SUTHERLAND RIFLES---THE LARGEST VOLUNTEER PIPE BAND IN THE WORLD

CHAPTER XX.

How Piping is Preserved.

" O, wake once more ! how rude soe'er the hand
 That ventures o'er thy magic maze to stray,
 O, wake once more ! though scarce my skill command,
 Some feeble echoing of thine earlier lay ;
Though harsh and faint and soon to die away,
 And all unworthy of the nobler strain ;
Yet if one heart throb higher at its sway,
 The wizard note has not been touched in vain.
Then silent be no more ! Enchantress, wake again ! "

—*Scott.*

The waking—Professor Blackie—Highland Society of Scotland—
 Highland Society of London—The system of competitions—The
 first competition—The venue changed—The gold medal—
 Present day competitions—Some suggestions—R. L. S.—Pipe
 bands—Examples from high life—Quality of music—The
 Pipes abroad—Sir Walter Scott.

THE verse of Scott's, quoted at the head of this
chapter, referred to the harp, but we may use it as
referring to the pipes, remembering at the same
time that there is little hope of these ever occupying the
position they once occupied. The waking must be to
another life altogether. Civilisation ousted the pipes from
the position of clan and war instrument of a native population, but it did not find them another. " Had the govern-

ing powers been anxious," says Professor Blackie, " to do
common educational justice to the sons of the brave fellows
who so freely shed their blood in our defence, the last thing
they would have suffered to be neglected in the Highland
schools was the national music. For national purposes
the " March of the Cameron Men," and scores of such heroic
lays in the true old Greek style, were worth all the Latin
grammars that ever were printed. But an evil destiny hung
over this noble foundation of national inspiration ; a blight
fell with deadening swoop over the brightness and the joy
and the luxuriance of Highland life." Professor Blackie
himself did more than any other man to remove this blight,
and to him in great measure is due the credit for the present
revival of respect for Highland literature and Highland
music. Other men of letters have, by writing of the Highlands, shown that the country has a past worth the attention of the romancist, and Scott, Stevenson, William Black,
Fiona Mac Leod, and Neil Munro have brought Highland
life into touch with the rest of the world better than centuries of ordinary " civilisation " could have done. But
Professor Blackie was the champion enthusiast, though even
he realised that if the harp of the Gael was to wake it must
wake to new conditions, and be prepared to live in a world
it knew not, and which, to a great extent, knew it not.
There is no room in the world for the piper of the olden
time ; there is room for the piper of the olden time when he
adapts himself to modern circumstances. That he has done,
and the result is that the pipes are more the national instrument of Scotland than ever they were.

Foremost among the agencies which have kept alive the
taste for pipe music are the Highland Society of London
and the Highland Society of Scotland. The latter, founded

in 1784, interested itself more particularly in agricultural matters and the general welfare of the people, but the former, established six years earlier for the special purpose of preserving the language, music, and literature of the Highlands, has done grand work. By deciding, on 12th July, 1781, "that a Pipe and Flag be given annually by this Society to the best Performer on the Highland Bagpipe, at the October Falkirk Tryst," it practically inaugurated the system of competitions which has done so much to encourage rising talent, and without which no young piper could hope in these days to come prominently before the public. Many other organisations in different parts of Scotland, and in different parts of the world, have done good work in the same cause, but the winning of the Highland Society of London's gold medal is still the highest honour coveted by the ambitious piper. The annual competition began with a salute to the Society by its own piper. This was followed by a dance. Then three or more of the competitors each played a pibroch. Then there was another dance and more pibrochs until the list of the competitors was exhausted. The judges then retired to consider their verdict, and by and by the prizes were distributed by the president. This, with a few alterations, may be said to be the programme at competitions to this day.

The Society's first competition was held in 1781, at Falkirk Tryst, the first prize being a new set of pipes and 40 merks Scots, and the second and third each 30 merks. Thirteen pipers competed, and the judges were so placed that they could hear, but not see, the players. Each competitor played four different tunes, and the winner of the first prize was Patrick MacGregor, piper to Henry Balnaves of Ardradour. The second was Charles Mac Arthur, piper to the Earl of Eglinton, and the third John Mac Gregor, a man of 73, piper to Lieutenant-Colonel Campbell of Glen-lyon. The winner of the first prize, curiously enough, wanted the third finger of the "upper" hand, but he was uncommonly clever at using the little finger instead. For this reason he was known as *Patrick na Coraig*. The competition was superintended by a "branch" of the Highland Society of London, which existed in Glasgow.

The competition was held at Falkirk until 1783, when the award of the committee caused so much dissatisfaction that a number of the candidates resorted to Edinburgh in quest of other patronage. There a new committee was formed and arrangements made for another competition. At this Mac Donald of Clan Ranald presided, and after the prizes had been awarded, the pipers, twelve in number, marched round St. Andrew Square playing "Clan Ranald's March." This revolt of competitors resulted in the formation, in 1784, of the Highland Society of Scotland, which afterwards co-operated with that of London in the matter of competitions. The 1784 gathering was held in "the Assembly Hall, back of the City Guard," better known afterwards as the Commercial Bank. In 1785 the place of meeting was rooms in West Register Street, long since pulled down, and among those present was "Professor" Mac Arthur, the last of the hereditary pipers to Mac Donald of the Isles. He opened the proceedings with a salute to the Society and closed with "Clan Ranald's March," both played in masterly style. There were twenty-five competitors, and fifty-two pieces were played. Afterwards the competition was held in various places, including a church, but at last the gathering found a home in what was then the Adelphi Theatre. From the first up till 1826 the gathering was annual. Then it became triennial, but whether the change was an improvement is questionable. It resulted, for one thing, in fewer first-rate performers presenting themselves. At all the competitions private rehearsals were held in advance, when those obviously unfit were weeded out and the programme thereby shortened. The first gold medal offered by the Highland Society of London was won in 1835 by John Mac Kenzie, piper to the Marquis of Breadalbane. Present day competitions differ only in matters of detail from those of former years. The plan of keeping the performers out of sight of the judges has been abandoned. That, too, was a questionable step. There is often a deal of heartburning over the decisions, and charges of partiality are often flung at the judges. The dissatisfaction of candidates has made itself felt most often at local competitions, where the judges knew all the men. There are, of course, many difficulties. The music is of such a peculiar character, subject to so few hard and fast rules, and leaving so much to the taste of the performer; it is, besides, produced in a continuous torrent, by quickly following players, many of whom are almost equal in skill. The ordinary auditor is simply bewildered, and remembers little beyond a confusion of noises, and with the judges themselves the final decision is often a matter of difficulty. But there are not many judges like those who presided over the piping competitions at the great Jubilee gathering at Balmoral in 1887. William Mac Lennan got all the firsts for open dancing, and as he was the only first-class piper present he felt sure of all the firsts for piping. But he only came in second. Whereupon he inquired of the judges what mistake he had made,

"Oh, nae mistake," they said. "Ye played capital."

"Surely, then," he asked, "I was entitled to first prize?"

"Maybe ye wis; but, ye see, ye had a' the firsts for dancing."

"But was I not the best dancer?"

"Nae doot aboot that."

"And was I not the best piper, too?"

"We're no sayin' but ye wis."

"But I thought the best piper ought to get the first prize!"

"Oh, nae doot; but we thocht ye had gotten plenty already."

Mac Lennan always told this story afterwards with great glee. "Do you know," he would say, "these judges were the most interesting men I ever met. I wonder what they would have done if the competitor was a hammer-thrower or a jumper. They could not say thirty feet was less than twenty-five feet.

Taken all over, however, the bigger competitions are honourably conducted, and the best men always come out first. These now competing are mostly the retainers of titled gentlemen, with a number of private individuals who unite to an ordinary occupation an enthusiasm for the pipes. There are several ways in which the gatherings could be improved and made more interesting to the general public and of more value to the devotees of the pipes. The names of the tunes played might be published with the list of results, as well as the names of the prize-winners; prizes might be offered for new tunes, and for essays on the history or merits of tunes; and thus composition would be stimulated; and, above all, the old plan whereby the player was kept out of sight of the judge might be reintroduced.

The judging at local competitions is often looked on as a joke, and not worth protesting against. Were the judges ignorant of the identity of the players, the charge of favouritism could not be made, and that in itself would be a great step gained. If pipers would form a society among themselves and insist on only thoroughly competent men being allowed to act as judges the charge of ignorance of the music would fall to the ground. And again, some attempt might be made to put a stop to the liberty which everybody seems to have to organise a competition, call it " amateur championship" or whatever he likes, issue medals of little or no value, and pocket the receipts. All the gatherings, say in Scotland, could be managed by one organisation, a pipers' society such as that suggested, or a more comprehensive Highland society of some kind, and a certain uniformity of grades in confined and open and amateur and professional competitions introduced which would give confidence to the competitors, make the principal prizes a known quantity, and interest the general public in the results. That, of course, would not preclude the holding of competitions under the auspices of well-known and accredited athletic or patriotic organisations.

The idea of competing with each other, even with no inducement in the way of medals or prizes, is an old one. It has given inspiration to the novelist, and Robert Louis Stevenson in one of the best passages of *Kidnapped* tells how Alan Breck and a son of Rob Roy exchanged a duel with swords for a duel with pipes, and finished very good friends indeed. " Robin Oig," said Alan, when the duel was over, " ye are a great piper. I am not fit to blow in the same kingdom with ye Body of me! ye have mair music in your sporran than I have in my head ; and though it still sticks in my mind that I could maybe show ye another of it with the cold steel, I warn ye beforehand—it'll no be fair ! It would go against my heart to haggle a man that can blow the pipes as you can." At swordsmanship it is certain that Alan would not have come off second best.

After competitions, perhaps the next potent force in keeping alive the music of the pipes is bands—regimental, volunteer, police, and private. Regimental bands have already been referred to at length, and of the others, although a good many exist, there is little to be said. The Glasgow Highlanders are said to possess more men who can play the pipes than any other volunteer battalion, and they have no less than four pipe bands in the regiment. The 1st Sutherland H.R.V. again have the strongest pipe band in the kingdom, if not in the world. There are seventy members, and although they live far from each other, scattered over an extensive and wild county, they are brought together regularly for training, and have reached a high degree of efficiency.

The only police band now in Scotland is that of Govan, which may be said to have been the first pipe band in connection with any police force. It was started in 1885, and is now more popular than ever, thanks to the encouraging care of Chief Constable Hamilton. The members of the force all take a thorough interest in the band, and when it plays in the public parks of Glasgow and neighbourhood it is always listened to by large crowds of the general public. The necessary funds are provided by two concerts annually, and the men cost the burgh nothing, either in the way of time lost from ordinary duty, or in the way of financial assistance. The tartan of the band is specially made to a pattern designed by the Chief Constable.

GOVAN POLICE BAND

The fact that " people of quality " keep pipers also helps wonderfully to preserve the music. The Sovereign's example in this respect has been followed by a great many of the old nobility, and even these men who rise from the ranks, and whose only claim for admission into aristocratic circles is their wealth, must needs do as the others do. In other words, it is now fashionable to keep a piper. Non-Highlanders have adopted the kilt—the once proscribed dress—and wear it while holidaying in the Highlands, and whether or not they appreciate pipe music, they have it. This results in a state of affairs not always pleasing to the true Highlander, but it does much to preserve what the true Highlander, if left to himself in these latter days, would certainly neglect. There is undoubtedly a lot of sham and affectation about the Highland sentiment of to-day, but that is inevitable, and so long as with it all the old customs are maintained, we ought not to grumble.

As to the quality of the music in these days of ours, it is to be feared that since the piper became a domestic servant he has found it to his interest to cultivate the tastes of strangers, and hence the warlike character of the pipes has been considerably toned down. The composition of salutes and pibrochs is still attempted, and with a certain degree of success, but pipers would gain quite as much credit by paying more attention to the first-rate works of their predecessors as by composing and playing tunes of their own. Where a musical ear is accompanied by scientific knowledge, the present-day piper has a great advantage over those of a hundred years ago, but the fact remains that there are no tunes like the old tunes, and their intrinsic merit is the pride of the piping fraternity. Present-day conditions are not conducive to the production of good music, and we should be glad that we have a race of men capable of adequately interpreting the old.

The emigration boom that existed before and after 1870 resulted in the music and language of Scotland being scattered all over the world. In all the British colonies there are Highland societies, and competitions are held periodically, at which bagpipe playing is a prominent feature. In consequence, the exportation of pipes from Scotland has increased, and is still increasing. But the long distances between townships in the colonies tells very severely on the efforts of the Highland clubs. In Sydney, New South Wales, for instance, there are from twelve to twenty pipers, and a pipe band in connection with the Sydney Scottish Volunteers, the members of which practice all the year round. There is a big gathering on New Year's Day, at which some 20,000 people usually assemble, and another similar gathering no less than 400 miles away. In November there is a gathering at Newcastle, sixty miles distant, and in January another at Goulburn, 130 miles by rail. So it is not easy for pipers to attend where prizes may be won. The only places, again, where pipes are made, or piping is taught, are in the towns of Sydney and Melbourne. Some of the native-born pipers are good players, having been taught by those who came from Scotland, and many of the old tunes are favourites, though the Colonials generally prefer the newer styles. The highest prize given is £5 for each event, but £3 for pibrochs, and £5, £4, £2, and £1 for marches, strathspeys, and reels grouped together is more common. Putting the three events together is a sore point with the Colonial pipers, and a strong effort is being made to restore the prize-list to its original form, giving three prizes for each event. The Pipers' Association of Sydney have already started a movement for obtaining a voice in the choice of judges, and have been so far successful that their nominee was appointed last year, with the result that there was general satisfaction. This might be particularly noted by home pipers.

In Canada, says the late Mr. Alexander Mac Kenzie, the jumping, tossing the caber, stone throwing, and various other Highland competitions, would do credit to some of the best athletes at home gatherings, although, he adds, "the pipe music was nowhere." Since he travelled through Canada, however, there have been great improvements, and the visits of leading pipers from home have borne good fruit. Canada now has her own Highland pipers and dancers, reared on her own soil but on the home model, not perhaps so good as the best at home, but better than the average. Scotland abroad is more Highland than Scotland at home, and the hope of the future of the language and music lies as much in Canada and Australia as it does in Argyllshire, Perthshire, or Inverness-shire.

It was Sir Walter Scott who wrote :—

" The Highlands may become the fairy ground for romance and poetry or subject of experiment for the professors of speculation, political and economical. But if the hour of need should come— and it may not perhaps be far distant—the pibroch may sound through the deserted regions, but the summons will remain un-answered. The children who have left her will re-echo from a dis-tant shore the sounds with which they took leave of their own.— *Cha till, cha till, cha till, sinn tuillie.*—We return, we return, we return no more,"

but the Wizard of the North hardly saw into the future so clearly as he might have done. Had he seen the latest war in

T

South Africa, he would not have put the " return no more " so strongly. The hour of need did come, the pibroch did sound, and from Canada, Australia, and New Zealand the answer came, in the shape of regiments of loyal Britons, who fought and died for the old land. There is now a far bigger Scotland than ever existed, or could exist, between Maiden Kirk and John o' Groats. Thus has good come out of evil.

CHAPTER XXI.

THE OLDEST PIPE TUNES.

" At present I'll content mysel',
A hamely Scottish tale to tell,
Whilk happened years and years back ;
An' says tradition its a fact :
Be't true or no I canna say,
I was nae up to see the day,
But took the story upon credit,
An' I shall gie it—as I had it."

Unreliability of tradition—Lost in antiquity—Occasions of tunes—
Interest of stories—The MacRaes' March—Story of "Suarachan "—Hal o' the Wynd—The MacIntosh's Lament—Two
different stories—*A Cholla mo run*—Duntroon's Salute—The
Campbell's are coming.

IT serves no good purpose to indulge in regrets for that
which is past, but one cannot help feeling sorry that
the story of our national music is so scrappy and so
unreliable. There is, indeed, a large quantity of material
of a kind, and on a cursory examination one may think the
stories of the origin of tunes are plentiful enough. But
when one begins to go deeper and trace each story to its
source, reconcile all its different versions and explain how
the same incident crops up in another place, under different
circumstances, perhaps even in connection with another

tune, it is then that the task of making intelligible, and at the same time trustworthy, stories for melodies that are now so well known, becomes difficult. Precise dates have been given for many tunes, but it is obvious enough that the writers giving them, though doubtless good pipers, were but little conversant with the facts of history. Very few, indeed, of the older tunes can be authenticated. With them it is truly a case of being lost in the mists of antiquity. It is too often assumed that a tune having a direct reference to a certain historical incident, is itself of the date of that incident, while the chances are that it was composed on that incident by a piper who lived many years after. Because Shakespeare wrote Macbeth we do not conclude that he lived in Macbeth's day. A composer, like a dramatist, has all history spread out before him, and can make his music on what he pleases. We have, for instance, a piece of pipe music called " The Battle of Harlaw," but, though we know that it is very old, we have no reason to think that, in its present form, it was in existence in 1411. So with very many others. When the events they celebrate took place, very few, if any, of the actors could write, and it was a long time after that the matters referred to became part of written history. When the tunes were composed must, therefore, be decided, when it can be decided at all, by other evidence—by historical data regarding the lives of their composers or by references in the authentic history of the country. Such data and references are, however, because of the lack of education in the times when the accurate information could be got, very scarce, and the result is that, although many of the older tunes have been first favourites from time immemorial, no one has any idea of how they came into being.

There was always a fine vein of poesy and music among the Celts, and they readily composed rhymes and tunes which powerfully affected the imagination. They had magnificent memories, cultivated, of course, by that very lack of written books to which I have referred, and into their tunes they compressed the sentiments of past centuries, and the troubles and joys of everyday life. Noted incidents induced commemoration. The birth of an heir to the ancient clan, the death of the chief, a victory in battle, the home-coming or departure of any notable personage, were all fit subjects for the genius of the clan piper, and were often utilised as such. Where we can prove that the tune was composed when the incident, of which we know the date, occurred, we are on sure ground. When we cannot we are none the wiser. Each clan had its own music, almost all of high antiquity, and all of the class common to the Gael, but we can no more fix the origin of the music than we can fix the origin of the clan. The Munros have a pibroch composed on the battle of *Bealach na Broige*, an event which took place about 1350, and there is the tradition in the Clan Menzies that their piper played at Bannockburn, but in neither case is the matter of any use as history. "The Desperate Battle of Perth" is alleged to date from 1395, "The Mac Raes' March" from 1477, and "Mac Intosh's Lament" from 1526. In each case, however, tradition is the only original authority, and to tradition a hundred years are often as one day, and one day as a hundred years.

But the fact that we cannot fix exact dates does not impair the value of the stories, as stories. And it is as stories, traditions if you will, that we wish to recall them now, if only to show the atmosphere in which our pipe

music lived and moved and had its being. The stories I
believe are true, though I would not like to vouch for the
accuracy of the names of characters and places in every instance, no more than for that of the dates. The incident
recorded may have taken place at some other time, in some
other place, and with some other people, and tradition may
have mixed up names and figures. But there must have
been such an incident sometime, somehow, somewhere in the
Highlands. So long as we know that it did not originate
in the imagination of the story-teller, it illustrates men and
manners just as well as if we could swear by all its details.
And as it throws light on the circumstances in which Highland music was so often composed, it lends a new interest to
the study of that music. I give, I need hardly add, in each
case, that version of the story which I consider best authenticated, told, whenever possible, in the form that is of
greatest interest.

Let us take the first two or three in the order of their
traditional dates :—

"THE MAC RAES' MARCH"

is the oldest known pipe tune. The Lord of the Isles in-
vaded Ross-shire about 1477 with a numerous army, and
laid waste the country of the Mac Kenzies, burning a chapel
at Contin. The Mac Kenzies took the field to protect their
lands and property, and in an endeavour to recover the
booty from the Mac Donalds they asked the assistance of
the Mac Raes. The Mac Raes joined them, and the Mac
Donalds were defeated with great slaughter. In the ranks
of the Mac Raes there fought Duncan Mac Rae, an orphan,
familiarly known by the name of *Suarachan*, a term of con-

tempt. His prowess on this occasion was remarkable, and fully entitled him to higher consideration. He slew a notable man in the Mac Donald ranks, and then calmly sat down on the body, as if no more was required of him. Mac Kenzie was astonished at the action of this ally of his, and exclaimed :—

" Why sit you so, when your help is so much needed ? "

" If paid like a man, I will fight like a man," replied Mac Rae. " If everyone does as much as I have done the day is yours."

" Kill your two and you shall have the wages of two," said the chief.

Suarachan obeyed, and again sat down on the corpse.

" Kill your three," shouted the Mac Kenzie ; " nay, fight on, and I will reckon with you for the dead."

Suarachan thereupon got up, and dealt fearful destruction among the Mac Donalds, killing sixteen with his own hand, and thus proved his worth. He was ever afterwards held in high esteem, and became a leading man in the clan, acquiring the honourable name of " Duncan of the Axe." It was an axe he wielded with such dread purpose on the field of battle. The pibroch was composed in his honour and in memory of the conflict, and has always been the march of the clan.

The resemblance between the story and that of Hal o' the Wynd in Scott's *Fair Maid of Perth* is too striking to pass unnoticed. Hal, at the battle on the North Inch of Perth, acted exactly as *Suarachan* did at Contin. Which is the original story, or whether the two are different stories it is hard to determine. It would be interesting to know where Sir Walter got the legend on which he based the Hal o' the Wynd incident.

"THE MAC INTOSH'S LAMENT,"

on the authority of The Mac Intosh himself, dates from
1550. Writing in 1885 the chief said :—"The tune is as
old as 1550 or thereabout. Angus Mac Kay in his pipe
music book gives it 1526, and says it was composed on the
death of Lauchlan, the fourteenth laird, but we believe
that it was composed by the famous family bard Mac Intyre,
on the death of William, who was murdered by the Coun-
tess of Huntly in 1550. This bard had seen, within the
space of forty years, four captains of the Clan Chattan meet
with violent deaths, and his deep feeling found vent in the
refrain :—

> ' Mac Intosh the excellent
> They have lifted.
> They have laid thee
> Low, they have laid thee.'

These are the only words in existence which I can hear of."
　　There is, however, another tradition connected with the
tune. There was a prediction, believed among the clansmen, that the Mac Intosh of that day would die through
the instrumentality of his beautiful black steed, whose
glossy skin shone as the raven's wing, and whose flowing
mane and tail waved free as the wind itself. But the chief,
whatever he felt, was determined to show his people that he
treated the prediction lightly, and so he continued to ride
his favourite, in spite of the entreaties of his friends. He
rode him on the day of his marriage, and on the way to
church the horse became more than usually restive. He
reared and plunged, and behaved so badly that the rider,
losing control of himself and his horse, drew his pistol and
shot the favourite dead. Another, a piebald horse, was

procured, and the company proceeded to church. After the ceremony they returned by the way they had come, the bride and her maids on white ponies, and the bridegroom and his friends following. The chief's horse, in passing, shied at the body of the black horse, which lay by the way-side, and the rider was thrown to the ground and killed on the spot. A turn of the road hid the accident from those in front, and the bride, unconscious of what had happened, went on her way. She is said to have composed and chanted the air as, at the funeral, she moved at the head of the bier, marking the time by tapping on the coffin lid all the way to the grave, where she had to be torn away as the body was being lowered in :—

" Oh ! my love, lowly laid, Oh ! my love, lowly laid ;
Oh ! my love, lowly laid, beside the fatal wall breach !

Wife am I, sorrowful in my weeds of deep woe,
Since I heard, with heart sore pained, that henceforth I must wear them.

Th' piebald horse laid thee low, th' piebald horse laid thee low,
The piebald horse laid thee low, beside the fatal wall breach.

Maiden waesome sad am I, whom scarce know they since the day
When he fixed the marriage ring then on my finger gaily.

Oh ! alas, I wasn't there, Oh ! alas, I wasn't there,
Oh ! alas, I wasn't there, by thy right hand to take thee.

Oh, I am filled with grief, tear-drops streaming down my cheek,
Mourning for my youthful chief, who newly rode the piebald.

Rider of th' bounding black, bounding black, bounding black,
Rider of th' bounding black, so mangled by the piebald.

To the feast I'll not go, nor where merriment fast flows,
Since in waking of the spring an arrow pierced me sorely.

> My young Hugh, lowly laid, lowly laid, lowly laid ;
> My young Hugh, lowly laid in debris of the wall breach.

I am sad, sore sad and wae, since in dust they low thee laid
My farewell I pray thee take, to stones in Dun high standing.

> My young Hugh lowly laid, lowly laid, lowly laid ;
> My young Hugh, lowly laid, alas ! and I not near thee.

Thou couldst dance with grace and glee, when they sang sweet
  melody ;
The grass blade scarce would bent down be by thy quick tread so
  lightly.

> Och an och ! lowly laid, och an och ! lowly laid,
> Och an och ! lowly laid, beside the fatal wall breach."

Another set of words were taken down in 1872 from the
singing of *Mor Nighean Alasdair Mhic Ruaraidh* in Barra.
The English here given is not, however, a translation of
this, but what is practically a third set, written by Mr.
Malcolm MacFarlane, Paisley, to give some idea of the
rhythm of the tune :—

> " Hark the pipes' piercing wail
> Sounding clear on the gale
> As they bear adown the vale,
>   My brave, my noble marrow.
> Pride of the Heilan's, chief of his clan,
> Ever in danger leading the van—
> Death ne'er laid a fairer man
>   Within his chamber narrow.

Day of dool! day of woe!
Day that saw Evan low,
Ne'er shalt thou from memory go
    While's life's dim lamp is burning.
In the morn a bride was I ;
Wife when noonday's sun was high ;
Ere its light had left the sky
    I was a widow mourning.

What is life now to me
Since they've ta'en ye frae me ?
What again can pleasure gie ?
    What dispel my sorrow ?
Life was sweet, I was gay
Love was short and joy's away ;
Grief has come, but grief will stay,
    Renewed with every morrow."

" A CHOLLA MO RUN."

One of the earliest recorded instances of the bravery of a
piper is contained in the annals of our own Highlands, and
is inseparably connected with the tune known as *A Cholla
Mo run*, referred to in a previous chapter. * It may be as
well to give the story here at full length. The hero was
the piper of Coll Kitto, or left-handed Coll, who landed in
Islay with the advance party of an expedition from Ireland,
with instructions to take the Castle of Dunivaig by surprise,
should he find that this could be attempted with any degree
of success. The Campbells, however, had heard of the
expedition, and they drew the party into an ambush and
made them prisoners. All were hung off-hand, except the
piper, who asked leave first to play a lament over his com-

* See page 92.

rades. The chief of the Campbells had heard of the fame of this piper, and, being himself fond of music, he granted the request, taking care, however, to put cattle in the way of those of Coll Kitto's people who might follow the advance party, which would distract their attention, while his men could fall on them as they did on the others. The piper saw and understood the arrangements, and adapted his pibroch to the occasion, so that the warning and lamenting notes could not fail to be understood by his comrades. The chief of the Campbells also understood, and on finding himself over-reached he plunged his dirk into the piper, who smiled proudly even in death, for he knew he had saved his friends. The lamenting notes represented in this tune by " We are in their hands, we are in their hands," and the warning notes represented by " leave the cattle, leave the cattle," are exceedingly touching, and Coll Kitto, when he heard the pibroch, at once knew that his advance party was in trouble, and that the piper wished him to keep away from the island. Accordingly he turned his *birlins*, that is, boats, and left for a less dangerous locality. The words, when translated, are far from having the power and beauty of the Gaelic, but they will serve to show somewhat how the old pipers were supposed to speak by their music to those who understood them :—

" Coll, array ; be ready, depart ;
Be ready, depart ; be ready, depart ;
Coll, array ; be ready, depart ;
We are in their hands, we are in their hands.

Leave the cattle, leave the cattle, leave the cattle,
Leave the cattle, leave the cattle, leave the cattle,
Leave the cattle, leave the cattle, leave the cattle,
We are in their hands, we are in their hands.

An oar, a baler, an oar, a baler,
An oar, a baler, an oar, a baler,
An oar, a baler, an oar, a baler,
We are in their hands, we are in their hands."

This was supposed to represent embarking quickly. A "baler" was a dish for throwing water out of the boat.

" The red hand, the red hand, the red hand,
The red hand, the red hand, the red hand,
The red hand, the red hand, the red hand,
We are in their hands, we are in their hands."

In this the piper hinted to his friends to call the Mac Donalds to their aid before attacking the Castle.

" Coll of my love, avoid the strait,
Avoid the strait, avoid the strait ;
Coll of my love, go by the Mull ;
Gain the landing place, gain the landing place."

This was a warning to " avoid the strait," and hasten to secure a landing place in the shelter of the Mull of Kintyre.

" Coll of my love, avoid the castle,
Avoid the castle, avoid the castle ;
Coll of my love, avoid the castle ;
We are in their hands, we are in their hands."

That is one version of the story. There are several others, all more or less similar. The tune is connected by tradition with two or three places in the Highlands, notably with two castles in Argyllshire—Duntroon, near Crinan (destroyed by fire in June, 1899), and, as already stated, with Dunivaig, in Islay. In 1647, another version of the story goes : Campbell of Calder was commissioned by Argyll to proceed against Mac Donald (Coll Kitto) and expel him

from Islay, where he had taken up his residence with some
followers.   Mac Donald, it seems, was a sort of thorn in the
flesh to Argyll, and continually troubled him.   In this case
Calder, assisted by several troops of Campbells and others,
razed the Castle of Dunad, where Coll was, to the ground.
but Mac Donald himself escaped to Dunivaig, where he was
again besieged.   Finding his forces too weak, he took boat
by night to procure assistance from Kintyre or Ireland,
leaving the castle in charge of his mother.   Calder having
discovered this, determined to increase his own strength, and
retired for that purpose, leaving his troops under the lady
of Dunstaffnage, a bold, masculine woman.   While the male
leaders were absent, the wooden pipe conveying water to the
castle was discovered, and the supply cut off, with the result
that Coll's garrison surrendered.   The night after, the
piper, whose profession ensured respect, recognised his
master's boat coming back, and that he might apprise him
of danger, he asked leave to play a piece of music he had
composed on the misfortunes of the party.   The request
was granted, and he played :—

> " Coll, O my dear, dinna come near,
>   Dinna come near, dinna come near,
>   Coll, O my dear, dinna come near,
>   I'm prisoner here, I'm prisoner here."

Coll Kitto at once recognised the warning, turned his
boat, and escaped.   The Lady of Dunstaffnage saw how she
had been out-witted, and she made the piper play on the
top of the highest hill in Islay tunes of the merriest kind,
and then ordered his fingers to be cut off so that he might
never play again.   The hill is known to this day as " The
Hill of the Bloody Hand."

In pretty much the same way the story is associated with Duntroon Castle, only there are no women in it, so it is difficult to say which is correct. But it is plain enough that the incident itself is authentic, although it is doubtless exaggerated, and tradition is somewhat hazy as to the proper location.

" DUNTROON'S SALUTE."

Another tune—" Duntroon's Salute "—is mixed up with *A Cholla mo run* in a rather peculiar way, a way that suggests that the origin of the one is somehow being attributed to the other. Sir Alexander Mac Donald, *Alister Mac Cholla Chiotaich*, so this story goes, made a raid on Argyllshire in 1644 (the dates are irreconcilable with the accepted facts of the two stories), and surrounded Duntroon Castle, with the object of cutting off every person inside in revenge for the murder of his father's piper. He himself, with a fleet of galleys, besieged the castle from the seaward side, and he ordered his piper to play the " Mac Donalds' March." Instead, however, the piper, on the spur of the moment, composed and played a war cry to alarm Duntroon. After saluting Duntroon and wishing him good health, he warned him of his danger, pointed out that the enemy were ready to attack him by sea and land, from right and left and front. The tune was understood on shore and also on board Mac Donald's boat, and the poor piper was instantly hung from the yard-arm. Mac Donald finding he could not reduce Duntroon, moved northward, following out his work of destruction. The tune composed and played on this occasion is still known as " Duntroon's Salute," and that there is some truth in the story is shown by the way in which it seems to represent the sound of waves breaking against rocks. The exact relations between its origin and that of *A Cholla mo run* would, however, do with a little clearing up. It may be mentioned as a fact that some years ago a body was found buried within Duntroon, which was evidently that of the piper referred to in the tradition. At anyrate his finger bones were awanting, a fact which goes to prove the second Dunivaig story. But how, then, did the piper come to be buried in Duntroon?

"THE CAMPBELLS ARE COMING"

dates so far back in the centuries that we fail to trace its origin. It has been the march of the clan for hundreds of years. There is an old Gaelic song sung to the air, which tradition says was the composition of a piper. This piper, in the course of his vocation, was at a wedding in Inveraray, where he was inhospitably treated. Smarting under a sense of injury, he composed the song :—

> " I was at a wedding in the town of Inveraray,
>   I was at a wedding in the town of Inveraray,
>   I was at a wedding in the town of Inveraray,
>   Most wretched of weddings, with nothing but shell-fish,"

thus mercilessly lashing his churlish host. The wedding evidently was so poor that all the company got was limpets, and the song is another hit at the poverty of Inveraray. Burns echoed it when he wrote :—

> " There's naething here but Highland pride,
>   And Highland scab and hunger ;
>   If Providence has sent me here
>   'Twas surely in his anger."

The tradition, by the way, was so implicitly believed in, that the playing of the tune at a wedding, up to a comparatively recent date, was regarded as a premeditated insult.

One curious story is told of the tune. Not very many years ago the steamer *Cygnet* was sailing in a Highland loch when a sailor's wife gave birth to twins. The fact was noticed more particularly because a few years before, in the same steamer, under the same captain, and at the same place, a similar event had taken place. On the first occasion the mother was a Mrs. Campbell, and, strangely enough, just when the twins were born, a piper on board happened to be playing vigorously " The Campbells are Coming," quite ignorant of the additions that had just been made to the passenger list.

The tune was played by the 78th Highlanders when coming to the relief of Lucknow, and was that heard by Jessie of Lucknow—if there was such a person—as she lay half asleep on the ground.

CHAPTER XXII.

Some World-Famous Pibrochs.

" Oh, heard ye yon pibroch sound sad on the gale,
  Where a band cometh slowly with weeping and wail,
  'Tis the chief of Glenara laments for his dear,
  And her sire and her people are called to the bier."
                                        —*Campbell.*

MacCrimmon's Lament—Best known of all pipe tunes—Its story—
    Blackie's poetry—Scott's—The war tune of Glengarry—A tragic
    story—The pibroch o' Donuil Dhu—Too long in this condition—
    Pipers and inhospitality—Oh, that I had three hands—Lochaber
    no more—Allan Ramsay's verses—An elated MacCrimmon—
    Rory *Mòr's* Lament—Clan Farlane pibroch—Pipers, poetry,
    and superstition.

THERE are several reasons why "MacCrimmon's
Lament" should be the best known of all pipe tunes,
but the most important is the fact that it is, and
must ever continue to be, inseparably associated with the
famous pipers of Dunvegan. The tune was composed by a
piper who was leaving home, and had a presentiment that
he would never return, but it has often been used in other
circumstances. In the evicting days, when Highlanders
were compelled to emigrate from their native shores, the
favourite air when they were embarking was

"CHA TILL MI TUILLE"

(I'll return no more), and on many other mournful occasions
the lament of the MacCrimmons was made the means of

expressing the feelings of Highlanders. It was composed in 1746 by Donald *Bàn* Mac Crimmon, then piper to Mac Leod of Dunvegan. Donald *Bàn* was considered the best piper of his day, and when the clan left Dunvegan to join the Royalists in 1746, he was deeply impressed with the idea that he himself would never again see the old castle. The parting of the clansmen with their wives and children was sad, and Donald *Bàn*, thinking of his own sweetheart, poured forth his soul in the sad wail of the Lament, as the Mac Leods were marching away from the castle. The clan afterwards took part in a skirmish, which, from the peculiar circumstances, is known to history as the " Rout of Moy," and Mac Crimmon was shot close by the side of his chief.

The Gaelic words usually associated with the lament are supposed to have been sung by Donald *Bàn's* sweetheart, but they are in all likelihood of much later date. The chorus, however, is probably as old as the tune, but the complete verses first appeared in print in 1835, in a collection of *Popular Gaelic Songs* by John Mac Kenzie, of the *Beauties of Gaelic Poetry*, where the words are said to have been taken from an old Skye manuscript. Translated into English they lose much of their plaintive melody, and make but a poor means of conveying an idea of the tune to the non-Gaelic reader :—

" The mountain mist flows deep on Cullin,
  The fay sings her elegy sorrowful ;
  Mild blue eyes in the Duin are in tears,
  Since he departed and refused to return.

      He returns not, returns not, returns not, Mac Crimmon,
      From war and conflict the warrior refuses to return.
      He returns not, returns not, MacCrimmon would not return,
      He will return no more until the day of the last gathering.

The winds of the wold among the boughs are wailing,
Each streamlet and burn is sad on the hills ;
The minstrels of the boughs are singing mournfully,
Since he departed and will never return.

    He returns not, etc.

The night is clouded, sorrowful and sad,
The birlin under sail, but reluctant to depart,
The waves of the sea have a sound not happy,
Lamenting that he departed and will never return.

    He returns not, etc.

Gather will not the tuneful race of Duin in the evening,
While echo with alacrity and joy answers them ;
The youths and maidens are without music lamenting
That he departed from us and will never return.

    He returns not, etc."

This is perhaps too literal a rendering. Let us try Professor Blackie's version. Blackie was an enthusiast for everything Celtic, and beautified everything in Celtic literature that his pen touched. A comparison of the two translations shows this :—

" Round Cullin's peak the mist is sailing,
The banshee croons her note of wailing,
Mild blue eyes with sorrow are streaming,
For him that shall never return, Mac Crimmon !

        No more, no more, no more for ever,
        In war or peace, shall return Mac Crimmon ;
        No more, no more, no more for ever,
        Shall love or gold bring back Mac Crimmon.

The breeze on the hills is mournfully blowing,
The brook in the hollow is plaintively flowing,
The warblers, the soul of the grove, are mourning
For Mac Crimmon that's gone with no hope of returning.

    No more, etc.

The tearful clouds the stars are veiling,
The sails are spread, but the boat is not sailing,
The waves of the sea are moaning and mourning
For Mac Crimmon that's gone to find no returning.

    No more, etc.

No more on the hill at the festal meeting
The pipe shall sound with the festal greeting,
And lads and lasses change mirth to mourning,
For him that's gone to know no returning.

    No more, etc."

The story of the origin of the tune which I have given is that generally accepted as historically accurate. There is, however, a tradition that after the passing of the Heritable Jurisdiction Bill in 1747 practically abolished the office of hereditary piper, Donald *Dubh* Mac Crimmon, the last of the race, who died in 1822 at the age of ninety-one, composed the lament on his departure for Canada. The sentiment is hardly that which one might expect from a departing emigrant, but rather what a piper might give expression to on leaving for the wars, a fact which tells against the tradition. Nevertheless, the tune has been turned into an emigrant's farewell on many occasions, and the last verse of Sir Walter Scott's composition connected with the tune, shows that the poet accepted the air as such, to some extent at least :—

MacLeod's wizard flag from the grey castle sallies,
The rowers are seated, unmoor'd are the galleys ;
Gleam war-axe and broadsword, clang target and quiver,
As MacCrimmon sings ' Farewell to Dunvegan for ever !
Farewell to each cliff on which breakers are foaming ;
Farewell each dark glen in which red deer are roaming,
Farewell lonely Skye, to lake, mountain, and river,
MacLeod may return, but MacCrimmon shall never !

' Farewell the bright clouds that on Quillan are sleeping ;
Farewell the bright eyes in the dun that are weeping ;
To each minstrel delusion farewell—and for ever—
MacCrimmon departs to return to you never !
The banshee's wild voice sings the death dirge before me,
The pall of the dead for a mantle hangs o'er me ;
But my heart shall not flag and my nerve shall not shiver,
Though devoted I go—to return again never !

' Too oft shall the note of MacCrimmon's bewailing
Be heard when the Gael on their exile are sailing ;
Dear land ! to the shores whence unwilling we sever ;
Return—return—return we shall never !

  ' *Cha till, cha till, cha till, sinn tuille !*
  Cha till, cha till, cha till, sinn tuille,
  Cha till, cha till, cha till, sinn tuille,
  Ged thilleas MacLeod, bheò MacCriomain.' "

Some stories, by the way, state that MacCrimmon himself composed the words to suit the air, and others that they
were composed by his sweetheart at Dunvegan on hearing
him playing the new lament when the clan was leaving the
castle.   Still others would have it that the sweetheart's song
was another, composed in response to that of MacCrimmon.

The phrase, *Cha till mi tuille*, is also associated with
the story of the piper who tried to explore a cave in Mull,

which was given in a previous chapter. The people of Skye claim the story, and say this piper was a Mac Crimmon, but the legend is not supposed to give the origin of the phrase. *Cha till mi tuille* was used on many occasions as an extempore expression of feeling on the part of a piper without any reference to the particular tune, " Mac Crimmon's Lament."

. If " Mac Crimmon's Lament " is associated with a departure for the wars, there is another tune associated very closely with war itself—so closely, indeed, that, according to the accepted story of its origin, it was composed while one of the most cruel deeds ever done in the name of warfare was being perpetrated.

" GILLIECHROIST " or " KILLYCHRIST "

is the war tune of Glengarry, and its origin—mythical according to some writers—is as follows :—

About the beginning of the seventeenth century there lived in Glengarry a famous character named Allan Mac Ranald, of Lundie. He was a man of great strength, activity, and courage, and, living as he did at a time when the feuds between the Mac Kenzies and the Mac Donalds were at their height, he invariably led any expedition that set out from Glengarry. In these fighting days young Angus Mac Donald, of Glengarry, anxious to distinguish himself, determined — though against the advice of his father — to lead a raid into the country of the Mac Kenzies. He surprised and defeated the Mac Kenzies, but on their way home by sea the Mac Donalds were in their turn attacked by the Mac Kenzies, and defeated with great slaughter. Angus Mac Donald was among the slain, and Allan of Lundie only escaped with his life by leaping into

the sea at Loch Hourn, where the battle took place, and
swimming ashore at another place. Allan was determined to
be avenged, and not long after he led a strong party of Mac
Donalds to the lands of Killychrist, near Beauly. He found
the Mac Kenzies totally unprepared, burned their lands, destroyed their crops, and finally mercilessly set fire to a church
in which a large congregation were worshipping, driving back
at the point of the sword all who attempted to escape.
Meantime he ordered Alister *Dubh*, his piper, to play so as
to drown the cries of the perishing people. Alister thereupon blew up loud and shrill, and, after making his instrument give utterance to a long succession of wild and uncon-
nected notes without any apparent meaning, he began his
march round the church, playing extemporaneously the
pibroch which, under the name of " Killychrist," has since
been used as the war tune of the Mac Donells of Glengarry.
For a short time the terrible sounds from the inside of the
church mingled with the music of the pipes, but they
gradually became fainter, and at last ceased altogether.

Allan and his comrades had little time to enjoy their
victory, for the Mac Kenzies soon gathered in overwhelming
numbers, and, finding the Mac Donells resting on a flat
near Mealfourvonie, known as " the marsh of blood," they
attacked them with great fury, and pursued them to Loch
Ness. Allan was again one of the few who escaped.

The story of the burning in the church has been altogether discredited, but it is admitted that there was a
raid, and that a large number of cottages, as well as the
manse of Killychrist, were burnt. None of the earlier
writers, however, mention the burning of the congregation. The music itself also contradicts somewhat the
traditional origin of the tune, for when it is properly

played the listener can fancy he hears the flames rustling and blazing through the timbers, mingled with the angry remonstrances and half-smothered shouts of the warriors, but there is no representation of the more feeble plaints of women and children, as there would surely have been had these been among the victims. However, I give the story for what it is worth.

"PIOBAIREACHD DHOMHNUILL DUIBH"

is one of the oldest and best known of pipe tunes. It is said to have been played at the Battle of Inverlochy in 1431, and it is first found on paper in Oswald's *Caledonian Pocket Companion*, published in 1764, where it is entitled *Piobaire-achd Mhic Dhonuill*. Afterward it appeared in the book compiled by Captain Mac Leod of Gesto, from which it was translated in 1815 into ordinary notation by the editor of *Albyn's Anthology*. Its first printed heading strengthens the title of the Mac Donalds, who claim the tune for their clan, but the words *Donull Dubh* are accepted as referring to Cameron of Lochiel, and the tune is known as " Lochiel's March." The chief of the Camerons bears the name *Mac Dhomhnuill Duibh*, or son of Black Donald. The air, which is the march of the 79th or Cameron Highlanders, is a call to arms, and is inseparably associated with Inverlochy, but whether composed and played on the field or only in commemoration of the battle cannot now be determined. The English words are by Sir Walter Scott, and first appeared in 1816 :—

> " Pibroch o' Donuil Dhu,
>   Pibroch o' Donuil,
> Wake thy wild voice anew,
>   Summon Clan Conuil ;

Come away, come away,
  Hark to the summons,
Come in your war array,
  Gentles and Commons.

Come from deep glen, and
  From mountain so rocky,
The war pipe and pennon
  Are at Inverlochy;
Come every hill plaid, and
  True heart that wears one;
Come every steel blade, and
  Strong hand that bears one;

Leave untended the herd, and
  The flock without shelter,
The corpse uninterr'd,
  The bride at the altar;
Leave the deer, leave the steer,
  Leave nets and barges;
Come with your fighting gear,
  Broadswords and targes.

Come as the winds come, when
  Forests are rended;
Come as the waves come, when
  Navies are stranded;
Faster come, faster come,
  Faster and faster!
Chief, vassal, page, and groom!
  Tenant and master!

Fast they come, fast they come;
  See how they gather!
Wide waves the eagle plume
  Blended with heather.

> Cast your plaids, draw your blades,
> Forward each man set !
> Pibroch o' Donuil Dhu,
> Knell for the onset ! ”

“IS FADA MAR SO THA SINN,”

which may be translated “Too Long in this Condition,” is an old pibroch, dating from about 1712. It was composed either by Donald *Mòr* Mac Crimmon or by Patrick, his son. Donald was compelled at one time, because of some depredations of his own, to flee for his life into Sutherlandshire. There he put up unrecognised at the house of a relative named Mac Kay, who was getting married that day. Mac Crimmon sat down in a corner almost unnoticed, but when the piper began to play he unconsciously fingered his stick as if it were the chanter. The piper of the evening noticed this, and asked him to play for them. Donald said he could not, and the whole company asked him, and he again refused. At last the piper said: “I am getting seven shillings and sixpence for playing at this marriage. I'll give you one-third if you will play.” Donald then took up the pipe and began :—

> “ Too long are we thus, too long are we thus,
> Too long in this condition,
> Too long lacking meat or drink,
> At Mac Kay's marriage am I.”

These lines he repeated three times, and concluded by adding—

> “ At the house of Mac Kay am I.”

He played so well that all present knew him to be the great Donald *Mòr* Mac Crimmon, and as he made his pipes speak to them they understood his complaint, and he was then royally entertained.

The pibroch is also said to have been composed by Patrick *Mòr* Mac Crimmon on his being taken prisoner, along with many others, at the battle of Worcester, and being left in a pitiable state. It is also associated with the same piper and the battle of Sheriffmuir, where he was left stripped of all his clothing, but it is impossible to say which, if either, is right.

Want of hospitality towards a piper gave rise to another tune. It is called

" THE MISERLY, MISERABLE ONE'S HOUSE,"

and its origin, as told to the late " Nether Lochaber" by an old Loch Awe-side piper, was as follows :—

Some two or three hundred years ago, when the great Clan Campbell was at the height of its power, the estate of Barbreck was owned by a Campbell, who was brother or cousin or something of another Campbell, the neighbouring laird of Craignish. Craignish kept a piper, but Barbreck did not. Barbreck could afford to keep one, but he grudged the expense, and his stinginess in this respect is commemorated in an Argyllshire saying—" What I cannot afford I must do without, as Barbreck did without a piper."

Barbreck one day was on a visit to Craignish, and as he was leaving he met the piper, and said to him—" The New Year is approaching. On New-Year's Day morning, when you have played the proper salute to my cousin, your master, I wish you would come over to Barbreck and play a New-Year's salute to me, for, as you know, I have no piper of my own to do it. Come and spend the day with us." This the piper promised to do, and on New Year's Day morning, after first playing his master into good humour, he went to Barbreck. He played and played until the laird was in raptures, but the piper became hungry and thirsty, and hinted as much to Barbreck. He got some food, but it was not satisfactory, either in quantity or quality. The drinkables were no better, and long before the sun set the piper was anxious to go home. "Give us one more tune before you go," said Barbreck. "That I will," said the piper, and there and then he struck up impromptu *Tigh Bhroinein*—the House of the Miserly One. The following are some of the lines attached to the tune from the very first, whether by the piper himself or by another is not known :—

> " I was in the house of the miserly one to-day,
> In the house of the miserly one was I ;
> I went by invitation thither,
> But I got no sufficiency (of meat or drink).
> I got a drink of meal gruel there,
> And got bad barley scones ;
> I got the leg of a hen there,
> And, by my troth, she was a poor and tough one.
> This is an invitation that has annoyed me,
> I will leave this to-night
> Without (I may say) food or drink
> I will leave thee, Barbreck ;
> Nor will I return any more
> To play thee a piobaireachd salute. "

The translation is too literal to be poetry, but one can imagine how Barbreck must have felt. He had better have done without that last tune.

" OH, THAT I HAD THREE HANDS ! "

is associated with at least two incidents in Highland history. Towards the end of the thirteenth century a dispute arose between *Mac Cailein Mòr*, chief of the Clan Campbell, and Mac Dougall of Lorne, chief of the Mac Dougalls, with reference to the boundaries of their estates. The parties met at a spot where two streams unite, and fell to recrimination and ultimately to fighting like tigers. The slaughter was terrible, and the streams ran with blood and were crowded with the bodies of the slain. Ultimately *Mac Cailein Mòr* was killed, and his followers ceased the fighting to carry off his body. Close to the battlefield there was a small conical hillock—called in the Gaelic *Tom-a-Phiobair*, the Piper's Hillock—on the top of which the piper of the Campbells stood and played while the battle raged. Sympathising with the Mac Dougalls, and regretting the havoc made among them, he composed on the spot a pipe tune, the purport of which was :—

" My loss ! my loss ! that I have not three hands,
　　Two engaged with the pipe and one with the sword,
　My loss ! my loss ! that I have not three hands,
　　Two engaged with the pipe and one with the sword ;
　My loss ! my loss ! low lies yonder
　Mac Dougall, with his pipe, whose sound was soft and sweet to me."

This hardly indicates whether the piper would, had he three hands, have fought with the Mac Dougalls against his own clan, but, at anyrate, the Campbells, seeing that this was not one of their own tunes, were so enraged that one of them ran to the piper and chopped off his head. It is said that the piper's fingers played three or four notes on the chanter while his head was toppling to the ground.

This story belongs to the same class as those relating to the battles of Philiphaugh and Bothwell Bridge, given in a previous chapter. The resemblance, indeed, is too striking to be a coincidence, and the three have probably at some time or other been one story. The other incident connected by tradition with the tune is that already related of a cave in either Skye or Mull, into which a venturesome piper entered. He never returned, but the last wailing notes of his pipes told that he was being hard beset with wolves, who threatened to tear him to pieces should he stop playing. So he played mournfully :—

> " Oh, that I had three hands !
> Two for the pipes and one for the sword,"

the inference being that in that case he could have kept on playing and fought the wolves at the same time.

The tune nearly always played at Highland funerals is

" LOCHABER NO MORE."

It was composed to Jane, daughter of Sir Ewen Cameron of Lochiel, by a young English officer on his being ordered back from the Highlands to join his regiment. Jane Cameron was afterwards married to Lachlan Mac Pherson of Cluny, thus bringing over the tune to the Mac Phersons. The traditional account is entirely different. According to it a party of marauders from Lochaber, consisting of forty to fifty men, reached, one autumn afternoon, the summit of a hill immediately above Glenesk, the most northerly parish of Forfarshire. They meant to make a raid on the valley, but lay down to rest until after dusk. They were, however, seen by some shepherds, who gave the alarm, and in the evening the inhabitants of the glen were all under arms for the protection of their property. After dusk the invaders descended, and in the battle that ensued five of the defenders were killed and ten taken prisoners. Prisoners and cattle were driven to the Highlands. The men returned next year after a ransom of fifteen merks had been paid for each, but the cattle were never seen again. A ballad giving these particulars was long popular in the glen, but nothing now remains of it except the last words of each verse— "Lochaber no more." Allan Ramsay wrote lines for the air, but they contain nothing of the spirit of the traditional origin. They are obviously based on the historical account :—

" Farewell to Lochaber, and farewell my Jean,
  Where heartsome with thee I've mony day been ;
  For Lochaber no more, Lochaber no more,
  We'll maybe return to Lochaber no more.
  Those tears that I shed, they're a' for my dear,
  And no for the dangers attending on weir,
  Tho' borne on rough seas to a far, bloody shore,
  Maybe to return to Lochaber no more.

  Tho' hurricanes arise and rise every wind,
  They'll ne'er make a tempest like that in my mind ;
  Tho' loudest of thunder on loudest waves roar,
  That's naething like leaving my love on the shore.
  To leave thee behind me my heart is sair pain'd,
  By ease that's inglorious no fame can be gained ;
  And beauty and love's the reward of the brave,
  And I must deserve it before I can crave.

  Then glory, my Jeanie, maun plead my excuse ;
  Since honour commands me, how can I refuse ?
  Without it I ne'er can have merit for thee,
  And without thy favour I'd better not be.
  I gae, then, my lass, to win honour and fame,
  And if I should luck to come gloriously hame,
  I'll bring thee a heart with love running o'er,
  And then I'll leave thee and Lochaber no more."

It is only fair to add that the tune, under another name, is said to have been a favourite Irish air in London in the time of Queen Elizabeth. If this was so, the explanation probably is that the Irish who came to Scotland, and the Scots who went to Ireland, each carried their music with them, and that there are many tunes common to both peoples.

" I HAVE HAD A KISS OF THE KING'S HAND."

Pipers of old times always had " a guid conceit o' themsel's," and Patrick *Mòr* Mac Crimmon, who flourished in 1660, was no exception to the rule. His master, Roderick Mac Leod of Mac Leod, went to London after the Restoration to pay his homage to Charles II., and was very warmly received. He had taken his piper with him, and the King was so pleased with his fine appearance and his music that he allowed Mac Crimmon to kiss his hand. Patrick was highly elated over this, and commemorated the honour that had been paid him by composing the tune *Fhuair mi pòg o laimh an Righ*, which, to those acquainted with the language and music, seems to speak forth the pride and gratitude of the performer, the words expressed by the opening measure being :—

> " I have had a kiss, a kiss, a kiss,
> I have had a kiss of the King's hand ;
> No one who blew in a sheep's skin
> Has received such honour as I have."

" RORY MOR'S LAMENT."

Sir Roderick Mac Leod of Dunvegan, who died somewhere about 1630, was a man of noble spirit, celebrated for great

military prowess and resource. His hospitality was un-
bounded, and he was in all respects entitled to be called
Mòr or great, in all the qualities that went to constitute
a great Highland chief and leader of men. The Gaelic
bards were enthusiastic in his praises, and his piper, Patrick
Mòr Mac Crimmon—the same Mac Crimmon presumably—
taking his death very much to heart, could not live at Dunvegan afterwards. Shouldering his great pipe, he made for
his own house at Boreraig, composing and playing as he
went *Cumha Ruaraidh Mhoir* (Rory *Mòr's* Lament), which
is considered the most melodious, feeling, and melancholy
lament known. The following are some of the words,
translated by " Fionn " :—

> " Give me my pipes, I'll home them carry,
> In these sad halls I dare not tarry,
> My pipes hand o'er, my heart is sore,
> For Rory Mor, my Rory Mor.
>
> Fetch me my pipes, my heart is breaking,
> For Rory Mor his rest is taking,
> He walks no more, and to its core
> My heart is sore for Rory Mor.
>
> Give me my pipes, I'm sad and weary,
> These halls are silent, dark, and eerie,
> The pipe no more cheers as of yore,
> Thy race is o'er, brave Rory Mor."

"THE CLAN FARLANE PIBROCH."

A Faust-like story is told of Andrew, chief of the Clan
Mac Farlane, and the supposed composer of the " Clan
Farlane Pibroch." Andrew and Alastair, chiefs of the Mac
Donells of Keppoch, were credited with having " the black
art." They were said to have sold their souls to the devil

in exchange for their supernatural powers. They seem to have driven a rather peculiar bargain, for the understanding was that the devil should get only one of their souls, the chiefs to decide between themselves which it would be. The appointed day and hour came on which the debt was to be paid, and still the chiefs, though they had come to the trysting place, had not decided which soul was to be given up. When the devil came he was in a desperate hurry, and at once exclaimed, " Well, and whose soul do I get ? " On the spur of the moment Mac Donell pointed to Mac Farlane's shadow, saying, " That's he," whereupon the devil snatched up the shadow and ran off with it. From that day Mac Farlane was never known to cast a shadow.

As to the tune itself, Sir Walter Scott supposes it had a close connection with the predatory excursions of the clan into the low country near the fastnesses on the western side of Loch Lomond. The pibroch, *Thogail nam bo*, seems to indicate such practices, the sense of the music being :—

> " We are bound to drive the bullocks,
> All by hollows, hirsts, and hillocks,
>   Through the sleet and through the rain ;
> When the moon is beaming low
> On frozen lake and hill of snow,
> Boldly, heartily we go,
>   And all for little gain."

The tune was almost lost, but about 1894 some enthusiasts gathered it from several who knew it, and committed it to paper, thus ensuring its preservation. The credit of this laudable effort, it should be added, is mainly due to Provost Mac Farlane of Dumbarton, who, with the help of Pipe-major J. Mac Dougall Gillies, Glasgow, had the complete tune taken down from the playing of John Leitch, an old man who lived in Glendaruel. The Faust-like story of its composer is also told of a Donald Mac Kay of Lord Reay's country, but not in connection with a tune.

"JOHN GARBH OF RAASAY'S LAMENT."

Connected with "John Garbh of Raasay's Lament," one of the most famous of pibrochs, and a favourite with most pipers to this day, there are stories of pipers, poetry, and superstition. John Garbh Mac Leod of Raasay met his death about 1650 at the early age of 21. He was a man of fine appearance and great strength. He had been to Lewis on a visit to a friend, and when he was returning home to Skye the day was so stormy that his crew were very unwilling to put to sea, being afraid they would lose their lives. Raasay thereupon exclaimed to the boatman in the Gaelic:—"Son of fair Muireil, are you afraid?" and the man at once threw his fears aside, and with the reply—"No, no, Raasay, we shall share the same fate to-day," began to prepare for the voyage. All went well until off Trotternish, the people of which anxiously watched the boat. The wind increased still more, and a heavy shower hid the vessel from their sight. When it cleared off the boat was nowhere to be seen. Mac Leod's untimely fate was deeply mourned, and Patrick *Mòr* Mac Crimmon commemorated the sad event by composing the famous and pathetic pibroch. A celebrated Skye poetess also composed a touching lament, and a sister of Mac Crimmon's composed an elegy, the English of which goes as follows:—

> " Sitting idly I sorrow,
>   Heavy hearted and ailing ;
> I am songless and cheerless,
>   I am weary and wailing.

Since the day of my sorrow
  I am weary with wailing,
Since the loss of the boatie
  Where the hero was sailing.

Since the loss of the boatie,
  Where the hero was sailing ;
Oh, strong was his shoulder,
  Though the sea was prevailing.

Oh, strong was his shoulder,
  Though the sea was prevailing ;
Now he lies in the clachan
  Whom I am bewailing.

Now he lies in the clachan
  Whom I am bewailing,
And a green grassy curtain
  His cold bed is veiling.

And a green grassy curtain
  His cold bed is veiling.
His sword in its scabbard
  The rust is assailing.

His sword in its scabbard
  The rust is assailing ;
His hounds on their leashes
  Their speed unavailing.

His hounds on their leashes
  Their speed unavailing ;
No more shall my hero
  His mountains be scaling.

No more shall my hero
  His mountains be scaling ;
Sitting sadly I sorrow,
  Heavy hearted and ailing."

Tradition says that John Garbh of Raasay was drowned through the machinations of a witch. She bore him a grudge, and while the boat was at sea she sat in her hut rocking a basin of milk in which there was a clam shell to represent the boat. When she sank the clam shell the boat sank, the story being that a crow alighted on the gunwale, and that Mac Leod, in trying to kill it with his sword, cut the boat to the waters' edge. There are several improbable things about this tradition, not the least obvious of which is the impossibility of knowing how the boat sank when no one was left to tell the tale. However, it is a tradition— that much at least is true.

CHAPTER XXIII.

SOME WELL-KNOWN GATHERINGS.

> " Ye voices of Cona, of high swelling power,
> Ye bards who can sing of her olden time,
> On whose spirits arise the blue panoplied throng
> Of her ancient hosts, who are mighty and strong,
> My bards raise the song."
>
> —*Ossian.*

A Tune with four stories—The Carles wi' the Breeks—The Mac Gregor's Gathering—Scott's verses—*Caber Feidh*—The Camerons' Gathering—Well-matched chiefs—The Loch of the Sword.

THE first tune to be noticed in this chapter is peculiar in this respect, that whereas to many are ascribed two origins, to this there are ascribed three or four. More than one cannot possibly be correct, unless we conclude that different pipers at different tunes in different places and without any co-operation, composed the same tune. That is rather too much, however, but we will give the stories as they are to be found in many books of Highland history and tradition.

In the first place, then, this tune has three names. It is known as

"THE BREADALBANE GATHERING"

(or March), " Wives of this Glen," and *Bodaich nam Briogais* (" The Carles wi' the Breeks "), and each name applies to the air as it is associated with a certain district of Scotland. As " Lord Breadalbane's March " it is noticed in an old hymn-book by *Iain Bàn Caimbeul,* first published in 1786, and afterwards in 1834. This book associated it with Coll Kitto, mentioned in a previous chapter, and gives a long story of raiding and plundering in which this worthy was engaged about 1644. At one stage in the exploits, when his enemies were fleeing, the Baronet of Lochawe ordered his piper to compose a march tune suitable for the occasion, and to keep playing all night. This the piper did, and his tune was *Bodaich nam Briogais.* There is certainly an air of authenticity about the story, and the details bear the stamp of probability if not of truth.

As the " Breadalbane Gathering " it is a Perthshire tune, and well known. The story is that it was played in 1762 at a battle in Caithness, in which the first Earl of Breadalbane was victor, but the air belonged to an earlier period, for *Seumas-an-Tuim,* the reiver referred to in the melody flourished at the beginning of the century :—

> " Ye women of the glen
> Ye women of the glen
> Ye women of the glen
> Ye women of the glen
> Is it not time for you to arise ?
> And *Seumas-an-Tuim* driving away your cattle."

The tune, then, although Breadalbane's raid into Caithness may have given it a new lease of life, under a new name, must have been in existence before that time. The raid itself, for that matter, is somewhat mythical, and the chances are that this is only a bowdlerised version of the next story, which is thoroughly authenticated.

It is as " The Carles with the Breeks " that the tune really hails from Caithness. Sir John Campbell of Glenorchy received in 1672 from George Earl of Caithness an assignment of all his lands and possessions on condition that he would take the name of Sinclair. Glenorchy agreed to this, and on the death of the Earl in 1676 he took the title. His right was, however, disputed by the heir male, George Sinclair of Kiess, and Sir John went to Caithness with a force of Campbells, and defeated the Sinclairs at Altimarlach, a spot on the banks of the Water of Wick, and a short distance from the county town. The Campbells, a Highland clan, of course wore the kilt, and like all true Highlanders—of that age—they despised those who did not. The Sinclairs, never a Highland clan, but only a county family at best, wore the trews, and when Findlay Mac Ivor, Glenorchy's piper, saw them wavering, he poured forth the voluntary :—

" The carles with the breeks, the carles with the breeks,
 The carles with the breeks are flying before us."

And to experts in pipe music the tune does appear to articulate very plainly the sentiments of *Bodaich nam Briogais*. Another set of words, given in the Killin collection of Gaelic song, seems more like a defying challenge to the Sinclairs than a song of victory :—

" Your cattle lifted are, lifted are, lifted are,
 Your cattle lifted are, your men sadly slain are.
 I'm Black John the sharp-eyed one, sharp-eyed one, sharp-eyed
   one,
 I'm Black John the sharp-eyed one, driving them safely.

Carles in trewses clad, trewses clad, trewses clad,
Carles in trewses clad, up and bestir you.
Carles in trewses clad, side dirk and mailed shirt,
Carles in trewses clad, flight we quick gave you.

Glenorchy's bold Mac Intyres, true shots that will not miss,
Bullets sure hitting that fast slay the carles.
There where the river bends, arrows that pierced you quick ;
Many's the house-head that rests without waking.

Carles in trewses clad, etc.

We made that morning start, morning start, morning start,
We made that morning start, when watching failed you.
Wives, mothers, in this glen, in this glen, in this glen,
Wives, mothers, in this glen, it's time you were waking.

Carles in trewses clad, etc."

Glenorchy, however, did not obtain a very firm hold in
the county, and the Sinclairs held the great bulk of the
lands until within the lifetime of the present generation,
when it seems to be drifting into other hands because of the
want of heirs male in the direct line. Neither did the contempt expressed by the piper do much to make the trews
unpopular, for the late Caithness Fencibles, raised and commanded by Sir John Sinclair, were dressed pretty much as
were their ancestors at Altimarlach. Caithness, of course,
was, and still is, not very Highland, except in the matter of
latitude, and it is very noticeable that the only pipe tune
associated with the county was played by a Perthshire piper
on a warlike excursion, fighting against the natives. Caithness has no pipe music of its own.

Again, the tune is known in Argyllshire as " Wives of
this Glen." Tradition says it was played by Breadalbane's
piper just previous to the massacre of Glencoe, in 1692, in

the hope of warning the Mac Ians of their danger, and that one Mac Ian wife heeded the warning and fled to the hills with her child, saving his life. Glencoe is one of the wildest places in the Highlands, gloomy and desolate, ten miles from any other inhabited district, and through it the Cona, a wild, rugged stream, on the banks of which Ossian is believed to have first seen the light, tumbles its way to the sea. Towards the north-west end the terrible tragedy, which left an ineradicable stain on Scottish history, took place, and there the piper is supposed to have stood when he played :—

> " Wives of wild Cona glen, Cona glen, Cona glen,
>> Wives of wild Cona glen, wake from your slumbers,
> Early I woke this morn, early I woke this morn,
>> Woke to alarm you with music's wild numbers.
> Slain is the cattle boy, cattle boy, cattle boy,
>> Slain is the cow-boy while you soundly slumbered ;
> Lifted your cattle are, lifted your cattle are,
>> Slain are your herdsmen, by foemen outnumbered.
> *Iain du Beeroch du, Beeroch du, Beeroch du,*
>> *Iain du Beeroch du* is off with the plunder.
> Wives of wild Cona glen, Cona glen, Cona glen,
>> Wives of wild Cona glen, wake from your slumbers. "

Iain du Beeroch du was a noted Highland cattle-lifter, and corresponds to *Seumas-an-Tuim*, of the Perthshire origin of the tune. Probably they were one and the same person under different names. The only theory on which the three stories can be reconciled is that the tune originally belonged to Perthshire, but was taken to Caithness and to Argyllshire by different pipers, accepted in each place as new, and given a new name. In those days, when communication between districts of Scotland which had nothing in common was very restricted, the tune could exist in one

county as new for many years without the people knowing
that it was familiar to those of another. And naturally
they contined to associate with it the circumstances in
which they themselves first heard it. It was this tune, by
the way, that on the morning of Quatre Bras, was played
through the streets of Brussels to wake the slumbering
Highlanders.

"THE MAC GREGORS' GATHERING."

Although the Clan Mac Gregor was one of the most
famous in Highland history, there is not very much even of
reliable tradition concerning the music of the clan. There
is—or, at least, was—enough of tradition; but as it does
not seem to have been committed to paper, it is now probably lost. Of the origin of "The Mac Gregors' Gathering" we know nothing beyond the fact that it was included
in Captain Mac Leod of Gesto's manuscript book of
pibrochs as having been taken down in pipers' language,
that "syllabic jargon of illiterate pipers" referred to at
length in a former article, from the performers, most likely
from the Mac Crimmons. From the Gesto book it was
translated in 1815 into ordinary notation by Alexander
Campbell, editor of *Albyn's Anthology*, and this gave it a
place in published pipe music. The notation of Captain
Mac Leod, says Mr. Campbell, he found, to his astonishment, to coincide exactly with regular notation, so it cannot have been such jargon after all. Scott thoroughly
caught the spirit of his tune in the song :—

> " The moon's on the lake, and the mist's on the brae,
> And the Clan has a name that is nameless by day !
>   Then gather, gather, gather, Gregalich !
>   Gather, gather, gather, etc.

Our signal for fight, that from monarchs we drew,
Must be heard but by night in our vengeful haloo !
  Then haloo, Gregalich ! haloo, Gregalich !
  Haloo, haloo, haloo, Gregalich, etc.

Glen Orchy's proud mountains, Caolchuirn and her towers,
Glen Strae and Glen Lyon no longer are ours ;
  We're landless, landless, landless, Gregalich !
  Landless, landless, landless, etc.

But doom'd and devoted by vassal and lord,
Mac Gregor has still both his heart and his sword !
  Then courage, courage, courage, Gregalich ;
  Courage, courage, courage, etc.

If they rob us of name and pursue us with beagles,
Give their roofs to the flame and their flesh to the eagles !
  Then vengeance, vengeance, vengeance, Gregalich !
  Vengeance, vengeance, vengeance, etc.

While there's leaves in the forest, and foam on the river,
Mac Gregor, despite them, shall flourish for ever !
  Come then, Gregalich ; come then, Gregalich ;
  Come then, come then, come then, etc.

Through the depths of Loch Katrine the steed shall career,
O'er the peaks of Ben Lomond the galley shall steer,
And the rocks of Craig Royston like icicles melt,
Ere our wrongs be forgot or our vengeance unfelt.

  Then gather, gather, gather, Gregalich !
  Gather, gather, gather, etc."

" CABER FEIDH."

One of the most stirring of pipe tunes is *Caber Feidh*,
composed by Norman Mac Leod, a native of Assynt,
Sutherlandshire. The Earl of Sutherland gave a commission to William Munroe, of Achany, who, with a large body

of retainers, descended on Assynt and carried off much
plunder. His excursion was in the latter end of summer,
when the cattle were grazing in distant pastures, and Achany
plundered the sheilings and stole a considerable amount of
butter and cheese. Indignant at this, Mac Leod composed
the tune and song which became the clan song of the Mac
Kenzies. He made it the vehicle of invective and bitter
sarcasm against the Sutherlands and Munroes. The
" victims " were very sore about the production, and
Munroe threatened the bard's life if they should meet.
They were personally unacquainted, but they did meet in
Ardgay Inn. Mac Leod was enjoying bread and butter and
cheese and ale, and he knew Munroe by the colour of his
bonnet, which was always grey, though Munroe did not
know him. Mac Leod drank to Munroe with great
promptitude, and then offered him the horn, remarking in
Gaelic :—

> " Bread and butter and cheese to me
> Ere death my mouth shall close,
> And, traveller, there's drink for thee
> To please the black Munroes."

Achany was pleased, drank the ale, and when he had
discovered who the courteous stranger was he forgave him
Caber Feidh, and ever after they were good friends. Years
later the poet's young son, Angus, then a licentiate, waited
on Achany relative to the filling up of a vacany in Rogart
Parish Church. " And so you really think," said Munroe,
" I would use my influence to get a living for your father's
son. *Caber Feidh's* not forgotten yet." " No, and never
will," replied Mac Leod, " but if I get the parish of Rogart
I promise you it will never be sung or recommended from
the pulpit there." " Thank you," said Achany, " that is

one important point gained. You are not so bad as your father after all, and we must try and get the place for you." And he gave young Mac Leod a letter to Dunrobin which got him the living.

"THE CAMERONS' GATHERING."

There is a good story associated with "The Camerons' Gathering:"—In the seventeenth century a dispute arose between Sir Ewen Cameron of Lochiel and the Earl of Atholl about their respective rights to grazing on lands on the borders of Rannoch. The two chiefs met at Perth, and it was agreed that the dispute should be settled amicably at a meeting on the ground in question. On the appointed day Lochiel started early, accompanied by a single hench-man and his piper, Donald Breac of Muirshiorlaich. On the way, however, he met an old woman—Gorm'uil Mhor of Moy—who warned him emphatically not to proceed further without more attendants:—" Go back, Ewen of Lochiel, go back! Take along with thee three score and five of the best men of thy name and clan. If their aid is required it is well to have them to appeal to, if not, so much the better. It is Gorm'uil of Moy that advises it; it is Gorm'uil of Moy, if needs be, that commands it." Lochiel went back and chose three score and five picked clansmen whom he took with him. Before meeting Atholl he con-cealed his men in a hollow within a few hundred yards of the trysting-place, and arranged with them that until they saw him turn his cloak, which was dark grey on one side and bright red on the other, they were to lie still. Whenever he turned his cloak it was a sign to them that Atholl was treacherous, and they were to come to their chief's assistance.

At noon the chiefs met, and after discussion they found that neither was disposed to yield his claims. The Earl at last threatened Lochiel, and at a signal fifty Atholl men sprang from a copse near by and awaited orders.

"Who are these, my lord?" demanded Lochiel.

"These," replied the Earl of Atholl, with a smile, "are only a few of the Atholl hoggets come across the hills with me to eat and grow fat on their own grazings."

Lochiel in the meantime had turned his cloak scarlet side out, and at the signal his three-score-and-five men rushed into view.

"And who are these, Lochiel?" said Atholl, rather taken aback.

"These, my lord," said Cameron, "are a few of my Lochaber hounds, sharp-toothed and hungry, and oh! so keen to taste the flesh of your Atholl hoggets."

The Camerons were nearer than the Atholl men, and could have made the Earl a prisoner before his own men could prevent them. So he gave in as gracefully as possible, and, drawing his sword and kissing it, he renounced there and then all claim to the grazings; and, in proof of his faith in Lochiel, he tossed the sword into the loch near by. The loch since then has been called the "Loch of the Sword."

Lochiel's piper meanwhile had been deeply interested in the scene, and the idea of the Lochaber dogs tearing the Atholl sheep inspired him to a new melody. Accordingly, he struck up and played for the first time *Cruinneachadh nan Camaronach*, "The Camerons' Gathering."

> "Ye sons of dogs, of dogs the breed,
> Come quick, come here, on flesh to feed."

The tune is considered one of the best pieces of pipe music extant ; and, in corroboration of the story, it is said that in 1826 a herd-boy fished out of the loch, then almost empty, a basket-hilted sword, but the men of Lochaber coming to hear of it, asked that it should again be deposited in its place, as it was a token and pledge of a very solemn transaction. So with due formality the sword was again thrown into the loch, the bard of the party repeating a Gaelic rhyme, which has been translated :—

> " The sword we've cast into the lake ;
>   Bear witness all the knolls around,
> Ours to the furthest stretch of time
>   Are hill and stream and pasture ground."

This story, on almost similar lines, is told of two other Highland chiefs, but in that case there is no pipe tune connected with it, and it is as the origin of " The Camerons' Gathering " that it is most generally accepted.

CHAPTER XXIV.

MORE STORIES AND A MORAL.

" Pipe of the simple peasant—still
    Through Caledonia's proud domains,
Thou cheer'st the rustic cottage hearth
    With thy enlivening strains.

" And in the far, far distant west,
    Where deep and pathless forests lower,
Thou sooth'st the drooping exile's breast
    Through many a lonely hour."

                    —*J. T. Calder.*

The Clan Stewart March—Mac Gregor of Ruaro—The Braes of the Mist—Episode at a Dunvegan competition—A Mac Crimmon surpassed—Mac Pherson's Lament—Burns and the story—Rob Roy's lament—The Mac Lachlans' March—*Gille Calum*—The Reel o' Tulloch—The Periwig Reel—Jenny Dang the Weaver —Mac Donald's salute—Mac Leod's Salute—Disappearing lore —Something to be done.

THE Royal House of Stuart should perhaps have been mentioned earlier, but, like other names famous in history, they did not leave much to posterity in the way of music or poetry. Enough has been composed and written about them, but that is another matter.

"THE MARCH OF CLAN STEWART"

is known in Perthshire as the "Sherramuir March," because it was played at that battle by the pipers of the clan.

According to tradition this tune was played both when the clan were marching to battle and in honour of a victory. It was played at Pinkie, Inverlochy, Sheriffmuir, and Prestonpans, and it was all along recognised as a tune peculiarly pertaining to the Stewarts. In accordance with Highland custom, the clansmen were in the habit of marching in the intervals of pipe music to improvised singing, and when or how the present words emerged from all previous improvisations and became a song it is impossible to say. At the battle of Pinkie in September, 1547, the clan was commanded by Donald Stewart, of Invernayle, the real chief being an old man. On the march homeward in October, when passing through Menteith, the clan found prepared at the house of one of the tenants a marriage dinner, at which the Earl of Menteith was to be present. Being hungry, Donald and his followers ate up the feast, and when Menteith arrived he was very angry, and instantly pursued the Stewarts. On overtaking them one of his men taunted them thus :—

> " Yellow-haired Stewarts of smartest deeds,
> Who could grab at the kail in your sorest needs,"

to which Stewart replied :—

> " If smartness in deeds is ours by descent,
> Then I draw, and to pierce you this arrow is sent,"

and he shot the man who had taunted his clan. A conflict ensued, in which the Earl and many of his men were killed, and then the Stewarts went off in triumph, their pipers playing the Stewarts' March. The words now in use are the composition of an *Iain Breac Mac Eanric* (Henderson), a celebrated piper of the time of Montrose, and a resident in the Glencoe district. There would probably be older

words, but those here given are those now associated with
the tune :—

"The heath-clad Ben we'll soon ascend,
Through Glen Laoigh we'll soon descend,
Our points of steel we'll swiftly send
    Thro' every loon that bars us.

        We will up and march away,
        We will up and march away,
        We will up and march away,
        Daring let of all men.

"O'er the hills we'll speed along,
Thro' Glencoe the march prolong ;
Our King the burden of our song,
    Asking leave of no man.

        We will up, etc.

"To Glengarry and Lochiel,
Ever with us true and leal,
Keppoch, too, who seeks our weal,
    Is there in spite of all men.

        We will up, etc.

"Mac Phersons come, in deeds not small ;
Mac Kenzies also at our call ;
Whose battle frenzy will appal
    And fill our foes with awe then.

        We will up, etc.

"Mac Gregors fierce when man to man,
Join with the Royal Stuart clan ;
Blow up the pipes, march in the van,
    Daring let of all men.

        We will up, etc."

The chorus is sung before the first verse, as well as after each. " Daring let of all men " means " Defying the hindrance of all men."

One of the most tragic of stories is associated with another Clan Mac Gregor air—

" MAC GREGOR OF RUARO."

The clan, as is well known, were terribly persecuted by the ruling powers. When, after the '45, most of the other Highland chiefs accepted Crown charters for their lands, the Mac Gregors refused, their clansmen backing them vigorously in their attitude. For this independence of theirs they were hunted like wild beasts, pursued by bloodhounds, and executed whenever caught. Even so early as 1603 the clan found themselves so persecuted and hemmed in that their chief, Mac Gregor of Glenstrae, considered it necessary to deliver himself and a score of his principal men to the Government, under promise of being allowed to leave the country. This promise was given, but ruthlessly broken, for they were all hanged at Edinburgh. In the group was Gregor Mac Gregor of Ruaro, the subject of the lament and the song. The author of neither is known :—

> " There is sorrow, deep sorrow,
>   Heavy sorrow down-weighs me ;
> Sorrow deep, dark, and lonesome,
>   Whence nothing can raise me.
>
> Yes, my heart's filled with sorrow,
>   Deep sorrow undying,
> For Mac Gregor of Ruaro,
>   Whose home was Glenlyon.

For the bannered Mac Gregor,
  So bravely who bore him,
With the roar of the war pipe
  Loud thundering before him.

His emblem the pine tree
  On mountain side swinging ;
His trim-tapered arrows
  The true bird was winging."

And so on in very much the same strain for other nine
verses.

There is another tune of the "Children of the Mist," as
the Clan Mac Gregor were known, that deserves mention.
It is a wild and melancholy pibroch, called *Cruachan a'*
Cheathaich, or

"THE BRAES OF THE MIST."

To it is sung a ballad, and connected with the air and song
there is an interesting story. The singer, a Mac Gregor,
concealed in her house her husband and two sons when some
bitter enemies of the clan were approaching. There was no
time for escape, and so she hid her friends in a bed, and,
sitting down by the fire, proceeded to sing :—

" I sit here alone by the plain of the highway,
  For my poor hunted kin, watching mist, watching byeway ;
  I've got no sign that they're near to my dwelling ;
  At Loch Fyne they were last seen—if true be that telling."

And so on, representing herself as waiting in solitude for
her persecuted kindred, and saying that as they had not
returned they must either be at Loch Fyne—as when she
last heard of them—or far away in the glens of the mist,
hunting and fishing, and compelled to pass the night in

some poor hut, where she had previously left some things for them. After a prayer for their safety—

" May the King of the Universe save you for ever
  From the flash of the bullet and the store of the quiver,
  From the keen-pointed knife, with the life-blood oft streaming,
  From the edge of the sharp claymore, terribly gleaming,"

she concluded with expressions of her own sadness on account of their dangers. The enemies stopped outside her cottage and listened to the song, and believing it to be from the singer's heart—as it was, but not in the way they supposed—they passed on without disturbing her, and her husband and sons were saved.

The Gaelic proverb, "The apprentice surpasses his master," or

" THE APPRENTICE SURPASSES THE MAC CRIMMON,"

is associated with two tunes. There was to be a piping competition at Dunvegan at which pipers from all parts of the country were to be present. The leading Mac Crimmon of the day, the head of the college—" Professor " he would now be called—and a nephew of his had " entered,"—if that formality was necessary in these days—and Mac Crimmon had taught his nephew all he himself knew, with the exception of one tune, which he hoped would give ·him the lead in the competition. The two of them, man and boy, on their way to Dunvegan, slept one night at a wayside inn, sharing a bed. When the old man slept he dreamed of the morrow, and in his dreams he seized the boy's arm and fingered on it the notes of the special tune he had reserved for himself. The youth was smart enough to realise that this meant something, and also smart enough to commit the notes to memory as his uncle fingered them on his arm. When the competition began he stepped out first and immediately played his uncle's tune, and carried off the principal honours of the day. Then, the story goes, the people began to speak of *An gille 'toirt bàrr air Mac Crimmon*—the lad that surpasses the Mac Crimmon.

But it is the other version of the story that is connected with the origin of a pipe tune. One of the Mac Crimmons, well known as *Padruig Caogach* or "Winking Peter," owing to his inveterate habit of winking while playing, once endeavoured to compose a new pipe tune. He managed two measures, which in time became very popular, but he could not for the life of him complete it. Two years elapsed, and still *Padruig's* muse had failed to come to his assistance, and the fragment began to be called *Am port leathach*—the half-completed tune. Then a young piper—*Iain Dall* it was—inspired with the music of the tune, set himself to complete it, naming it *Lasan Phadruig Chaogaich,* and renouncing all share in the honours of authorship. But *Padruig* did not like being outstripped in this way by Mac Kay, who was but a beardless boy, and, in his anger, he persuaded the other students at the college to make away with his rival. He succeeded the better in his scheme that Mac Kay had previously given great offence to his classmates by his proficiency, of which they were jealous, and with which the master piper taunted them. So one day as they were all walking together at *Dun Bhorraraig,* they came to a rock twenty-four feet in height, over which they pushed the blind "apprentice." But he alighted on his feet without sustaining much injury, and the spot over which he was thrown was known for a long time after as *Leum an doill*—the leap of the blind. *Iain Dall* ultimately returned to

Gairloch and succeeded his father as family piper to the Mac Kenzies of Gairloch, dying at the age of ninety-eight.

will always be associated with Burns's song and with the noted Highland freebooter who in 1700, after holding the counties of Aberdeen, Banff, and Moray in fear for a long time, was captured, tried before the Sheriff of Banffshire, along with certain gipsies taken in his company, and executed on the Gallow Hill of Banff. But it is not generally known that Burns's words can hardly be called original. As a matter of fact, Mac Pherson himself, tradition says, composed both the pibroch and a set of words wonderfully like those afterwards composed by Burns. The pibroch he composed long before his capture, and the words he gave to the world when he was executed, under the name of " Mac Pherson's Farewell." Here they are :—

> " My father was a gentleman
>   Of fame and lineage high,
> Oh! mother, would you ne'er had born
>   A wretch so doomed as I !
>   But dantonly and wantonly
>   And rantonly I'll gae,
>   I'll play a tune and dance it roun'
>   Below the gallows tree.
>
> The Laird o' Grant, with power aboon
>   The royal majesty,
> He pled fu' well for Peter Brown,
>   But let Mac Pherson die.
>   But dantonly, etc.

But Braco Duff, in rage enough,
  He first laid hands on me ;
If death did not arrest my course,
  Avenged I should be.
    But dantonly, etc.

I've led a life o' meikle strife,
  Sweet peace ne'er smiled on me,
It grieves me sair that I maun gae
  An' nae avenged be.
    But dantonly, etc."

Burns, on his tour through the Highlands, probably learned the air and the tradition of how Mac Pherson, when in prison under sentence of death, wrote the song, sang and played it on the scaffold, and concluded by breaking his violin to pieces because no one would accept it as a present, and promise to play the tune over his body after his execution. Neither the old version nor the words of Burns have much of the ring of a lament about them, but both are in accordance with the notorious character of the man. Burns, by the way, perpetrates a rather curious Irishism in first saying Mac Pherson

"	Played a spring and danc'd it round
  Below the gallows tree ; "

and immediately afterwards making him say—

" Untie these bands from off my hands
  And bring to me my sword."

How a man could play a spring and dance it round while his hands were tied, he does not take the trouble to explain.

" ROB ROY'S LAMENT."

Rob Roy himself, the most celebrated of all the clan who had " a name that was nameless by day," had a lament specially composed by his wife, Helen Mac Gregor, on an occasion when the family were compelled by the law to leave their fastnesses and take refuge in Argyllshire. Helen was a woman of fierce and haughty disposition, and, feeling extreme anguish at being expelled from the banks of Loch Lomond, she gave vent to her feelings in a fine piece of music, still known as " Rob Roy's Lament." "I was once so hard put at," Scott makes Rob say, " by my great enemy, as I may well ca' him, that I was forced e'en to gie way to the tide and remove myself and my people and my family from our native land, and to withdraw for a time into *Mac Cailein Mòr's* country—and Helen made a Lament on our departure, as well as Mac Crimmon himself could hae framed it—and so piteously sad and waesome that our hearts amaist broke as we sat and listened to her—it was like the wailing of one that mourns for the mother that bore him—the tears came down the rough faces of our gillies as they hearkened —and I would not have the same touch of heartbreak again, no, not for all the lands that ever were owned by Mac Gregor."

" THE MAC LACHLANS' MARCH."

A touch of the romantic is found in the story of *Moladh Mairi*, a well-known Mac Lachlan tune. Angus Mac Kay, son of *Iain Dall*, the blind piper of Gairloch, attended a competition in Edinburgh on one occasion, and the other competitors were so jealous of him and afraid of his superior talents that they conspired together to destroy his chances.

They obtained possession of his pipes and pierced the bag in several places. When Mac Kay began to practise on the day of the competition he discovered the injury, and was in despair. But he had a fair friend of the name of Mary who quickly procured for him a sheep's skin, from which, undressed as it was, they between them formed a new bag. With this the piper carried off the first prize, and in gratitude to his helper Mac Kay composed *Moladh Mairi.*. He afterwards married a Mary Fraser of Gairloch, but we have nothing to show that this was the same Mary. In a proper story it certainly would have been.

Another, and a more probable, story is associated with this tune. A daughter of Mac Lachlan of Strathlachlan, chief of the clan, made a present of a wether's skin to the family piper to make a bag for his pipes. He was delighted with the present, and composed the tune in her honour. This story is the more likely, inasmuch as it is well known that pipers always had a high sense of honour, as they still have, and would never think of treating a competitor in the way the first story says Mac Kay was treated.

"GILLE CALUM,"

or "The Sword Dance," is one of the best known of pipe tunes. There is the jocular story to the effect that it made its first appearance in the world after the Deluge, when the Ark had landed on Ararat, and Noah expressed his joy by dancing over two crossed twigs. That the tune, or at anyrate the dance, is an heirloom from the ancients, is highly probable, as the sword dance in a modified form was the special antic of the priests of Mars. The real *Gille Calum,* however, is said to have been *Callum a' chinn mhoir*—Malcolm Canmore, who incurred the displeasure of the Highlanders by removing the ancient Court from Dunstaffnage Castle, in Argyllshire, to Dunfermline, by marrying the Saxon Princess Margaret, which led to the change of Court language from Gaelic to English, and also by having added to the coinage a very small coin, the bodle, equal in value to one-third of our halfpenny, and so small as to be contemptible in the eyes of his Highland subjects. The translation, by " Fionn," of the Gaelic associated with the name shows considerable wit and a pretty strain of sarcasm :—

> " Gillie-Callum, twa pennies,
> Gillie-Callum, twa pennies,
> Twa pennies, twa pennies,
> Gillie Callum, ae bawbee.
>
> I can get a lass for naething,
> I can get a lass for naething,
> Lass for naething, lass for naething,
> My pick and wale for ae bawbee.
> Gillie-Callum, etc.
>
> I can get a wife for tuppence,
> I can get a wife for tuppence,
> Wife for tuppence, wife for tuppence,
> A useless ane for ae bawbee.
> Gillie-Callum, etc."

" THE REEL O' TULLOCH "

has two alleged origins, but one at least is discredited by the known character of the people concerned. It was on a wild Sunday in the parish of Tulloch, Aberdeenshire, that the minister, thinking his people would not venture out, stayed at home. His congregation, however, to whom the kirk was a trysting-place, turned up as usual. For a time they waited patiently enough, but by and bye, moved by

the stormy weather and their minister's absence, they proposed refreshments. The collection ladle was sent round,
and the proceeds invested in "yill" at the neighbouring
changehouse. As the liquor took effect the fun grew more
furious, and at last a dance was suggested. The enthusiasm
rose even to this height, the village cobbler mounted the
pulpit, the blacksmith from the precentor's box roared out
the ditty "John, come kiss me now," and the floor rang with
the flying feet of the dancing congregation. The fiddler,
impressed for the occasion, allowed his bow to get more and
more into the spirit of the gathering; it went madder and
madder as the excitement increased, and at last, in a sudden
burst of inspiration, he improvised the dance tune of all
dance tunes—"Reel o' Tulloch." Tradition is silent as to
what befel the revellers in so sacred a place, as well it may.
It is hardly possible to imagine a company of Scottish
Established Church people looking at a fiddler on the Sabbath, much less dancing in church to his music.

Strathspey also claims the tune, and in competition with
Deeside, it has a fierce tradition on the subject. The district of Tulloch lies at the back of the Abernethy forest,
and here is said to have occurred the incident that inspired
the maddest of Highland reels. A certain John Mac
Gregor, commonly known as *Iain Dubh Gearr*, was at
Killin at a market held somewhere between 1550 and 1580.
In the house of call there, known as "Streethouse," he was
set upon by eight men, but being powerful and a splendid
swordsman, he discomfited all his adversaries, killing some
and wounding others. Then he fled to Strathspey, where
he married a woman named Isabel Anderson (one version of
the story has it that Mac Gregor got into trouble with some
Robertsons through having married this Isabel, who was

sought by a Robertson, and that these and not market acquaintances were his enemies). His foes followed him, and one night thirteen of them arrived at his house, determined to take him dead or alive. John was sleeping in the barn when they came, and when he was wakened and told of his danger he determined to fight it out. Isabel and he had a gun and a pistol and plenty of ammunition, and they defended the barn against all comers. John fired the weapons one after the other alternately through crevices in the walls, and Isabel kept them loaded. The thirteen outside, handicapped as they were by the shelter from which the defenders worked, were very soon all wounded, whereupon John sallied out and cut off their heads. Then Isabel in her glee gave him a big draught of beer, which he drank, and seizing his spouse by the waist they improvised and danced those reel steps which have ever since been so popular. The music must have been old, but the words are of the date of this incident :—

> " At Streethouse at *Feill Fhaolan,*
>   On him they made an onset dead ;
>   And were he not most manly brave,
>   Eight sturdy men had mastered him.
>   From Tullechin to Ballechin,
>   From Ballechin to Tullechin ;
>   If beer we don't in Tullechin,
>   We'll water get in Ballechin."

The song then, at considerable length, tells the story until :—

> " Says Black John, turning towards his bride,
>   ' Since I did what I meant to do,
>   Give me a drink of beer to quaff,
>   And we will dance the Tullechin.'
>   From Tullechin, etc."

The story has two traditional endings. In the one John became a peaceable and prosperous man, and as his name appears in authoritative documents of date 1568, it is the more likely to be true. The other is tragic. Mac Gregor's enemies, according to it, still hunted the couple, and Isabel was thrown into prison. Then Mac Gregor himself was shot, and his head brought to Isabel. At the sight she was so struck with sorrow that she suddenly expired.

It may not be inappropriate to conclude these stories of tunes with two which are associated with ministers.

"THE PERIWIG REEL"

can always be depended on to provoke laughter when well played. It is probably the composition of Mr. Fraser of Culduthal. This gentleman was at a baptismal " entertainment " at the house of Fraser of Knockie, where the presence of a very old and venerable minister could not restrain him from exciting mirth. He sat next but one to the minister, and found means over his neighbour's shoulder to tickle below the parson's large wig with a long feather or a blade of corn. As the glass went round the old man became uneasy, but suspected nobody. At last he got into a rage, dreading an earwig or spider, and shook out his wig over a blazing fire, which unfortunately got hold of it. It was too greasy to admit of its being saved. Amid great laughter, it simmered in the fire till it had almost suffocated the company. The minister's bald head produced more laughter at his expense, in which he himself joined, and he enjoyed the joke thoroughly when it was told to him. The real name of the air is " The Fried Periwig."

The other tune is

"JENNY DANG THE WEAVER,"

and its story is somewhat interesting. Rev. Mr. Gardner, minister of the parish of Birse, in Aberdeenshire, was well known for his musical talents and his wit. One Saturday he was arranging his ideas for next day's service in his study, which overlooked the courtyard of the manse. Outside his wife was beetling potatoes for supper. To unbend his mind a little, Mr. Gardner took up his fiddle and begun to run over the notes of an air he had previously jotted down, when suddenly an altercation arose between Mrs. Gardner and Jock, the minister's man, an idle sort of weaver fellow from the neighbouring village of Marywell, who had lately been engaged as man of all work about the manse. "Here, Jock," cried the mistress as Jock came in from the labours of the field, "gae wipe the minister's shoon." "Na," said Jock, "I'll dae nae sich thing. I came here to be yir ploo'man, but no yir flunkey, and I'll nae wipe the minister's shoon." "Deil confound yir impudence," said the enraged Mrs. Gardner, and she sprang at him with a heavy culinary implement, and giving him a hearty beating, compelled him to perform the menial duties required of him. The minister, who viewed the scene from his window, was hugely diverted, and gave the air he had just completed the title of "Jenny Dang the Weaver." This is supposed to have occurred in 1746. There is a well-known Gaelic song entitled "Trousers for meagre shanks, and bonnets for the bald," sung to the air.

OF OTHER CLAN TUNES

there are not many stories of general interest. The tunes

are there, but whence they came, or when they came, must
ever remain a mystery. " Mac Donald's Salute" and
" Mac Leod's Salute" were composed by Donald *Mòr* Mac
Crimmon on the reconciliation of the Mac Leods and the
Mac Donalds after the battle of Bencuillein in Skye, and
played when the chiefs met at Dunvegan. There had been
a feud between the clans, in the course of which much blood
was spilt. This feud at last became so notorious that in
1601 the Privy Council interfered and requested the chiefs
concerned to disband their forces and leave Skye. It being
known that both intended to " mass togider grit nowmeris
and forceis of thair kin and freindschip," and pursue each
other " with fyre and sword and other hostilitie by say and
land," they were required to release peacefully all prisoners,
and to observe the King's peace. Ultimately a reconciliation was effected, on which the chief of the Mac Leods invited the chief of the Mac Donalds to a banquet at Dunvegan
Castle. When Donald Gorm *Mòr* Mac Donald appeared
in sight of the castle, he was met by Mac Leod's famous
piper, Donald *Mòr* Mac Crimmon, who welcomed him by
playing " Mac Donald's Salute," which he had composed
for the occasion. In connection with the same banquet
he composed and played for the first time " Mac Leod's
Salute."

The stories I have given are, after all, but the merest
pickings from the wealth of lore which has now almost disappeared from the Highlands. It irritates one considerably
to find here and there fragments of what were once fine
tales, with perhaps important bearings on social life or current history, and to realise the impossibility of ever obtaining
them complete. For this we have to thank the Sassenach
over-running of the Highlands, which resulted in the

extinction of clan bard and clan piper—who between them took the place of a literature—and did not even try to introduce in their stead the blessings of that wider education which preserves the life of a nation by better means, until after much of what was worth preserving had vanished into a misty past. We have, for instance, the " Lament for the Harp Tree," connected either with some tree on which the bards were wont to hang their harps, like captives in Babylon of an even earlier age, or with the disappearance of the harp itself, or, as the tune is called *Bean Sith* in the North, with the fairies in some way or other ; *A mhic Iain mhic Sheumais*, which celebrates some battle between the Mac Donalds and the Mac Leods; another on *Blar léine*, or the "Shirt Battle," fought at Kinloch Lochy between the Frasers of Lovat and the Mac Donalds of Clan Ranald, and so called from the parties having stripped to their shirts; " The Sister's Lament for her Brothers "; a lament expressive of the aged warrior's regret that he is no longer able to wield his sword ; " Grim Donald's Sweetheart," a salute of very ancient origin ; *A Ghlas Mheur*, an ancient pibroch composed by *Raonull Mac Ailean Oig*, a Mac Donald of Morar, to which there is supposed to have been a wild story attached ; *Cogadh na Sith*, " war or peace," one of the best known of tunes, and one which, as its composition indicates a determination either to obtain an honourable peace or engage in immediate war, must have had a story ; and any number of others, around which stories of love or adventure or war must at one time have clustered. Tunes of later generations have no stories to speak of. They have been composed on special occasions, or in honour of certain people, but that is all. It is the old tunes we would know more about, and the old stories. Several writers, notably

Mr. J. F. Campbell, of Islay ; Alexander Mac Kenzie, of
Inverness ; Angus Mac Kay, and Hector Mac Lean, of
Ballygrant, Islay, did much good work by gathering at first
hand Highland legends and traditions ; and in our own day
Henry Whyte, (" Fionn "), the *Celtic Monthly*, and others,
are doing a great deal to preserve what is left to us of
Highland life and story.   But there is much yet to do, and
to do quickly, for the generation that knows of these things
is fast passing away.   This volume makes no claim to
originality.   It is only a gathering together of material
that is common to Highland tradition and Highland
literature, but if it shows what an amount of such material,
even on one side phase of Highland life, really exists, it will
have served a good purpose.   In every hamlet in the Highlands there is surely some individual patriotic enough to
take an interest in its folk-lore, and intelligent enough to
see the necessity for saving still more of it, and these people
can do more to preserve it, if only by giving it a place in
the columns of the weekly papers, than any one collector or
writer.   And why should there not be a Highland Publishing Society, which would sell every known book on the
Highlands, take the financial risk of gathering material for
new books, and publishing them, and do the educational
and other work now being attempted by various societies ?
There are already enough of county societies and clan
societies working only for their own county or clan.   Such
distinctions have been broken down by the march of civilisation, and with the intermixing of the clans and the free
movement of the people all over the country, the societies
have little more than the sentiment of the past, a sound
enough reason, no doubt, to justify their existence.   But
there is the Highlands and the language and the music,

the scattered literature and half-Anglicised people, and if
Highlanders with a craze for organising will but think on
these things and build up some organisation that will
become the natural rallying point of everything Highland,
it is not yet too late to let the world see that the Scottish
Highlands has a history and a literature worthy of a far
higher place among the nations of the earth than the earth
has yet given them. As to its music :—

" Long may its lays be heard on Scotia's hills,
　Which call no more her clans in fray to meet,
　And dye with kindred blood their native rills ;
　And, as blythe echoes the shrill notes repeat,
　May Scottish hearts with kindling raptures beat ;
　For valour's throb no more obeys the call,
　Than laughs the eye with mirthful jollity
　When the pipe sounds at village festival.
　Such power, loved pibroch, has thy magic minstrelsy.

　Thee from her hall let heartless fashion spurn,
　For softer warblings of the Italian string ;
　Let luxury or wantoned dalliance burn,
　Yet into hearts that round our Scotia cling,
　With thy dear lays shall patriot raptures spring ;
　And he who can o'er faded glory sigh,
　Who to oppression's children gives the tear,
　Will say, while awful transport lights his eye,
　No generous soul is theirs, unmoved thy strains who hear."

APPENDIX.

It was at first intended that the Appendix to this book should contain a tutor to the bagpipe. It was, however, seen that to do this would not only be departing from the avowed character of the undertaking—the production of a thoroughly untechnical book, and one that would appeal to players and non-players alike—but it would also be encroaching on the preserves of the publishers of pipe music, nearly all of whom preface their volumes with a tutor. Other, and it is hoped, equally interesting matter has been substituted.

Appendix.

I.—THE SCALE OF THE PIPES.

BY JOHN MAC NEILL, LANGHOLM.

In making a few observations on the scale of the bagpipe (*Piob-mhorna h-Alba*) it is not necessary to go deeply into the evolution of instrumental music, but it' may be well to state shortly that the earliest instruments devised for expressing musical sounds, that is sounds having a definite relation to one another, were of two distinct orders, the first probably being the reed or pipe, made of various materials, such as straw, reeds, bone, wood, or metal, blown by the mouth and giving a single note which varied in pitch according to the diameter and length of the tube or pipe through which the wind escaped. The second order was a stringed instrument wherein cords varied in length and thickness were fixed at both ends upon a suitable frame, and the sound was produced by plucking with the finger and allowing the cord to vibrate freely.

The next stage was to make vents or holes in the pipe, arranged so that they could easily be covered by the fingers, and as the sound always escaped by the hole nearest the reed, it was easy to produce a series of sounds by removing one or more fingers in succession. In a somewhat similar way, a series of sounds were obtained from the vibrations of a single cord by pressing, or merely touching, it at certain points, and thus shortening the portion which was allowed to vibrate.

The primary object of all music is to give pleasure through the ear by imitating, or reproducing, more or less

correctly, the sound of the human voice, and other natural
sounds, so we find that as early instruments began to be
improved they were so constructed as to produce various
notes having the same intervals between them as are found
between the tones of the human voice. In this way instruments with a fixed scale were obtained, and we know that
in course of time various nations improved the instruments
they had in use, the ancient Greeks especially bringing the
art of music and their favourite stringed instrument, the
lyre, to a high degree of perfection.

The great defect of all the more ancient instruments was
their limited compass, most of them containing from five to
ten notes only, thus rendering it impossible to play anything
upon them except by the same series of notes and at the
same pitch. This was gradually remedied, both as regards
wind and stringed instruments, by adopting various devices
whereby their compass was extended, and by introducing,
with more or less accuracy, new notes called semi-tones between the original notes. The modern method of tuning
musical instruments by " equal temperament " was unknown
until the time of Johann Sebastian Bach (1685-1750) who,
disregarding the custom which had prevailed until his day,
of writing in a few keys only, and tuning instruments so as
to render these keys nearly perfect at the expense of the
rest, himself tuned the instruments on which he played in
" equal temperament." When he first began to play music
on the harpsicord, tuned in the old way, in other than the
keys in which it was originally composed, the effect was
almost unbearable, and it thus became necessary to alter
the relation of the notes throughout the whole scale by
framing a complete chromatic scale having exactly the
same interval between each semi-tone. In this way every
note was slightly altered from the true natural scale, but
not to such an extent as to seriously offend the ear.

It is obvious that to have a perfect chromatic scale a
separate string or pipe is required for each note in such instruments as the organ and pianoforte, while it is obtained
in those of the flute and oboe class by making additional

holes in the tube at the correct intervals and covering them with close-fitting pads with levers (keys) within convenient reach of the fingers. (Having mentioned the oboe, it may be remarked in passing that its tone has been called " bagpipe music sublimated.") Various attempts have been made to adapt similar appliances to the chanter of the bagpipe, but the results have not been satisfactory, and its scale remains practically the same as it was two centuries ago. It will be shown, however, with the aid of the table of vibrations appended to this article, that it does not differ so widely from the natural or " equal temperament" scales as the critics allege.

The scale of the bagpipe closely resembles what is known as the Greek scale, having a flat seventh, if we take it as running from A to A¹, with a supplementary note G (the lowest on the instrument). While this is true, a reference to the table of vibrations shows that other scales can be rendered with a fair amount of correctness. A great deal has been written on this subject, much of it tending to show that the bagpipe is hardly, if at all, entitled to be considered a musical instrument. One writer starts with the assumption that the first or lowest note is the keynote of its scale, and thereby, very easily, comes to the conclusion that all the rest of the notes are out of tune. As well might it be asserted that the lowest note in any piece of music is the keynote of such piece; and it is obvious that taking the highest note on the bagpipe for the keynote and descending, quite a different result would be arrived at. There are various other writers who seem unable to distinguish between the Great Highland Bagpipe and the Italian and French bagpipes. With these it has hardly anything in common except the name.

It is pretty certain that the pipe chanter was at first used without a bag, and blown directly from the mouth, as a practising chanter still is, and that its key was D, thus giving an equal number of notes above and below. Afterwards two drones were fitted into the bag along with the chanter, probably in unison with one another, and with the

lower A on the chanter, the key of the Greek scale already
referred to. The instrument remained in this form for a
long period. In the seventeenth century probably a third
and longer drone (*dos mor*) was added, tuned an octave
below the others. The drones form a fixed bass, and,
according to the well-established principle in music that the
bass always ends with the keynote, this may furnish very
good ground for saying that the true scale is A, with which,
indeed, a very large proportion of pipe music ends. But
taking the note D on the chanter as the keynote, it is found
that the notes *above* it are nearly in perfect tune, as can be
easily observed by playing any well-known air in that key
that falls within the compass of the *piob mhor*. Of course, it
can be seen at a glance from the table of vibrations annexed
that the scale of D is very nearly the same as that of A with
a flat seventh. The use of this flat seventh descending is so
common in minor scales as to form, after the minor third,
one of their chief characteristics; and it does not greatly
offend even the critical cultivated modern ear, when not an
accented note nor leading directly to the key note. According to the principle mentioned already, that the bass always
ends with the key note, it must be assumed that A is really
the key note of the bagpipe scale, seeing the drones are
tuned to that note; and starting from that point we find
that A, C, E, A¹ are Do, Mi, So, Do¹ of the scale of A.
Taking the higher Do of this scale and descending a fifth,
we find D (Fa), and taking this as the key of a new scale,
we find that D, F, A¹ , A are Do, Mi, So, So₁ of the scale of
D. In the same way, taking the fifth below D—that is, G
—we find that G, B, D, G¹ are Do, Mi, So, Do¹ of the scale
of G. On referring to the table of vibrations it will be
seen that all these notes are very nearly correct in the
scales mentioned, whatever their Sol-Fa names, the only
differences being that B should be a little sharper in the
key of A than in D and G, and that E should be a little
flatter in the key of G than in D and A. For comparison
there is a column inserted in the table giving the vibrations
according to "equal temperament" of the chromatic scale

from G to A¹ . None of the notes of the bagpipe admit of being sharpened or flattened except the upper G, which can be slightly sharpened by opening the F hole along with G and E. The notes D, C, B can be slightly flattened by lifting one finger only, with all those below it closed, but passages requiring this fingering are hardly met with except in pibrochs (*Ceòl mor*). The scale given in the annexed table is, I venture to submit, the true scale of the bagpipe. It is as perfect as can constructed upon an instrument of such limited compass without the aid of valves, and places it much on a level with the other instruments in use up to the time of Bach, already referred to, whereby the approximate correctness of a few keys was obtained by the sacrifice of all the others. It is possible that pipe chanters may not always be bored with perfect accuracy, and that in the case of very old instruments the holes may get enlarged by wear so as to be more or less out of tune, but I think that the true " bearings " are as I have stated.

Is is to be noted that but very few of the airs of our Gaelic songs can be played on the bagpipe, a fact which we think goes far to prove that the instrument was designed and used for martial purposes in the open air. Indeed the *timbre* of the instrument renders it unsuitable for playing in concert with the human voice.

It is, I think, a matter of great satisfaction to all Highlanders and to those who love the race, that so many intelligent and praiseworthy efforts are being made at the present time to preserve and cultivate our national music.

The following is the table of vibrations of musical scales forming the foundations of the scale for the bagpipe :—

Notes on the Staff.	Sol-fa Names with Vibrations in				Equal Temperament.	True Pipe Scale.	
	C	G	D	A		Staff.	Vibrations.
A	1 880	r' 891	so 891	do'891	891		891
G sharp				t 835⁺	841		
G	so 792	do'792	f 792		794		792
F sharp		t 742½	m 742½	l 742½	750		742½
F	f 704				706		
E	m 660	l 660	r 668¼	so668¼	666		668¼
D sharp					627		
D	r 594	s 594	do 594	f 594	592		594
C sharp			t,556⅞	m 556⅞	559		556⅞
C	do 528	f 528			528		
B	t, 495	m 495	l, 495	r 501⁺	499		495
A sharp					471		
A	l, 440	r 445½	so,445½	do445½	445½		445½
G sharp				t,417⁺⁺	420		
G	so,396	do 396	f, 396		397		396

NOTE.—These calculations are made assuming that C in the middle of the staff has 528 vibrations, but of course whatever pitch be taken the relative proportion of the notes remains the same. Fractions, except in the case of one note, are omitted in the scale of equal temperament.

II.—PRACTICAL HINTS.

BY PIPE-MAJOR A. D. CAMPBELL, BONAR BRIDGE.

I.—CARRIAGE OF THE PIPES.

If the player is standing the body should be perfectly upright, head erect, and eyes carelessly fixed on some object as high as himself. Great care should be taken that the shoulder on which the big drone rests is not allowed to rise, or yield in any way to the weight or blowing of the pipes; the head must not incline towards the big drone or droop backwards or forwards; the chest must be kept inflated and the shoulders square.

If the player is marching the shoulders should be allowed to swing to and fro, the motion proceeding from the haunches only and not exceeding what will suffice to give a free and easy step. His bearing should be stately and lofty in accordance with the warlike instrument on which he plays. In playing marching tunes the performer should never stand, if possible, and when marching should beware of taking short stilted steps. He should also practise reels in marching time, and play over irregular ground, in order to gain confidence and command over his instrument.

II.—BLOWING THE PIPES.

In blowing the bagpipe, the cheeks must never be inflated nor the face distressed in any way. There is really no hard work required, only a little careful practice, and everything should be done as easily and freely as possible. The bag does not at all times require to be filled to its full extent, a little more than three-fourths being usually sufficient. The player must not expend all his breath without resting, as by so doing he will not only hurt but disable himself. The arm should be pressed lightly on the bag, but allowed to yield gently to the wind as it comes from the mouth, the pressure being gentle and steady and according to the strength of the reeds. The player will at first find some little difficulty in satisfactorily managing the bag, but when he has succeeded he will be able to play in a free and commanding style, and will have surmounted a difficulty which is a great bugbear to all inexperienced players.

III.—TUNING THE PIPES.

When the pipes are first struck in, the big and outer drones should be stopped by placing a finger over the hole of the bell of each. In doing this or at any time when only one hand holds the chanter, the E note should be sounded. The centre drone being nearest to the ear should, as a rule, be tuned first. Should this drone not be in tune with the chanter reed, a discord between them will ensue, and to get a chord the point of the drone must be moved up or down, as the case may require. By carefully listening to the chanter reed and moving the joint at the same time, the player will easily discover whether the sounds are assimilating or the discord increasing, and be able to suit his action accordingly, until the sounds blend into one. The low A must now be sounded, and the drone tuned to that note. (We may, however, tune to E, high G, or in fact any note, providing the chanter reed is true to all the notes, but in order to prove the reed and tune the pipes at the same time, low A is generally preferred.) Afterwards sound high A to prove whether the chanter reed is properly set, and true from low to high A. If it is, the drone also will be in perfect chord with the latter note. But should this not be the case and the drone cannot be brought to the exact pitch with both notes. The discord, however slight, must be divided between the two notes, and not left wholly on either. If the pipe or the reeds are not defective, this should never occur, and the reeds if properly fitted should tune about the centre of the joint. After the centre drone is properly tuned, the outer should be begun by placing the finger on the air-hole of the bell, or suddenly easing the arm. This drone is not tuned to the chanter reed but to the drone already tuned, in the same manner as that was tuned to the chanter reed. The big drone is tuned to the other two in a similar manner.

After the centre drone has been tuned to the chanter reed, raising the others to the same height in the tuning joint or in line with it, does not always put the drones in tune. The reeds may differ materially in tone, and they must be brought to the same pitch by studying the sounds only. When the pipes are in tune all four reeds will chord. One may be stronger or harsher than another, and still chord with it. It is sometimes difficult for the learner to find the tuning mark, as it is very exact. Care and practice makes it easy.

Young pipers should never play with their instruments out of tune, as this will accustom their ears to discords, and they will eventually be unable to tell when their pipes are in tune and when they are not. Suddenly moving the joints up or down to their full extent will be found capital practice for the beginner, as he cannot then fail to distinguish discords. He should then move them cautiously back as if feeling for something, and he will hear the jarring sounds gradually dying away until they blend in chord. In tuning, care must be taken that the pressure of wind on the reeds is exactly the same as when playing, otherwise discord is inevitable.

Beginners should use reeds in the centre and big drones only, as the pipes will then be easier blown, as well as easier tuned. The practice can be discontinued when the player is able to blow freely. The further down the drones are tuned the sharper the sound becomes, and the further up the flatter or deeper. So if the chanter should have a sharp sound the drone must also be made sharp, or *vice versa.* All new reeds are generally sharp, and become flatter the longer they are played on.

IV.—REEDS AND THEIR DEFECTS.

Reeds have many defects, and nothing but experience combined with care will make a piper thoroughly at home in dealing with them.

A new reed before being put into the chanter should be placed in water for a few minutes. If it has lain past for some time it should be left in the water longer, as the wood may have shrunk or the blades become too open or close. New reeds can never be thoroughly depended on, as they alter more or less with use. They should therefore never be cut or interfered with before being tried. They are also, as a rule, harder to blow than reeds which have been in use for some time; and, if after a fair trial, they are still found to be too strong, they may then be weakened at the discretion of the player. When a reed has a "dirling" sound on the low hand (generally A or G), it is either too weak or too lightly built. In the latter case, it will, combined with the "dirling" sound, have a want of fulness of tone, and cannot be readily improved. Should it be only too weak, it can be easily strengthened by being opened carefully and gradually with a specially made implement of some kind until it has a firm sound. This, of course, has to be done with great care, or the reed may be rendered useless. When a reed is too flat, the staple should be lowered into the chanter until the correct sound is produced. If the staple is as far down as it can be got a hairsbreadth may be cut from the point of the reed and the staple raised or depressed as required. If after this the reed becomes too strong, the blades may be slightly reduced with sandpaper. If the blades are already sufficiently thin, but the point of the staple too open, it can be made considerably closer by inserting a tapered instrument into the staple, and giving the latter a slight tap with a small hammer. In this, care must be taken that the instrument used is shaped as like the inside of the staple as possible. In the event of the reed being too sharp, the staple should be raised in the chanter as high as possible, when should it still prove too sharp, it may be opened in the way already described. This, however, should only be done when the staples or blades are too close, as although the tone is rendered flatter by the process the reed is more or less strained, which is apt to give it a sound insufficiently full, and render the playing laborious without any object being gained.

The player should always bear in mind that the longer reeds are in use the flatter they become. In cases where a reed is not very much out, it can be toned down by frequent playing, rather than by experimenting with it. When it is too strong and not too open in staples or blades it may be partly because it contains too much wood, a matter which can be easily rectified with fine sandpaper. A reed that is too strong owing to its being too open in the blades can be made considerably closer and easier to blow by taking a common cork, making a deep cut in the end of it, and inserting the blades of the reed into the cut, then tying a piece of cord round the cork sufficiently tight to close the blades, and leaving it in that position for a few days. The width of the staple should, however, be tested before this is done, as if it is too open making it closer by the process already explained will make the blades closer also, and save the trouble of using the cork.

It should be noticed that when chanter reeds have certain false notes, such as a sharp high A or a flat high G or E, this is caused by the reeds being improperly fitted, the points of the blades being too thin or the sides of the reed being too thick. Care must therefore be taken, when fitting a reed, that all the different notes are true, after which it should never again be touched except when actually requiring attention.

The beginner may find some difficulty in distinguishing the true sound when the chanter reed is in his mouth. He should therefore put it unto the pipe and sound it, when he will be better able to judge, as he will hear the sound from a greater distance. The chanter reed should always have a clear, distinct, shrill sound, accompanied with a full and firm tone in every note.

V.—DRONE REEDS.

The small drone reeds should sound smooth and firm, with a clear humming sound, and the big drone reed deep and bass, and strong enough to bear the pressure of wind required for the chanter reed. New reeds are often hard to " strike in," and have a rough or sharp tone. This is owing to their newness and dryness, and goes away with playing. They are also frequently inclined to close or stop. This is caused by the steam of the breath swelling the wood, and causing it to fall into its natural set. In this case, the tongue of the reed should be raised as high as it will admit of without straining, and the centre pressed down. Should it after this become too rough or flat, it can be rectified by bringing the tuning string a little towards the point of the tongue. Should this make it too weak for the strength of the chanter reed, the best plan is to raise the tongue and put a hair (out of the head) between the tongue and body of the reed, and as far back as the tuning string will permit.

When a drone tunes too far up, that is when the tuning mark is higher than the joint can be raised, it will be too sharp to admit of its chording with the chanter reed. In that case the reed should be lowered—*i.e.*, given a smaller catch in the joint or drone. Should it still prove too sharp, the tuning string should be moved backwards towards the end placed in the joint. This ought to correct any ordinary reed. Should it fail, the reed must be too short and cannot be amended except by altering the chanter reed, which should never be done for such a purpose, the chanter reed being always first set and the others set to it.

When the tuning mark is too far down for the joint, and the tone cannot be rendered sufficiently sharp, the required sound will in most cases be produced by moving the tuning string towards the point of the tongue. Should this fail, the reed may be put further into the joint of the drone, or a very little cut off the end which goes into the joint.

When reeds have a rough, roaring sound they may be rectified by bringing the tuning string nearer the point of the tongue, as before described.   A reed may have a burring, squealing, or double tone when blown up to the full pitch of the chanter reed.   This may be caused by the tuning string being too tight, or it may be caused by the tongue being too heavy, in which case the proper note may be obtained by cutting one or more notches across the tongue. This will weaken the false sound, and with regular playing it will disappear.

It must be remembered that over-blowing a reed will cause it to " dirl," and half covering any of the holes will cause the reeds to squeal.   In blowing, also, if the regular strength of wind is withheld from the reeds, even for an instant, they will stop, or " hiccough," as pipers term it. The results of these mistakes must not be attributed to the reeds.

An old reed may be made to wear much longer by putting one or more hairs under the tongue where the tuning string is placed and using a new tuning string.

A reed is said to be " water-locked " when it has become soft through continuous use.   Drone reeds only are liable to become water-locked, and should never be over-played. When the mischief is done they must be laid aside until properly dry.

Wet reeds should be taken out before the pipes are laid past, and the water blown out of them.   They should then be rolled between the hand and knee and the tongue slightly lifted, after which they should be replaced in the joints.   Reeds should not be exposed to the air to dry.   A common bottle makes an excellent receptacle for them.

Young pipers should on no account tamper or experiment with their reeds, unless they are perfectly certain of what they are to do, why they are to do it, and what the result will be.

VI.—THE BAG, AND HOW TO KEEP IT.

For making the bag tight a paste composed of resin, beeswax and sweet oil boiled together is here recommended. This, when cool, should be slightly thicker than cream.

After the stocks have been inserted a few spoonfuls of this paste should be put in (lukewarm), then the stocks stopped up and a little wind left in the bag to prevent its sides sticking. The skin should be rubbed and wrought until it becomes impregnated with the paste.

When pipes are much used, and the bag draws a good deal of water, the reeds will always be damp. To remedy this, a little salt may be put into the bag, which will cause the damp to be discharged through the skin. This, however, might make an old bag give way altogether. Water should never on any account be put into the bag.

The bag should always be soft and pliable. This can be managed in several ways. After being dried, say half a teacupful of melted brown sugar may be passed into it, and worked with the hands, the skin being then hung up overnight for the surplus sugar to run out.

VII.—KEEPING THE PIPES IN ORDER.

Pipes as a rule should be cleaned thoroughly at least once a month, and if much played on once a week. Cocoa-nut oil will be found to serve the purpose best. When the pipes are to be cleaned the reeds should first be removed, and either placed in a bottle or rolled in a damp rag. The different joints should then be detached and the pieces cleaned outside and inside with an oily rag, a long feather saturated with oil being passed through the joints. If not required immediately, and after the reeds have been reinserted, the instrument should then be laid past in its oily state for a few hours. Before being used, the reeds should be again abstracted and all the parts carefully cleaned. Care must be taken that the warping on the joints is never allowed to get ragged or soaked with water, as this will cause the joints to crack, or swell the hemp, and render them difficult to move. The player cannot be too particular in satisfying himself that none of the joints are too tight. New pipes, especially in hot weather or warm climates, should before being used be laid up for a few days in cocoa-nut oil and exposed daily to the sun ; care, however, being taken that they are not allowed to dry and that they are frequently turned and well wetted with oil. This will season the wood, and lessen the danger of splitting.

The young piper must not forget that it is the practice chanter that makes the piper, and he should never attempt to play a tune on the full set until he can play it thoroughly on the chanter. Quick and careless playing should always be avoided. Also, the player should endeavour to get into the spirit of the music by understanding the circumstances under which each particular tune was composed and the feelings it is meant to express. No man other than a Highlander can fully appreciate the *piobaireachd* or do justice to the wild, though majestic, strains. The histories of the various tunes, with the words to which they are set, would be invaluable to the player, and it is to be hoped that the present volume will do something towards emphasising all the grand old associations that cling round the Highland Bagpipe, and thus enable the public to appreciate it all the more and pipers to play it all the better.

III.—BIBLIOGRAPHY OF PIPE MUSIC.

THE list of books of pipe music is not very long, but the difficulties of making it complete and accurate are more than may at first appear. The principal difficulty is in the matter of dates, publishers, no doubt for good reasons, nearly always refraining from giving on their title page the year in which the book was first issued. Some of the older books, too, are now very rare, and there are not many people who have anything like a complete set. The following list has been compiled with every possible care :—

1784—MAC DONALD—A collection of Highland Vocal Airs with a number of Country Dances or Reels of the North Highlands, a few Bagpipe Strathspeys and Reels set for the Violin, and also four Pibrochs, viz. :—Mac Intosh's Lament, Mac Crimmon's Lament, The Finger Lock, and Peace or War. Compiled and published by Rev. Patrick Mac Donald, minister of Kilmore, Argyllshire. Out of print.

1803—MAC DONALD—A Treatise on the Theory, Principles and Practice of the Great Highland Bagpipe, to which is added one pibroch for a beginner ; prepared by Joseph Mac Donald, Sutherlandshire, and published by his brother, Rev. Patrick Mac Donald, Kilmore. Out of print.

1818—" AMATEUR "—A Preceptor for the Great Highland Bagpipe, with a few favourite simple airs ; written and edited by " An Amateur," and published by Oliver & Boyd, Edinburgh. Price 3s. Out of print.

1822—MAC DONALD—A collection of the Ancient Martial Music of Caledonia, called *Piobaireachd*, consisting of 23 pieces, as performed on the Great Highland Bagpipe. Now also adapted to the pianoforte, violin and violincello ; with a few old Highland lilts purposely set for the above modern instruments ; to which is prefixed a complete tutor for attaining a thorough knowledge of pipe music. Respectfully dedicated to the Highland Societies of London and Scotland by Donald Mac Donald, and published by Alex. Robertson & Co., Edinburgh. Republished in 1855 by Messrs. J. & R. Glen. Price £1 1s.

1828—MAC LEOD—*Canntaireachd*, a collection of twenty *Piobaireachd* or pipe tunes, as verbally taught by the Mac Crimmon pipers in the Isle of Skye to their apprentices ; published as taken from John Mac Crimmon, piper to the old Laird of Mac Leod and his grandson, the late John Mac Leod of Mac Leod. Edited by Captain Neil Mac Leod of Gesto. Reprinted in 1880 by Messrs. J. & R. Glen, Edinburgh.

1829—Mac Donald—A collection of Quicksteps, Strathspeys, Reels and Jigs, consisting of 120 tunes, arranged for the Highland Bagpipe. Edited and published by Donald Mac Donald & Son, pipe makers, Edinburgh. Republished by Messrs. J. & R. Glen in 1848 and frequently afterwards. Now in fifth edition. Price 2s.

1838—Mac Kay—A collection of Ancient *Piobaireachd* or Highland Pipe Music, consisting of sixty-one tunes, many of them adapted to the pianoforte, with instructions for learners of pipe music, sketches of the principal hereditary pipers, and historical and traditional notes respecting the origin of the various pieces. Edited and published by Angus Mac Kay, piper to the Queen. Second Edition published in 1839, also by Mac Kay. Price, £1 15s. Reprinted in 1899 by Logan & Co., Inverness. Price, £1 1s.

1841—Mac Kay—The Complete Tutor for the Great Highland Bagpipe, with a compendious selection of Marches, Quicksteps, Strathspeys, Reels, and Jigs, consisting of 100 tunes. The whole selected and arranged specially for the instrument by William Mac Kay, piper to the Celtic Society of Scotland. Published by Alexander Glen, Edinburgh. Corrected and improved by Angus Mac Kay in 1843 and republished by Mr. Glen. Price 4s. Out of print.

1843—Mac Kay — The Pipers' Assistant, a collection of Marches, Quicksteps, Strathspeys, Reels, and Jigs, consisting of 155 tunes. Edited by Angus Mac Kay, piper to the Queen. Edinburgh, published by Alexander Glen, bagpipe maker, 30 West Regent Street. London, by Angus Mac Kay. Price 8s. Out of print.

1847—Gunn—The Caledonian Repository of Strathspeys, Reels, Jigs, and Quicksteps, consisting of about 200 pieces. Edited and published by William Gunn, piper, Glasgow. Enlarged by about a dozen tunes in 1867, and republished by Gunn. Republished in 1892 and 1889 by Peter Henderson, Glasgow. Price 6s.

1853—Mac Lachlan—The Pipers' Assistant, containing 120 tunes. Compiled by John Mac Lachlan, piper to

Neil Malcolm of Poltalloch, and published by Alex. Glen, Edinburgh. Price 6s. Out of print.

1860—GLEN—The Caledonian Repository of Music for the Great Highland Bagpipe, consisting of Marches, Strathspeys, Reels and Quicksteps to the number of 120 tunes. Edited and published by Alexander Glen, Edinburgh. Revised and republished by David Glen in 1882. Price, 6s. Out of print.

1869—ROSS—A collection of Marches, Strathspeys, Reels, and Pibrochs, consisting of 243 pieces. Edited and published by William Ross, piper to the Queen. Several editions since published, and book now contains 41 pibrochs and 437 marches, etc. Republished in 1900 by Mrs. Ross. Price, £1 10s.

1870-1871—GLEN—Parts I., II., and III. of Glen's collection for the Great Highland Bagpipe, consisting of about 160 tunes. Edited and published by J. & R. Glen, Edinburgh. Price, originally 3s. each part, now 1s.

1876-1901—GLEN—Parts I. to XVII. of a collection of Bagpipe Music, consisting altogether of about 1000 pieces. Edited and published by David Glen. Edinburgh, at different times between 1876 and 1901. Price, each part, 1s ; complete volume, with tutor, £1.

1876—MAC PHEE—A selection of Music for the Highland Bagpipe, consisting of about 150 Quicksteps, Marches, Strathspeys. Reels, etc., with a complete tutor. Edited and published by Donald Mac Phee, Glasgow. Price, 6s., in cloth 7s. Republished in 1895 by Messrs. Logan & Co., Inverness, in two volumes, at 2s. each.

1880—MAC PHEE—A collection of Pibrochs, consisting of 37 tunes. Edited and published by Donald Mac Phee, bagpipe maker, Glasgow. Republished in 1885 by Messrs. Logan & Company, Inverness. Price, 8s.

1880-1899—GLEN—Parts I. to IV. of a collection of Ancient *Piobaireachd* or Highland Pipe Music, consisting altogether of 55 tunes ; arranged, revised, and published by David Glen, Edinburgh, at different times between 1880 and 1899. Price 4s. each part.

1881—GLEN—David Glen's Highland Bagpipe Tutor, with a selection of Quicksteps, Strathspeys, Reels, and Jigs, amounting to 50 tunes. David Glen, Edinburgh. Price, 3s. Now in 13th thousand, price, 1s.

1887—MAC KINNON—A collection of Highland Pipe Music, consisting of Marches, Strathspeys, and Reels to the number of 82 tunes, with a complete Tutor. Edited and published by Robert Mac Kinnon, bagpipe maker, Glasgow. Republished by Mr. Mac Kinnon in 1898. Price 4s.

1888 — HENDERSON — Henderson's Bagpipe Collection of Marches, Strathspeys, and Reels, extending to 138 tunes. Edited and published by Peter Henderson, bagpipe maker, Glasgow. Price 5s.

1891—HENDERSON—Henderson's Bagpipe Tutor and Collection of Marches, Strathspeys, and Reels, to the extent of 56 pieces. Price 2s.

1899—BETT—A Collection of Pibrochs, Marches, Strathspeys, and Reels, consisting of 198 tunes. Edited and published by James Bett, Strathtay. Price, £1 1s.

1899—LOGAN—A collection of Marches, Quicksteps, Laments, Strathspeys, Reels, and Country Jigs, consisting of sixty pieces. Logan & Co., Inverness. Price 1s.

1900—GLEN—The Music of the Clan Mac Lean, consisting of 25 pieces, compiled under the auspices of the Clan Mac Lean Society of Glasgow. Edited and published by David Glen, Edinburgh. Price, in paper, 5s., in cloth gilt, 7s. 6d.

1900—HENDERSON—Henderson's Tutor for the Bagpipe and collection of Marches, Strathspeys, Reels, Country Dances, Jigs, etc., consisting of 197 pieces. Peter Henderson, Glasgow. Price 7s. 6d.

1900—THOMASON—A collection of *Piobaireachd* as played on the Great Highland Bagpipe—*Ceol Mòr*—compiled, edited, and rendered in a new and easily acquired notation by Major-General C. S. Thomason, R.E. (Bengal). Published by C. S. Thomason, c/o S. Sidders & Co., 17 and 19 Ball Street, Kensington, London, W.

IV.—GOLD MEDALISTS OF THE HIGHLAND SOCIETY OF LONDON.

In 1781, the Highland Society of London instituted competitions in pibroch playing. It was not, however, until 1835 that the gold medal now so well known as the highest honour attainable by pipers, was first awarded. The following is a list of the first prize winners and gold medalists so far as it has been found possible to obtain them. Unfortunately for the absolute authenticity of the list, the records of the Highland Society were lost in a fire sometime ago, and the secretary, therefore, could not supply them officially. It has, however, been carefully compiled from Angus Mac Kay's book of pipe music, the files of the *Glasgow Herald* and those of the *Inverness Courier*, and it may be relied on as thoroughly accurate :—

1781—Patrick Mac Gregor, Ardradour, Perthshire.
1782—John Mac Allister, West Fencible Regiment.
1783—Neil Mac Lean, Airds.
1784—John Mac Gregor, senr., Fortingall.
1785—Donald Mac Intyre, senr., Rannoch.
1786—Roderick Mac Kay, North Berwick.
1787—Archibald Mac Gregor, Glenlyon.
1788—John Mac Gregor, Strathtay.
1789—Duncan Mac Nab, Lorne.
1790—Robert Mac Intyre.
1791—Donald Mac Rae, Applecross.
1792—John Mac Kay, Raasay.
1793—John Mac Gregor, Breadalbane Fencibles.
1794—Angus Cameron.
1795—Peter Mac Gregor.
1796—Donald Fisher, Breadalbane.
1797—Alexander Mac Gregor, Glenlyon.
1798—Donald Mac Earchar.
1799—Dugald Mac Intyre.
1800—George Graham.
1801—William Forbes.

1802—John Buchanan, 42nd Highlanders.
1803—Donald Robertson, Edinburgh Volunteers.
1804—Malcolm Mac Gregor.
1805—Duncan Mac Master, Coll.
1806—John Mac Gregor, London.
1807—Donald Mac Nab.
1808—John Mac Gregor, 73rd Regiment.
1809—Peter Forbes, Foss.
1810—Allan Mac Lean, Mull.
1811—John Mac Gregor.
1812—Donald Mac Gregor.
1813—Finlay Mac Leod.
1814—Robert Mac Kay. Sutherlandshire.
1815—John Mac Kay, Sutherlandshire.
1816—Donald Mac Kay, Glasgow.
1817—Donald Mac Donald, Argyllshire.
1818—Allan Mac Donald.
1819—John Campbell.
1820—William Mac Kay, piper to Celtic Society.
1821—Adam Graham.
1822—Donald Mac Kay.
1823—John Mac Kenzie.
1824—Donald Scrimgeour.
1825—Donald Stewart.
1826—John Gordon.
1829 (First triennal competition)—John Mac Nab, 92nd
    Highlanders.
1832—Roderick Mac Kay, Abercairney.
1835 (First competition for gold medal)—John Mac Kenzie,
    piper to the Marquis of Breadalbane.*
1838—John Mac Beth, piper to Highland Society of London.
1841—Donald Mac Innes, late piper to Colonel Mac Neill of
    Barra.
1844—Donald Cameron, piper to Sir James J. R. Mac
    Kenzie of Scatwell.

---

* In Chapter XIX., page 278, the date 1838 is given by mistake instead of 1835, as the year of this competition. Also, on page 284, it is stated that John Bane Mac Kenzie and Donald Cameron were the only players who held the title of "King of Pipers." That there were at least two others is, however, shown by this list.

There is a blank between 1844 and 1859 which it has not been found possible to bridge. In 1844 we leave the competitions being held triennally at Edinburgh; in 1859 we find the Gold Medal being competed for at the Northern Meeting, Inverness, as "a new feature." Several other competitions are reported during these fifteen years, and well-known names are given as prize-winners, but there is no mention of the Highland Society's Gold Medal. It would be interesting to know if the competition was discontinued during these years.

1859 (First competition under auspices of Northern Meeting, Inverness)—Donald Cameron, piper to Seaforth.
1860—Alex. Mac Lennan, pipe-major, Inverness Militia.
1861—D. Mac Kenzie, 25th Borderers, Shorncliffe.
1862—Alex. Cameron, Greenock Rifle Volunteers.
1863—Ronald Mac Kenzie, 78th Highlanders.
1864—Alex. Mac Donald. piper to Mac Pherson of Glentruin
1865—Colin Cameron, piper to Mr. Malcolm of Glenmarog.
1866—Wm. Mac Kinnon, 74th Highlanders, Limerick.
1867—John Mac Lennan, piper to the Earl of Fife   Donald Cameron, piper to Mr. K. W. S. Mac Kenzie, of Seaforth, was this year "Champion of Champions."
1868—Andrew Gordon, piper to the Earl of Seafield, Balmacaan. Glen-Urquhart.
1869—Wm. Mac Donald, piper to the Prince of Wales.
1870—Alex. Cameron, piper to the Marquis of Huntly.
1871—Malcolm Mac Pherson, piper to Cluny Mac Pherson.
1872—Donald Mac Kay, piper to Sir George Mac Pherson Grant, Bart., of Ballindalloch.
1873—Duncan Mac Dougall, piper to the Earl of Breadalbane. Champion of Champions, Ronald Mac Kenzie, 78th Highlanders.
1874—John Smith, 93rd Highlanders, Lochgilphead.
1875—Ronald Mac Kenzie, piper to Neil Mac Donald of Dunach.
1876—John Mac Kenzie, Royal Caledonian Asylum, London. Champion of Champions, Duncan Mac Dougall, piper to the Earl of Breadalbane.
1877—John Mac Bean, piper to Lord Middleton.
1878—Lewis Grant, piper to the Earl of Seafield.

1879—William Mac Lennan, Dundee.
1880—John J. Connan, piper to John H. Dixon, Inveran.
1881—Angus Mac Rae, piper to Mr. E. H. Wood of Raasay.
1882—Angus Mac Donald. South Morar.
1883—A. D. Longair, 2nd A. and S. Highlanders.
1884—John Mac Coll, Oban.
1885—Pipe-Major J. Mac Dougall Gillies, Glasgow.
1886—R. Meldrum, 93rd Sutherland Highlanders.
1887—Alex. Fletcher, Invermoriston.
1888—William Boa, piper to Mr. Dixon of Inveran.
1889—John Mac Kay, 4th A. and S. Highlanders.
1890—John Mac Donald, Glentromie Lodge, Kingussie.
1891—Colin Thomson, 3rd Seaforth Highlanders.
1892—John Cameron, 2nd Cameron Highlanders.
1893—Pipe-Major Matheson, 3rd Highland Light Infantry.
1894—Pipe-Major D. Campbell, Scottish Rifles.
1895—Murdo Mac Kenzie, piper to Mr. A. G. Butter of
    Fascolly.
1896—Alec. Mac Kenzie, Resolis, Invergordon.
1897—Wm. Campbell, second piper to the Queen.
1898—Murdoch Mac Kenzie, Church Street, Inverness.
1899—D. C. Mather, Lochcarron.
1900—W. G. Meldrum, Moy Hall.

The Highland Society of London, have also, since 1875,
presented a gold medal at the Argyllshire Gathering, to be
competed for under the same conditions as that at the
Northern Meeting. The two medals are of about equal
value, and, though neither can be won twice by the same
competitor, one piper may win both. The following are
the prize winners at the Argyllshire Gathering, as kindly
supplied by the secretary, Mr. Alexander Sharp, Oban:—

1875, Sept. 8.—John Mac Bean, Culloden.
1876, ,, 13.—Malcolm Mac Pherson. Cluny.
1877, ,, 12.—John Mac Bean, Culloden.
1878, ,, 11.—William Mac Lennan, Inverness.
1879, ., 10.—George Mac Donald, South Morar.
1880, ,, 15.—Pipe-Major Robert Mac Kinnon, Skipness.
1886, ,,   8.—Pipe-Major Robert Meldrum, Argyll and
    Sutherland Highlanders.

1887, Sept. 14.—Pipe-Major John Mac Kay, 4th Argyll and
Sutherland Highlanders, Paisley.
1888, „ 12.—Kenneth Mac Donald, Braemar.
1889, „ 11.—John Mac Pherson, Cluny.
1890, „ 10.—Norman Mac Pherson, Loch Lomond.
1891, „ 9.—D. C. Mather, Loch Carron.
1892, „ 14.—A. R. Mac Coll, Oban.
1893, „ 13.—Pipe-Major Wm. Robb, 91st Highlanders.
1894, „ 12.—Pipe-Major George Ross, Black Watch.
1895, „ 11.—John Mac Kenzie, Glasgow.
1896, „ 9.—Gavin C. Mac Dougall, Aberfeldy.
1897, „ 8.—John Mac Donald, Kingussie.
1898, „ 14.—Farquhar Mac Rae, Glasgow.
1899, „ 13.—Murdo M'Kenzie, Inverness.
1900, —— No Gathering.

From 1880 till 1886 no Medal was given.

V.—DIRECTORY OF BAGPIPE MAKERS.

The making of bagpipes is almost, if not quite confined
to Scotland. One or two firms in London profess to be
makers, but they either make very little or get the instruments from Scotland. There are no makers abroad, but a
large trade is done by Scottish makers with colonial customers. The following is a list of all the makers of any
professional standing :—

ABERFELDY—
Gavin Mac Dougall.

DUNDEE—
David Thow, 45 and 47 Gellatly Street.

EDINBURGH—
John Centre & Sons, 12 Grove Street.
David Glen, 8 Greenside Place.
J. & R. Glen, North Bank Street.
J. & W. Hutcheon, 3 Niddry Street.

GLASGOW—
Peter Henderson, 100 Renfrew Street.
Robert Mac Kinnon, 59 Renfrew Street.

VI.—THE LARGEST KNOWN LIST OF PIBROCHS.

The following list of pibrochs, which is the index to Major-General Thomason's *Ceol Mor*,* is the most complete that has ever been published. With the exception of three new tunes included in *The Music of the Clan Mac Lean*, and one or two others, it contains all the pibrochs known to present day players, while the particulars as to composers' names and dates of origin are more full than anyone else has attempted :—

ENGLISH.	GAELIC.	AUTHOR AND DATE.
Abercairney's Salute...	*Fàilte Aberchàrnaig*	
Aged Warrior's Lament, The	*Cumha Chlaibh*	
Allan, Lament for Young ...	*Cumha Ailein Oig*	
Altearn, The Battle of ...	*Blàr Allt-Eire*	1645.
Anapool, Lament for Lady ...	*Cumha Ban-tighearna Anapuil* ...	
Antrim, Lament for the Earl of	*Cumha Iarla Antruim*... ...	
Argyll's Salute	*Fàilte Marcus Earraghaidheal*	
Army, The Red Tartaned ...	*An t-arm breac dearg*	
Athole, The Battle of ...	*Blàr Athol*	
Athol Salute, The	*Fàilte Dhiuc Athol*	
Away to your tribe, Ewen, or Lochiel's Salute	*Gu do bhuidheann Eoghainn* ...	
Balladruishaig, The Battle of	*Blàr Bhaile Dhruisheig*	
Battle of the Bridge (or Inch) of Perth, The	*Ceann drochaid Pheairt*	
Battle of Doirneag, The ...	*Blàr nan Dòirneag*	
Battle of Glenshiel, The ...	*Blàr Ghlinn Seile*	J. D. Mac Kay.
Bealach na bròige, The Battle of	*Blàr Bealach na bròige*	
Beinn na Greine	*Beinn na Gréine*	
Bells of Perth, The	*Cluig Pheairt*	
Beloved Scotland, I leave Thee gloomy	*Albainn bheadarach's mise 'gad fhàgail*	
Berisdale Salute, The	*Fàilte Morair Bhurisdail*	A. Mac Lennan.
Bicker, The	*Port a' Mhràdsair*	
Big Spree, The, or You're drunk and had better sleep	*An Daorach mhor (Tha'n daorach ort 's feairrd thu cadal)* ...	
Black Donald of the Isles, March of	*Piobaireachd Dhomhnuill Duibh*	
Black Watch's Salute, The ...	*Fàilte an Fhreiceadain Duibh*..	J. Mac Donald, 1730
Blind Piper's Obstinacy, The	*Crosdachd an Doill*	J. D. Mac Kay.
Blue Ribbon, The (the Grants)	*Riobain Gorm nan Granndach*	
Blue Ribbon, The (Isle of Mull)	*Riobain Gorm an Eilein Mhuilich*	
Boat Tune, The	*Port a' Bhàta*	

* See page 110.

ENGLISH.	GAELIC.	AUTHOR AND DATE.
Boisdale Salute, The	... *Fàilte Fir Bhaosdail*	...
Borlum's Salute, The Laird of	... *Fàilte Thighearna Bhorluim* ...	...
Breadalbane, Lament for Lord	... *Cumha Morair Braidalbainn* ...	...
Brothers' Lament, The ...	... *Cumha nam Bràithrean*	...
Cameron, Donald, Lament for	... *Cumha Dhomhnuill Chamaroin*	. K. Cameron, 1893.
Camerons' Gathering, The ...	... *Cruinneachadh nan Camaronach*	...
Campbell, G., of Calder's Salute	... *Fàilte Sheòrais òig Tighearna Chaladair*	
Campbell of Kintarbet's Salute, Lachlan MacNeill	*Fàilte Mhic Néill Chinn-tairbeart*	...'J. Mac Kay, Snr., 1837.
Carles wi' the Breeks, The ...	... *Bodaich nam Briogaisean*	
Carles of Sligachin, The ...	... *Bodaich Shligeachain*	
Catherine's Lament	... *Cumha Chatriona*	
Catherine's Salute	... *Fàilte Chatriona*	
Castle Menzie or Fraser's Salute	... *Caisteal a' Mheinneirich—Piobaireachd Uaidh, Fàilte Cloinn Shimidh*	
Charich's, Alastair, March ...	... *Spaidsearachd Alastair Charaich*	...
Cheerful Scotland	... *Albainn Bheadarach*	...
Children, The Lament for the	... *Cumha na Cloinne*	... P.M. Mac Crimmon.
Chisholm's Salute	... *Fàilte 'n t-Siosolaich*	...
Chisholm of Strathglass's Salute	... *Fàilte Siosalach Srath-Ghlais* ...	...
Choaig, Patrick, A Satire on	... *Lasan Phadruig Chaoig Mhic Cruimein*	D. M. MacCrimmon.
Ciar, Lament for John ...	... *Cumha Iain Chéir*	
Ciar, Salute for John... ...	... *Fàilte Iain Chéir*	
Clan Chattan, The Gathering of	... *Cruinneachadh Chloinn Chatain*	...
Clan Ranald's Salute... ...	... *Fàilte Chloinn Raonuill* ...	...
Claverhouse, Lament for ...	... *Cumha Chléibheir*	...
Cleaver, General, Lament for (?) Claverhouse	*Cumha Chléibheir*	1689.
Comely Tune, The	... *Ant-Ailteachd*	...
Company's Lament, The ...	... *Cumha na Cuideachd*	...
Contullich, Lament for the Laird of	*Cumha Fir Chontullaich*	1714.
Craigellachie, The Grants' Gathering	*Creag Ealachaidh*	...
Crunluath Tune, The ...	... *Port a' Chrunluaith*	...
Daughter, Lament for the ...	... *Cumha na h-ìghne*	...
Davidson of Tulloch's Salute	... *Fàilte Tighearna Thulaich* ...	...
Dead, Lament for the ...	... *Cumha nam Marbh*	...
Desperate Battle Cuchulin, The	... *Cath fuasach Chuchulinn* ...	...
Donald Gruamach's Lament for his elder Brother	*Spaidsearachd Dhomhnuill Ghruamaich*	D. Gruamach.
Doyle's, Lady, Salute ...	... *Fàilte Bain-Tighearna Dhoile*	.. J. Mac Kay.
Drizzle on the Stone	... *Ceòb air cloich*	.. R. Mac Dougal.
Duke of Perth's March, The	... *Spaidsearachd Dhiùc Pheairt*	... Finlay *Dubh* Mac Rae, 1715.
Duncan Mac Rae of Kintail's Lament	*Cumha Dhonnachaidh Mhic Iain*	...
Duntroon's Salute	... *Fàilte Dhùntròin*	...
Duntroon's Warning	.:. *Caismeachd Dhuntroin* ...	...
Dunyveg, Lament for the Castle of	*Cumha Caisteal Dhun-Naomhaig*	.. 1647.

ENGLISH.	GAELIC.	AUTHOR AND DATE.
Earl of Ross's March, The ...	... *Spaidsearachd Iarla Rois* ...	...D. M. Mac Crimmon, 1600.
Earl of Seaforth's Salute ...	... *Fàilte Uilleam Duibh Mhic Coinnich* ...	Finlay *Dubh* Mac Rae, 1715.
Elchies Salute, or MacNab's Salute,	*Fàilte Elchin, na Fàilte Chloinn an Aba*	
End of the Great Bridge, The ...	*Ceann na Drochaide mòire*	
End of Isheberry Bridge, The ...	*Ceann Drochaid Iseberri*	
End of the Little Bridge ...	*Ceann na Drochaide bige*	1645.
Ewen of the Battles	*Eoghan nan cath*	
Extirpation of the Tinkers, The ...	*Sgrios nan Ceàird*	
Fair Honey	*A mhil bhraonach*	
Fairy Flag, The	*A' bhratach Shìth*	
Fare thee well, Donald ...	*Soiridh leat a Dhòmhnuill* ...	
Finger Lock, The	*A' Ghlas Mheur*	
Finlay's Lament	*Cumha Fhionnlaidh*	
Forbes, Lament for Colonel...	*Cumha Chorneil Forbes*	D. Fraser.
Frenzy of Meeting, The (or Lament for Brian O'Duff)	*Faoin Bhaile na Coinneimh* ...	J. Mac Kay, or Donald Mac Dougal.
Frisky Lover, The	*An Suiriche stogach*	
Fuinachair	*Fiunnachair*	
Glen is mine, The	*'S leam fhein an Gleann*	
Glengarry, Lament for ...	*Cumha Mhic-Alastair*	A. Munro.
Glengarry's March	*Cille Chriosda*	
Gordon's Salute, The... ...	*Fàilte nan Gordonach*	
Gower, Lament for Lord Fred Leveson	*Cumha Morair F. L. Gobhair* ...	
Grain in Hides and Corn in Sacks ...	*Grain an Seicheannan 's siol am pocannan*	
Great Supper, Lament for the ...	*Cumha na Suipearach mòire*	Mac Dougal.
Groat, The	*An Gròta*	
Gunn's Salute...	*Fàilte nan Guineach*	
Hail to my Country	*Fàilte do m' dhùthaich*...	Ed. June, 1896.
Half-Finished Piobaireachd, The ...	*Am Port leathach*	P. M. Mac Crimmon and J. D. Mac Kay.
Hamilton, Lament for the Duke of	*Cumha Dhiùc Hamiltoin*	
Harp Tree, Lament for the ...	*Cumha Craobh nan teud*	
Hen's March o'er the Midden, The	*Glocail nan cearc*	John Dall Mac Kay.
Hey! for the old Pipes ...	*Dastriom gu'n seinnam piob*	
Highland Society of London's Salute, The	*Fàilte Comunn Gaidhealach Lunainn*	John Mac Kay.
Highland Society of Scotland's Salute, The	*Fàilte Commun Gaidhealach Albainn*	Prof. Mac Arthur, 1796.
I got a kiss of the King's hand	*Fhuair mi pòg o laimh an Righ*	..D. M. Mac Crimmon, 1651.
Inveraray, Salute to	*Fàilte Ionaraora*	
Inverness	*Inbhirneis*	

ENGLISH.	GAELIC.	AUTHOR AND DATE.
Islay, Farewell to the Laird of ...	*Soraidh Tighearna Ileath* ...	... A. Mac Kay, 1840.
Isle of Skye	*Eilean a' Cheo*	... a Mac Crimmon.
James VI.'s Salute	*Cumha Righ Seumas an seathamh*	
King George III., Lament for ...	*Cumha Righ Seoras a tri*	...
King James' Departure, Lament for	*Siubhal Sheuma's*	1688.
King's Taxes, The	*Màl an Righ*	...
Kinloch Moidart's Salute	*Fàilte Fir Cheannloch-Muideart*	...
Kinloch Muideart—Lament for Mac Donald of...	*Fàilte Fir Cheannloch-Muideart*	...
Laggan Salute, The	*Fàilte Lagain*	... D. Mac Kay, 1871.
Laird of Anapool, Lament for the ...	*Cumha Fir Anapuil*	...
Lament for Abercairney ...	*Cumha Aberchàrnaig*	...
Leaving Kintyre	*Fàgail Chinntire*	...
Leigh, Col., Farewell to ...	*Soraidh Chòirneil Leigh* ...	... C. S. Thomason, 1893.
Little Finger Tune, The ...	*Port na Lùdaig*...	...
Little Spree, The	*An Daorach bheag*	...
Little Supper, Lament for the ...	*An t-Suipear bheag*	...
Loch Carron-point, The Battle of ..	*Blàr an t-Srian*...	1602.
Lord Lovat, Lament for ...	*Cumha Mhic Shimidh* ...	...
Mac Cruimein, Donald Ban, Lament for	*Cumha Dhòmhnuill Bhain Mhic Cruimein*	...
Mac Cruimein, Patrick Og, Lament for...	*Cumha Phàdruig Oig Mhic Cruimein*	J. D. Mac Kay.
Mac Cruimein will never return ...	*Cha till, cha till, cha till mi tuille*	... D. B. Mac Crimmon, 1746.
Mac Cruimein's Sweetheart ...	*Mal Dhonn*	...
Mac Donald of the Isles, Lament for Sir James...	*Cumha an Ridire Seumas Mac Dhomhnuill nan Eilean*	C. Mac Arthur.
Mac Donald of the Isles, Lament for Sir James...	*Cumha an Ridire Seumas Mac Dhomhnuill nan Eilean*	W. Mac Donald of Vallay.
Mac Donald of the Isles Salute ...	*Fàilte Mhic Dhòmhnuill nan Eilean*	
Mac Donald of the Isles, Sir James, Salute	*Failte an Ridire Seumas Mac Dhòmhnuill nan Eilean*	
Mac Donald, Lament for Lady ...	*Cumha Bain-tighearna Mhic Dhomhnuill*..	Angus Mac Arthur, 1790.
Mac Donald, Lord, Lament for ...	*Cumha Morair Chloinn Dhomhnuill* ...	A. MacArthur, 1796
Mac Donald of Morar, Ronald, Lament for	*Cumha Raonuill Mhic Ailein òig*	...
Mac Donald's, Angus, Assault ...	*Ionnsaidh Aonghais Bhig Mhic Dhomhnuill*	...
Mac Donalds are simple, The ...	*Tha Clann Dòmhnuill socharach*	...
Mac Donalds of Clanranald's gathering at Sheriffmuir	*Cruinneachadh Chloinn Raonuill (Sliabh an t-Siorra)* ...	1715.
Mac Donalds of Clan Ronald, The Gathering of the...	*Cnocan Ailean Mhic Iain* ...	...

ENGLISH.	GAELIC.	AUTHOR AND DATE.
MacDonald's, Lady Margaret, Salute	*Fàilte Bain-tighearna Mairearad* ...	
Mac Donalds, March of the... ...	*Spaidsearachd Mhic Dhòmhnuill* ...	
Mac Donald's Salute, Lady Margaret	*Fàilte Bain-tighearna Mhic Dhomhnuill*	
Mac Donalds' Salute, The	*Fàilte Chloinn Domhnuill*	D. M. MacCrimmon
Mac Donalds, The Parading of the...	*Uaill Chloinn Dòmhnuill*	
Mac Donald's Tutor	*Oide-ionnsachaidh Mhic Dhòmhnuill*...	
Mac Donell, Alex., of Glengarry's Lament	*Cumha Alastair Dheirg*	
Mac Donell of Laggan's Lament, ...	*Cumha Dhomhnuill an Lagain* ...	
Mac Dougall, Lament for Captain ...	*Cumha Chaiptein 'Ic Dhughaill* ...	Ronald MacDougall
Mac Dougall's Salute, The	*Fàilte Chloinn Dughaill*	R. Mac Dougall.
Mac Duffs' Gathering, The... ...	*Cruinneachadh Chloinn Duibh* ...	
Mac Farlanes' Gathering, The	*'Thogail nam bò*	
Mac Gregors' Gathering, The ...	*Cruinneachadh nan Griogarach* ...	
Mac Intosh, Lament for	*Cumha Mhic an Toisich*	
Mac Intoshs' Banner, The ...	*Bratach Mhic an Toisich*	
Mac Intyre's Salute	*Fàilte Mhic an t-saoir ...* ...	
Mac Kays' Banner, The ...	*Bratach Chloinn Mhic Aoidh* ...	
Mac Kay's, Donald Dugal, Lament, or Lord Reay's Lament,	*Cumha Dhomhnuill Dhughail Mhic Aoidh* ...	D. M. Mac Crimmon
Mac Kays' March, The ...	*Spaidsearachd Cloinn Mhic Aoidh* ...	
Mac Kenzie of Applecross's Salute...	*Fàilte Tighearna na Coimirich* ...	A. Mac Kay.
Mac Kenzie, Donald—his Father's Lament for	*Cumha Dhòmhnuill Mhic Coinnich (le 'Athair)*	
Mac Kenzie of Gairloch's Lament,...	*Cumha Tighearna Ghedrloch ...* ...	J. Mac Kay.
Mac Kenzie of Gairloch's Salute ...	*Fàilte Thigearna Ghedrloch*	
Mac Kenzie, Lament for Colin Roy	*Cumha Chailein Ruaidh Mhic Coinnich*	
Mac Kenzie's, Capt. D., Lament ...	*Cumha 'Chaiptein D. Mhic Coinnich...*	
Mac Kenzies' Gathering, The ...	*Tulloch Ard*	
Mac Kenzies' Gathering, The—Tulloch Ard	*Cruinneachadh Chloinn Choinnich (Tulloch Ard)*	
Mac Lean, Great John, Lament for	*Cumha Ian Ghairbh Mhic Illeathain*	
Mac Lean of Coll, Lament for Sir John Garve	*Cumha Iain Ghairbh Mhic 'Illeathain*	
Mac Lean, Lachlan Mor, Lament for	*Latha Sron a' Chlachain*	
Mac Leans' Gathering, The ...	*Cruinneachadh Chloinn Ghilleathain...*	
Mac Leans' Gathering, The...	*Spaidsearachd Chloinn Ghilleathain ...*	
Mac Lean's, Hector, Warning ...	*Caismeachd Eachnin Mhic Ailein nan Sop*	1579.
Mac Leans' March, The ...	*Spaidsearachd Chloinn Ghilleathain ...*	
Mac Lean, Lament for Hector Roy,	*Cumha Eachainn Ruaidh nan cath* ...	A. Mac Lean, 1650.
Mac Leod, A Taunt on ...	*Port Gedrr Mhic Ledid*	
Mac Leod of Colbeck, Lament for ...	*Cumha Mhic Ledid Cholbec*	J. Mac Kay.
Mac Leod, dispraise of, ...	*Di-moladh Mhic Ledid*	
Mac Leod of Gesto's Salute ...	*Fàilte Fir Gèosta*	
Mac Leod John, Lament for, ...	*Cumha Iain Mhic Iain Ghairbh* ...	
Mac Leod of Mac Leod, Lament for	*Cumha cinn-cinnidh nan Leddach* ...	D.M.Mac Crimmon, 1626.

ENGLISH.	GAELIC.	AUTHOR AND DATE.
Mac Leod of Mac Leod's Rowing Pibroch or Salute	*Port Iomram Mhic Leòid, na Fàilte nan Leòdach*	D.M. Mac Crimmon,
Mac Leod, Mary, Lament for ...	*Cumha Màiri Nic Leòid*	
Mac Leod of Raasay, John Garve, Lament for	*Cumha Iain Ghairbh Mhic Gille Chaluim*	P.M. Mac Crimmon, 1548 (?).
Mac Leod of Raasay's lament ...	*Cumha Mhic Gille Chaluim Rathasadh*	D.M. Mac Crimmon, 1648.
Mac Leod of Raasay's Salute ...	*Fàilte Mhic Gille Chaluim Rathasadh*	A. Mac Kay, Gairloch
Mac Leod, Roderick More, Salute at Birth of	*'Nann air mhire tha sibh?* ...	P.M. Mac Crimmon, 1715.
Mac Leod of Tallisker's, Mrs., Salute	*Fàilte Bain Tigearna Thailasgear*	...
Mac Leod of Tallisker's Salute ...	*Failte Tighearna Thailesgear*	...
Mac Leod's Controversy ...	*Iomradh Mhic Leòid*	D.M. Mac Crimmon, 1503.
Mac Neill of Barra's Lament ...	*Cumha Mhic Nèill Bhara* ...	...
Mac Neill of Barra's March...	*Spaidsearachd Mhic Nèill Bhara*	...
Mac Neill of Kintarbert's Fancy ...	*Aon tlachd Mhic Nèill*... ...	...
Mac Phees, The Rout of the ...	*Ruaig air Cloinn a Phi* ...	...
Mac Pherson's March, Cluny ...	*Spaidsearachd Thighearna Chluainidh*	
Mac Pherson's Salute, Cluny ...	*Fàilte Fir Chluainidh*	...
Mac Raes' March, The ...	*Spaidsearachd Cloinn Mhic Rath* ...	1491.
Mac Suain of Roaig, Lament for ...	*Cumha Mhic Shuain à Roaig*... ...	
Maolroy, The Battle of, or Isabel Mac Kay	*A mhuinntir a chàil chaoil thugadh am bruthach oirbh*	
Mary's praise for her Gift ...	*Moladh Màiri*	
Massacre of Glencoe ...	*Mort Ghlinne Comhann*	
Melbank's Salute ...	*Fàilte Fir Bhlabhne*	
Menzies' Salute, The ...	*Fàilte 'Mhèinneirich* ...	
Men went to drink, The ..	*Chaidh na fir a dh'òl*	
Middling Spree, The ...	*An Daorach mheadhonach*	
Monroe' Salute, The	*Fàilte nan Rothach*	
My dearest on earth, give me your kiss	*Thoir domh pòg, a luaidh mo chridhe*	
My King has landed in Moidart ...	*Thàinig mo Rìgh air tir am Mùideart*	
Old Sword's Lament, The ...	*Cumha an tseana Chlaidheimh* ...	
Old Woman's Lullaby, The...	*Crònain na Cailliche*	
Only Son, Lament for the ...	*Cumha an aona mhic*	P. M. Mac Crimmon.
Park, Battle of ...	*Blàr Pairc Shruithleith*	1477.
Pass of Crieff, Battle of the...	*Cath bealach Chraoibh*... ...	
Perth, The Desperate Battle ...	*Cath fuathasach, Pheairt*	1395.
Perth, Lament for the Duke of ...	*Cumha Dhuic Pheairt*	
Piper Samuel, Lament for ...	*Cumha Shomhairle Dhuibh* ...	
Piper's Farewell to his Home, The	*Soraidh piobaire da dhachaidh* ...	
Piper's Salute to his Master, The ...	*Fàilte a' Phìobaire d'a Mhaighstir*	
Piper's warning to his Master, The	*A Cholla mo rùn*	
Praise of Marion	*Moladh Màiri*	
Pretty Dirk, The	*A 'Bhiodag bhòidheach*	
Prince Charles' Lament ...	*Cumha Phrionnsa Teàrlach* ...	Capt. M. Mac Leod, 1746.
Prince's Salute, The	*Fàilte' Phrionnsa*	J. Mac Intyre, 1715.

ENGLISH.	GAELIC.	AUTHOR AND DATE.
Queen Anne, Lament for	*Cumha Ban-Righ Anna* ...	...
Red Hand in the Mac Donald's Arms, The	*Lamh dhearg Chloinn Domhnuill*	...
Red Hill, The Battle of the... ...	*Fir nam breacan dubha* ...	...
Red Ribbon, The	*An riobain dearg* ...	...
Robertson's Salute, Strowan	*Fàilte Thighearna Struain* ...	...
Rout of Glen Fruin, The ...	*Ruaig Ghlinn Fraoine*	1602.
Rout of the Lowland Captain, The	*Ruaig a'Chaiptein Ghallda* ...	...
Sauntering, The	*A Chracaireachd*	...
Scarce of Fishing	*Spiocaireachd Iasgaich*... ...	...
Sheriffmuir, The Battle of ...	*Blàr Sliabh an t-Siorra* ...	... J. Mac Intyre, 1715.
Sinclairs' March, The ...	*Spaidsearachd Mhic na Ceàrda*	...
Sisters' Lament, The... ...	*Cumha na peathar*	...
Sobieski's Salute	*Fàilte shobia-gaidh*	...
Smith's, Mrs., Salute ...	*Fàilte Bean a'Ghobha*	.. J. B. Mac Kenzie.
Strone, The Battle of Castle	*Blàr Chaisteal Stroine*	...
Stuarts' White Banner, The	*Bratach Bhàn nan Stiubhartach*	...
Sutherlands' Gathering, The ...	*Cruinneachadh nan Sutharlanach*	...
Tallisker, The Battle of Waternish	*Blàr T'hailengeur*	...
Thomason's, Miss Mabel, Salute ...	*Fàilte na h-òighe Mabal nic Thòmais*	K. Cameron, 1894.
Thomason's Salute, General ..	*Fàilte an t-seanaileir Mhic Thòmais*	...A. Paterson, H.L.I., 1893.
Too long in this condition ...	*'Sfada mar so tha sinn*... ...	... P. M. Mac Crimmon, 1715.
Tune of Strife, The	*Port an Strìth*	...
Union, Lament for the ...	*An Co-chomunn*...	...
Unjust Carceration, The ...	*An ceapadh eucorach*	... J. Dall Mac Kay.
Vaunting, The	*A'Bhòilich*	... Rd. Mac Donald of Morair.
Waking of the Bridegroom, The ...	*Dùsgadh Fir-na-Bainnse* ...	...
War or Peace	*Cogadh na sith*	...
Waterloo, The Battle of ...	*Blàr Bhaterlù*	... J. Mac Kay, 1815.
Weighing from Land... ...	*Togail bho tìr*	...
Welcome Johnnie back again	*Slàn gu'n till Eoinachan* ...	...
Writer, Lament for the ...	*Cumha 'Chleirich*	...
Young King George III. Salute ...	*Fàilte Sheòrais òig*	1760.
Young Laird of Dungallon's Salute	*Fàilte Thighearna Oig Dhungallain*	...
Young Neill's Salute... ...	*Fàilte Neill Oig*...	...
You're welcome, Ewin Lochiel ...	*Is e do bheatha Eòghain* ...	...

With nineteen pibrochs, of which name and date and composers are all alike unknown.

VII.—THE GARB OF OLD GAUL.

(From the *Glasgow Herald*, April 7, 1900).

" Oh first of garbs ! garment of happy fate,
    So long employed, of such an antique date,
    Look back some thousand years till records fail,
    And lose themselves in some romantic tale ;
    We'll find our god-like fathers nobly scorned
    To be by any other dress adorned."

                —Allan Ramsay.

THE " quelt," as very ancient writers called it, is one of the few things that are left to remind Scotland of its once distinctive nationality. Together with the Gaelic and the pipes, it makes Scottish history peculiar among the histories of countries. In no other land have the distinguishing marks of a nationality that, as a separate kingdom, has ceased to exist been retained in almost all their original purity. Of the three things, the kilt is perhaps the most interesting. The language and the music have been, and are, confined to the people of the Highlands, either in or out of the Highlands ; but the kilt, while no longer the every-day wear of Highland people, has found its way into non-Highland circles, and the tartan has become a fashionable dress. But still, and this is a peculiar thing, it remains the Highland garb, and must, wheresoever seen, be associated with a distinctive country and a distinctive people.

The kilt is the most ancient of all garments. It is the development of the fig leaves of our first parents. Primitive man wrapped himself round with a piece of cloth, when he had cloth, caring little about the niceties of cut or fashion. When the cloth didn't hang properly he, quite naturally, tied it round his waist with a string, and in so doing transformed his wrappings into a belted plaid, the immediate predecessor of the plaid and kilt. It was certainly not a sense of delicacy but a desire for outward show that led primitive man to clothe himself. Cæsar found the Britons with their bodies painted with woad, and they appeared naked in public. Afterwards they clothed themselves with skins of animals and with woollen garments, the latter of which was undoubtedly the string-bound plaid of the well-to-do Highlander.

The earliest bit of evidence regarding the antiquity of the Highland dress in anything like its present form is a piece of sculpture which was dug in 1860 from part of the ruins of the wall of Antoninus, built in A.D. 140. It shows figures representing very clearly the plaid and kilt, presumably in one piece. Another sculptured stone, found at Dull, Perthshire, gives the bonnet and shield of the Highlander; while a third, discovered at St. Andrews, shows the arrangement of the belted plaid or full dress of the ancient Gael. Both the latter, now in the Museum of Antiquaries, Edinburgh, are of unknown antiquity. Then in A.D. 204 we find Herodian, a classical writer, saying that the Caledonians were only partly clad; and in A.D. 296 a Roman writer, in a eulogy of the Emperor Constantinus, calls the Picts *hostilibus seminudis*, half-clad enemies. European historians, as a matter of fact, almost always called the Gael of Alban half-naked. Besides, we have Gildas, the earliest of British writers, saying that the Picts were dressed only with cloth round the loins, a rude form of the plaid evidently. And, while both Cæsar and Tacitus assure us that the Britons were precisely the same people as the Gauls, in manners, religion, appearance, and customs, we also read, in other writings of the same date, that the Gauls " wore coats stained with various colours." Also as a very ancient writer on Scotland tells us :—

" The other pairt Northerne are full of mountaines, and very rud and hornelie kind of people doeth inhabite, which is called Reid Sohankes, or Wyld Scottish. They be clothed with ane mantle, with ane schirt fachioned after the Irish manner, going bare-legged to the knie."

These things all indicate a people partially clad in cloth which was not all of one colour, and it is not stretching the inference very far to identify the garb with the latter-day dress of the Scottish Highlander.

Let us come now to times of which more or less authentic history treats. The first historical reference we find is contained in the Icelandic Sagas. When the death of Malcolm Canmore plunged Scotland into anarchy, Magnus Olafson, King of Norway, was ravaging the west coast and securing a firm hold of the Hebrides for his own country. On his return from that expedition in 1098, the Sagas relate, he adopted the costume of these western lands, and "his followers went bare-legged, having short kirtles and upper wraps, and so men called him ' Barelegs.'" The seal of Alexander I., whose reign began in 1107, shows him in Highland dress, and as the same seal was used by David I. (1124) and Malcolm IV. (1153), we are quite justified in concluding that these monarchs actually wore what they were represented on their seal as wearing. Such a dress must certainly have existed at that time.

Then, dating from 1350, we have a sculptured representation of a chief attired finely in Highland dress, and in 1471 John, Bishop of Glasgow, treasurer to King James III., in an account for tartan for the use of the King, gives the following item :—" For a yard and a half, £1 10s. (Scots of course), and the colour blue." Half a yard of " double tartane" for the Queen cost 8s. James V. made a hunting expedition into the Highlands in 1538, and a Highland dress was provided for the occasion. The account of the King's treasurer shows that it consisted of " a short Highland coit," hose of " tertane," and a "syde Heland sarkis," all for the " Kingis Grace." The last article was presumably an unusually long shirt.

John Lesley, Bishop of Ross, writing in 1578, says the garments of his day consisted of a short woollen jacket and a covering of the simplest kind for the thighs, more for decency than for protection from cold. About 1580 a writer with a turn for rhyming described the dress of the Highlanders thus :—

" Their shirtes be very straunge,
  Not reaching past the thigh,
  With pleates on pleates they pleated are,
  As thick as pleates can lie,"

which was a very good and concise description of the plaid
as it then was. Another writer, in *Certayne Mattere Concerning Scotland*, published in London in 1603, says the
Highlanders " delight in marbled cloths, especially that have
long strips of sundrie colours . . . . with the which, rather
coloured than clad, they suffer the most cruel tempests that
blow in the open fields, in such sort that, in a night of snow
they sleep sound." From *A Modern Acccunt of Scotland*,
printed in 1679, also in London, we learn that " the Highlanders wear slashed doublets, commonly without breeches,
only a plad tyed about their wastes, thrown over one
shoulder, with short stockings to the gartering place ; their
knees and part of their thighs being naked ; others have
breeches and stockings all of a piece of plad ware." A
writer of 1710 supplements this by saying, " they wear
striped mantles of divers colours called plaids"; a statement
which brings the evidence to a date so recent as to render
the calling of further witnesses unnecessary. That the kilt
is a pure outgrowth of Scottish life there is no gainsaying.
It could have been imported from Ireland only, and that it
was not is proved by the two facts, that the colony of Irish
Scots who settled in Argyllshire never overran Scotland, and
that the checkered plaid was worn in Scotland at dates
earlier than it can be proved to have been worn in Ireland.

The complete outfit of a Highland chief in the middle of
the eighteenth century makes rather a formidable list.
Here it is :—

Full-trimmed bonnet.
Tartan jacket, vest, kilt, and cross-belt.
Tartan belted plaid.
Pair of hose, made up from cloth.
Tartan stockings, with yellow garters.
Two pairs of brogues.
Silver-mounted purse and belt.
Target with spear.

Broadsword.
Pair of pistols and bullet mould.
Dirk.
Knife and fork.

The garb was completed by a feather, or, in the case of the common people, a tuft of heather, pine, holly, or oak, in the bonnet. Personal decoration was always considered a more important matter than home decoration or even home comforts.

Hair was used for making clothing at one time, for we are told Ossian Fin Mac Coul was " arrayed in Hieland plaidis of hair," but wool was the general material, and so long as wool was worn, so long—it is said—was rheumatism unknown in the Highlands. In colours green and black predominated, with an occasional stripe of red. The number of colours indicated the rank of the wearer, a King or a Chief having seven, a Druid six, and other nobles four, while the very poor people had their plaids plain. The dyes were got from herbs, and the colours are said to have been so " fast " as to keep for two hundred years. The Celts were proud of the grandeur of their tartans, and an old song makes one of them, when wooing a Lowland lass, say :—

> " Bra sall the sett o' your braid tartan be
> If ye will gang to the Highlands wi' me."

The rigorous Disarming Act, passed in 1747, created what was perhaps the most critical time in the history of the tartan. The pipes and the tartan were banned as treasonable things, and marks of extreme disloyalty to the House of Hanover. The law expressly enacted that "neither man nor boy, except such as are employed as officers and soldiers, shall, on any pretence, wear or put on the clothes commonly called Highland clothes, viz., the plaid, philabeg or little kilt, trowse, shoulder-belts, or any part whatsoever of what peculiarly belongs to the Highland garb, and that no tartan or party-coloured plaid or stuff shall be used for greatcoats, or for upper coats, on pain of imprisonment for six months, without the option of a fine, for the first offence, and transportation for seven years for the second." This was stringent enough, and it nearly strangled all that was peculiar to the Highlands. But, thanks principally to the patriotic exertions of the then Duke of Montrose, the ban was removed in 1782, and the Highland garb restored to favour. It is now worn by five British regiments. The Gordons wear the Gordon tartan, the Camerons the Erracht-Cameron, the Seaforths the Mac Kenzie, the Argyll and Sutherlands the Sutherland, and the Black Watch a special tartan closely resembling the Sutherland. Both battalions of the Gordons, and one each of the other four regiments, are now in South Africa.

The Highland garb as we have it to-day is a compound of three varieties, all of which were worn in the seventeenth century. There was first the dress worn by the gentry—a shirt died with saffron and a plaid of fine wool tartan, with colours assorted so as to give the best possible effect. Then there was the dress of the common people—a shirt, painted instead of dyed, with a deerskin jacket above it, and the plaid, not always of tartan, worn over the shoulders instead of belted about the body. The third variety was the trews, but this cannot be traced farther back than 1538. It probably came from Ireland, where it was the dress of the gentry from the earliest periods.

The plaid proper consisted of a long piece of tartan carefully plaited in the middle and bound about the waist in large and very particularly-adjusted folds. While the lower part came down from the belt to the knees, the upper, after various wrappings so as to cover the whole body, was fixed to the left shoulder with a brooch, leaving the right arm at liberty. In wet weather the plaid was thrown loose, and formed a complete covering for the body. The headdress, when there was any, was a round, flat bonnet, the stockings were cut from the web of tartan, and the shoes were made of skin shaped in the best possible way to the form of the foot. The original of the sporran was a large piece of goat's or badger's skin profusely ornamented, which hung in front, and served as a pocket.

There seems to have been a time, before the dress
developed into its present form, when the belted plaid and
the trews were worn together. In 1656 a certain Thomas
Tucker, who reported on the settlement of the revenues
of excise and custom in Scotland, says one of his collectors,
in order to avert the antipathy of the natives to an excise-
man, " went clad after the mode of the country, with belted
playde, trowses, and brogues." " In sharp winters," says a
writer of 1680, " they wear close trouzes, which cover the
thighs, legs, and feet ; " while at the Battle of Killiecrankie,
in 1715, " there were several of the common men died in
the hills, for, having cast away their plaids at going into
battle, they had not wherewith to cover them but their
shirts ; whereas many of the gentlemen that instead of short
hose did wear trewis, though they were sorely pinched, did
fare better in their short coats and trewis than those that
were naked to the belt."

By and by, however, the belted plaid and the trews gave
way to the plaid and the kilt as we now have them. It
cannot be said, indeed, that there ever was a period in
which the trews held anything like universal sway. The
transition was rather from the original form of the loosely
wrapped plaid to the present form of the dress. There is a
story to the effect that an English tailor named Parkinson
or Ralliston invented the kilt in 1715 or 1745—it is a
somewhat vague story—and both Pennant and Sir John
Sinclair accept it as truth. Pennant, himself an Englishman, may be excused, but the man who edited the *Statistical
Account of Scotland* might have known better. The Earl
of Moray of Charles I.'s day wore the kilt, and Lord Archibald Campbell, in *Records of Argyll*, shows two pictures,
one of 1672 and one of 1693, in both of which the kilt can
be plainly seen. Besides, the Highlanders wore it in the
rebellion of 1715. It is carrying conjecture a bit too far to
contend that the Saxons, who were able to introduce very
few of their customs among the Celts, introduced the
national dress. The simple fact seems to be that the
change from the belted plaid, with the plaid and trews here

and there, to the plaid and kilt, took place when the altering circumstances of the people made continuous labour a necessity, and also, therefore, a convenient and inexpensive working outfit.

It gives one an insight into the habits of the times to read that the managers of the piping competition held in Edinburgh in 1783, apologised to the public for the deficiency in dress. The competitors, they said, having no prospect of appearing " before so magnificent and great a company," had nothing in view in quitting their distant dwellings but the competition at Falkirk, where their instruments alone were essential. In 1785, however, candidates were warned to appear "in the proper Highland habit," which has since held good. Pipers' dress was sometimes stylish enough even in the middle of the eighteenth century, for we read that in a procession of the Royal Company of Archers in Edinburgh in 1734 there was " one Highland piper who was dressed in scarlet richly laced."

In the present-day dress, as is well known, the upper part of the plaid is disjoined from the lower, and made up so as to resemble the ancient form. The kilt itself is plaited so as to resemble the lower half of the plaid, but as a matter of fact, it is always too well plaited to be more than a far-off imitation. When properly made, the garb is certainly one of the most picturesque in the world. It is not so well adapted for the hillside as the old was, having been "improved" too much, but it is remarkable as showing how closely mankind clings to habits and costumes which experience has proved suitable, and which is entwined into the history and traditions of their particular race. As to its suitability for war, a great deal has been said in connection with the present operations in South Africa, and it has been laid to the charge of the tartan that it not only betrays the presence of the wearer, and makes him a target for the enemy's sharp-shooters, but also exposes the soldier to all sorts of chills, and the attacks of all the vermin that crawl over the ground on which he has often to sleep. There is no use denying the fact that there is a great deal of truth in this, and if the Government press their proposals for the reform of Army dress, and include in these proposals the abolition of the kilt as a fighting garment, it seems as if there will not be one half the outcry there would have been in the same circumstances before the war begun. The campaign has undoubtedly revealed the short-comings of the kilt as a part of active service dress, but that is no reason why it should be altogether abolished. Sentiment can be satisfied by retaining the kilt for parade purposes and garrison duty, while common-sense will indicate that sentiment, unless it can be proved to be very strong indeed, must have little voice in deciding what is best in the face of the enemy. It would certainly be bad policy to totally dissociate the Highland regiments from their distinctive tartans. Recruiting in Scotland is not what it might be, and when the Highland regiments cease to be distinctively Highland it will decline still further. If the authorities wish to foster the military enthusiasm of Highlanders they cannot do better than foster all that pertains to their part of the kingdom. Besides, the tartan is not now the badge of a rebellious remnant, but of a race that is loyal to the empire of which it is a worthy part, and considering the high position the kilted regiments hold in the British army, it is not too much to expect that their peculiar dress should be left to them, for use in all possible circumstances.

The war has given a decided impetus to the general trade in tartans. The demand from the regulars remains practically stationary, as the number of men wearing the Highland uniform is always the same. Among Scottish Volunteer regiments, however, the kilt is coming more and more into favour, and quite a number of additional "Highland companies" have been formed recently. The 6th V. B. Gordon Highlanders is the only battalion in the Highland Brigade unprovided with the national garb, the Government having, owing to "financial difficulties," declined to supply the dress. The honorary colonel, Mr. J. Gordon Smith, has, however, now given the regiment £1500 to enable the men to wear their territorial uniform, and it is almost certain that the Government will supply the regiment with the kilt in the future. But it is from fashionable civil life that the bulk of the increased demand comes. The headquarters of the kilt-making industry—for it is an industry—are in Glasgow, but the principal market is in London. The demand in the Metropolis for the Highland dress is very extensive, and the biggest firm of Glasgow manufacturers are kept continually employed fulfilling orders from the South. The favourite tartans are, naturally, those of the kilted regiments, but the fashionable Highland dress consists of the kilt with an ordinary dinner jacket above it— the full outfit would be too Highland for London drawing-rooms. In Scotland the formation of clan societies has, in the cities, revived interest in the different tartans, but in the real home of the kilt, the fastnesses of the Highlands, the dress is practically extinct. A few old men wear it, as well as some of the better class residents, visitors sometimes wear it, while retainers wear it as a sort of livery ; but among the people themselves it is, to all intents and purposes, obsolete. The garb of old Gaul has ceased to be the at-home dress of the Highlander, and become the evening dress of the fashionable who would ape a Highland connection, and the mark of the Highland wanderer, who far from home stands by home customs out of patriotic love for his home land. We may regret the turn of events, but there is no use blinking simple facts.—W. L. M.

Index.

411

CPSIA information can be obtained at www.ICGtesting.com
Printed in the USA
LVOW111406081211

258423LV00001B/163/P